What They Don't Teach You in Deer River

Navy Memoirs of a Small Town Girl

Julia A. Maki

To Madison
Remember you
can do anything!
~Julia
5-27-17

TM

TACTICAL.

What They Don't Teach You in Deer River
Copyright © 2015 by Julia A. Maki

First Edition

Because of the dynamic nature of the internet, any web address or links contained in this book may have changed since publication and may no longer be valid.

Brand names, trademarks, and service marks appearing in this book are the intellectual property of their respective owners.

The views expressed in this work are solely those of the author and do not necessarily reflect the views of the publisher, and the publisher hereby disclaims any responsibility for them.

Published by Tactical 16, LLC
Colorado Springs, CO

eISBN: 978-1-943226-04-7
ISBN: 978-1-943226-07-8 (hc)
ISBN: 978-1-943226-08-5 (sc)

Printed in the United States of America

This book is dedicated to the amazing little town of Deer River, Minnesota, and all of the wonderful people with whom I grew up; for I would not be who I am without them.

It is also dedicated to all of the men and women who have ever served their country - especially to those whom I have worked next to during those amazing years in VP-8 (Tiger Tiger!) And of course to all of my big brothers (and sister) on Combat Aircrew Nine - undeniably the best aircrew in the VP Navy.

Many I may never see again but they will always have a special place in my heart. Thank you for all of the wonderful memories and life's lessons. I can only hope life is treating you well, my fellow sailors, wherever you may be!

"Good friends are hard to find, harder to leave, and impossible to forget." ~Author Unknown

The Crew. (Left to Right) Stimpy, Algae, Farr, Big Lovin', Burke, Chief, Dave, Rugged, Knuckles (Me), Deena, Big 'Ol

FORWARD

The following stories were written from emails, journal entries, and inputs from various nights and days of drinking and story-swapping; but mostly from sheer memory. I have tried to the best of my knowledge to get complete details of the various adventures in history straight. It was written strictly from my point of view and opinion, which was that of a small town girl exposed to the vicious and authentic, but rewarding life of a United States Sailor and Aircrewman. If I had to do it all over again, I would without a moment of hesitation. Well, maybe about thirty seconds of hesitation...

There is no greater honor than to serve so that others may live free.

CHAPTER 1

Children were playing kickball in a snowy park near the side of the winding road that had few travelers. One of the kids stopped for a moment, glancing up at us and as our eyes met for that brief moment, it felt as if he was looking right through me, no doubt wondering what we were doing. Or perhaps he already knew, as this bus passed this way up the mountainside every three weeks or so and then back down again a week later, carrying with it changed people.

How I wish it were a time when I was playing kickball instead of the fate that lie before me. At this moment, I knew the next week was going to be grim, and my bones were weighted with a feeling of dread. I longed for my freedom as I already was taken as prisoner, off to fulfill my sentence.

Deer River, MN
June 1997

He was the only kid to have a mustache when facial hair was not cool. I liked that about him. He laughed a lot and though his ego was as big as any high school jock, he also was very kind and respectful to his elders. All of our teachers loved him. His parents were crazy eccentric, but likeable. My friends and I always enjoyed hanging out at their house. They had two Great Danes that ate baby rabbits as afternoon snacks. In the two years we were together during our crazy influential teenage years, we were inseparable. He taught me many things. How to drive a stick shift at the price of his transmission. How to shoot a sawed-off shotgun. How to fancifully eat artichokes. And how to solve for $e=mc^2$. Though some things I did not retain as much as others.

He also taught me that stop signs with a white ring around them were optional, that boys did not really jerk off, and that I was the only one for him and that he would marry me someday. Turns out, like most teenage boys, he lied.

If I had known it was going to be the last time I would see him for the next decade, I may have said something more profound. "Were you able to finish hauling all the firewood today?" I sniffed as he hugged me.

He smiled, nodded and brushed a strand of loose hair behind my ear. "You know, I'll see you soon. We just need to get through this very small piece of our lives. Then we'll be able to get stationed together. Thirteen weeks is such a short time in the whole scheme of things, Babe." He was the first person who ever called me Babe. To me it was a sign of true love. Turns out my mechanic also calls me Babe.

Then, just as quickly as we jumped on that train, it had passed. Our high school chapter had come to a close. And what a ride it was. He was on the football team and I was on the high school dance team, performing at half time of the football and basketball games. Our town loved its sports, and our graduating class was a close one. We were all friends and I genuinely cared about all of my classmates. We did all of the typical things seniors did together; homecoming, pep-fests, proms, and class trips. We had cabin parties and gravel pit parties. We camped often-and I mean real camping without electronics, where you stink badly, have to bathe and brush your teeth in the lake, and cook hotdogs from a stick over a fire. It all had gone by in a second, a blink of an eye, and it was over. So quickly, that it was a short wonder if it was real or not, or just a long dream or a movie that played "We Are the Champions" during the closing credits.

Dillon (aka Mr. Mustache) was my life. He was the one I leaned on through my parents' divorce when I was sixteen. He helped me take care of my two younger sisters. Together we focused on our goals for the future in the military. He was my refuge, and today I was saying goodbye to him. I had to believe in my heart that it would be okay - that I was making the right decision.

I had watched him all week go around saying goodbye to everyone in our small town. It was gut-wrenching. It was even more difficult to know that I would be doing the same thing in just two more weeks.

They all had their own words of advice. Some thought it was great that we were getting out of this small town. They said there was nothing here for us. Meanwhile others expressed their opinion very freely as they told us we were making the biggest mistake ever.

"Don't you know we're going to be getting a Subway soon," they would say.

"A subway? Like a train?"

"Nah, man. Like the sandwich shop. We're actually getting a Subway in Deer River."

And that is how the great rumor of a subway coming through Deer River started.

Why ever would we want to leave such a beautiful place? After all, with crystal-blue lakes (10,000 of them according to the license plate), and densely wooded lands, this was truly "God's country." There was undoubtedly nothing better out there, still mostly untouched by man. Still in the middle of nowhere. And yet, I believed it held no possible future for someone like me.

I was born with a sense of urgency in the pit of my stomach. The urgency only grew louder with each passing year. I had to see the world-before it was too late-as if the world would not wait for me. There had to be something more than just placid lakes and enduring trees. I needed action, adventure. I wanted the life I saw on the television of far off places with bright lights and buzzing cities that never slept. I wanted to travel the world, and the military seemed like the best way for a kid right out of high school to do so.

And then there was the moment when I was ten years old. The fighter jets flew over our farmhouse on Memorial Day, in formation, headed to do a ceremonial flyover over the cemetery. I could feel the power in their deafening engine blasts. The windows shook and the rumble gave me chills of excitement. *It was the sound of freedom.* Instantly, I was hooked. I wanted nothing more than to fly in one of those powerful machines. I could not think of a bigger adventure.

On that last Sunday before Dillon left, and two weeks before I did, our old Scandinavian Lutheran Church prayed for us. My mom, who played the piano for church, selected the song "Eternal Father Strong to Save" in honor of us leaving for our separate boot camps. Me, the Navy, and Dillon, the Marines. My mother sat next to us and wept. My father, who was a holidays-only churchgoer, also attended that day - so I knew it was important.

World War II and Korean veterans patted my shoulder with pride. They knew the world would go on, and this was simply the circle of life. Somebody had to do it. At the time I thought they were just proud. Looking back, I suppose they were, but they also knew we were leaving behind our innocence as we left this small town. We would come back changed. It was unavoidable. The day was surreal - like watching your own funeral.

"I'll write you every day," he promised, squeezing my hand. "I love you so much. We'll be together soon."

"I love you too! Be strong."

Then he pulled me in tighter. I inhaled him-memorizing his scent. And with one quick last kiss, I watched him jump into his old, red F-150 pick-up truck and drive away down our gravel driveway. The tires popped over the rocks as he made his final exit.

I should stay and wait. It would be the easy route to take. We could get married now and I could follow him everywhere around the world. I could be a Marine wife. It could be very fulfilling if I made it so. We would be able to be together. I wanted to get married, didn't I?

My heart and my head were like Israel and Palestine - in pretty much any decade. It was a constant battle, neither one listening to reason over the other. The pull in my stomach became greater. Every day it grew. I was restless. I knew I would always look back if I did not go and wonder 'what if.' It would grow into resentment. I had to follow my own dreams- not follow his. I had to go. There was no question about it. It was going to suck. But if I did not go now, I knew I never would. Besides, Dillon and I would make it work. That had always been the plan. We would be stationed together. I was going to be Mrs. Mustache. And we would have lots of little hairy babies running around.

Saying Goodbye

Rain fell on a cool Minnesota morning two weeks later. As it refreshingly cleansed the atmosphere, it also cast a dark gloom over the Earth and its life below. It was the kind of rain that allowed for a lazy summer afternoon indoors, without the guilt and expectations that a beautiful day will bring.

My family and I all sat in silence during the hour-long ride to the nearest bus stop. If a word had been spoken, it was irrelevant, and quickly cast aside. Everyone's minds were preoccupied with a shared sensation of the expected loss that was about to come. For me, my life and freedom as I knew it. After what seemed like an eternity, but in reality was all too quickly, the car finally came to a halt at its dreaded destination. More silence followed and the air hung thick. "Well, this is the place." My dad spoke the obvious.

I had never actually been to a bus stop before, and this one just seemed incredibly lonely. *Why was I doing this again? I could turn around and forget it all….*

First, I said goodbye to my vulnerable and impressionable younger sisters. They looked like little baby ducks that I was trying to release back into the wild. Their heads cocked to the side as they looked up at me, pleading with their eyes for me not to turn away from them. I knew I was unable to shelter them any longer. I felt selfish when I thought of the burdens they were to bear in the near future. I could only hope that someday they would understand why I had to go and forgive me. I kissed them on the head as they squeezed my waist and cried openly, uninhibited.

There is nothing more humbling than seeing your father cry. This was my father. He was my protector. He kept the monsters away when I was little. And now he cried. It was confusing, scary, and heartbreaking. I felt guilt.

Again, my dad reminded me, "If it's about the money, we'll find a way to get you through college. It's not too late, you know."

"No, Dad." I shook my head and looked into his crinkled eyes. It was not about the money. He would have offered me the world at that moment if I just would say I would stay. But I could not stay. I hugged my mother, who had been sobbing all morning. She kissed me and promised to write every day.

I climbed onto the bus and peered out the window- fighting back the tears. This was not the place to cry. I watched my family until the very last second as they slowly disappeared in the rainy distance. *Wait, just one more look…* but it was too late.

CHAPTER 2

Bus Station, Minneapolis, MN

Approximate distance from Deer River: 200 miles

And so the adventure began. Now I don't know if God was trying to distract me from my homesick heartache, or if it was merely a coincidence. Whatever it was, it worked like sliced bread. It just so happened that I ended up sitting on the bus in a seat behind what "appeared" to be two men who were-I can hardly say it- I had to double check without being obvious. Yup-they were actually *making out* with each other! In fact, they were all over each other.

An important fact to slip in here: The year was 1997. We still believed Pluto was a planet. Al Gore had just invented the Internet. Phones still had cords or gigantic pull-up antennas. It was a very different time.

I'd never seen anything like this before, and tried with great failure not to stare. I was purely and utterly shocked. One of them *had* to have been a female. Attempting to be inconspicuous, I peered around the seat to see if there were any 'female' characteristics on either of them. It was a challenge as they kept moving all over the place. Limbs were intermingled. It looked like an octopus salad.

After about a half an hour or so of this "nonchalantly glancing," my findings revealed that they were both, in fact, completely flat in the chest region. They both had short, spiky-like hair. They both also had several piercings in each ear, so that didn't help me much. Wasn't it if the right ear was pierced that meant they 'batted for the other team'? I couldn't remember. Still, it was impolite to stereotype.

Soon enough, they began talking and slapping their hands in the air. Even their voices were hard to distinguish as they fell somewhere in between a high and low, lispy pitch. It wasn't until I got a good look and saw that, by God, they *DID* have some stubble on their face. *Holy smoking Joes! They were two boys. They were gay boys making out in the seat right in front of me. In front of every-one! And they didn't care if anyone saw them!*

Now understand, while homosexuality had begun revealing itself to the world around or before this time-it hadn't quite made it up to Deer River just yet. At least not openly. **Ellen** had just came out. It was only a few years later when I began to hear of people "coming out of the closet" back home- but oh what a scandal! This was the first time I'd ever seen anything like it. I knew in that first glimpse of the world moment, my life was sure going to be different from everything I once knew.

Stranger Danger

I rode the bus for four hours down to "The Cities" (aka Minneapolis/St. Paul) where I arrived in the bus station. I had never been to a real bus station before. No one had warned me about bus stations.

As I got off the bus into the jumble of people hustling about, I stood out like a platinum blond in South Africa. I wandered in circles trying to figure out the direction to the street that led to the hotel in which I was to stay. Now I'm not sure if it was the smell of diesel exhaust and urine, or the fast food wrappers and mice droppings laying all about. Maybe it was the creepy dude selling CDs out of pockets sewn into a trench coat. Perhaps it was a combination of all of the above- but I soon began to feel short of breath and waves of anxiety in the form of nausea started to creep through my body. *I think I made a huge mistake.*

After a few minutes of trying to read a map, and searching through the crowd of apathetic faces, I was approached by an older, straggly-looking man. His face was furrowed and black with grease smears. He had a white beard and a tattered shirt. His left arm appeared to be missing as his stained, frumpy shirt hung limp and empty to his side. And as he opened his mouth to speak, his chapped lips produced a thick strand of saliva, never allowing them to completely separate.

"Are you lost, little girl?" His voice crackled. I peered at him, trying to decide how much I should reveal. He seemed nice enough and concerned. Still I felt uncomfortable, and wanted to puke all over him. I quickly dismissed the feeling and told myself not to be so judgmental. *"Just because the guy doesn't have an arm doesn't make him scary,"* I told myself. Though I knew it wasn't about the arm.

"Actually, I think I'm okay. Just looking." At this point, I didn't even know what I was trying to say.

"Don't worry, Honey, I can help you. I'm Amish." Now, I knew who Amish people were, as we had them down near where my grandma lived in Wadena, Minnesota. They would ride their dark, horse-drawn buggies into town. They were somewhat of a novelty for us kids as we always loved to see horses, and marveled at the fact they could live without a television. I found them to be incredibly fascinating. This guy did not appear Amish. *Perhaps there were different 'types' of Amish people?*

"I can show you around. Where you going?"

"Um, I'm going into the Navy. I'm leaving for boot camp tomorrow," I replied politely.

"Wow. The Navy, huh?" He repeated. "I wanted to go into the Navy. But I'm Amish."

I wasn't quite sure what to say to that. Or really what to do. *Should I apologize? Why does he keep emphasizing that he's Amish?* I just wanted to be left alone and away from this man. It was time to get direct.

"Here, let me take you to your hotel." He began to lean into me and with his good arm reached for my bag. Red flags were going off all over. I was about to vomit. I had to get out of there now.

I yelled, "no thanks!" I snatched my suitcase and began a semi-jog in the opposite direction, out onto the street, flooding myself into a sea of strangers, hoping to get away and blend in. I jogged without looking back for about two blocks. Out of breath, I quickly asked a vendor for directions to my hotel, which was another few blocks up. I ran the rest of the way to my hotel, lugging my bags behind me.

When I got to my room, I locked the door, set my alarm clock to awake at 4am and felt the most alone I had ever felt in my life. I called my mom and told her to come and get me. She didn't. She performed her usual reassuring talk that always calms me down, and allows me to be rational. She's always so rational. It has never been my strong point.

At some wee hour into the night, I was finally able to quiet my mind and sleep eventually found me.

The Airplane

I should have known from the beginning that pain was ahead, as it was prefaced by my flight (my first real flight ever) being delayed six long hours. It wasn't nicely delayed either- if there is such a thing- as in *"we're delayed, go sip sodas and have fun for six hours, and come back at your own leisure."* No, we were actually in the plane, waiting for our take-off clearance, when all flights headed into Chicago O'Hare airport (where I'd be flying into for boot camp in Great Lakes, IL) were grounded as President Clinton's plane landed there. For security reasons, they had to ground or put all flights on hold for about fifteen minutes. This began a chain-reaction of delays that resulted in a smash-your-head-into-the-tray-in-front-of-you, six-hour back-up.

Honestly, I was not too bothered by this. This was six more hours of freedom for me. However, I could only imagine how excruciatingly painful it was for everyone else on that plane that actually yearned to get to their happier destinations.

You couldn't have paid me all the money in the world to be one of the flight attendants that just happened to have the unfortunate luck of being on duty this day. Hot and fatigued, they were doing everything in their power to ease the travelers' discomfort and anxiety. They offered food, alcohol, pillows, alcohol, and alcohol all to no avail. They had nothing left to give. It was a perfect catastrophe.

When finally the hour came that Mr. Clinton was safe (rest assured), and we actually could proceed to take off, there was a multitude of tremendously anxious sighs of relief all around.

I should have tried to sleep. I knew sleep was going to be a hot commodity in the next weeks, but I just couldn't bring myself to do it. This was the first time I was actually flying! And somehow, I always knew it would be this amazing. I didn't know why- but *this! This* was what I had always wanted. I felt elated, excited, nervous, and a bit nauseous.

I eagerly hung on every word the flight attendant spoke as she demonstrated the various emergency procedures. My seatbelt was tightly secured. Check. I made a mental note of where my nearest exit would be. Check. I examined the tray in front of me, ultimately keeping it in the upright position as instructed. Check. I closed the air vents as they were annoyingly blowing cold air on my head. I glanced around me. NOT A SINGLE PERSON WAS PAYING ATTENTION TO THE FLIGHT ATTENDANT. *What was happening? Did they already have their plan in case of an emergency?* Quickly, I grabbed the safety emergency card in the seat pocket in front of me. I realized if there was a real emergency, it was up to me to get these people out quickly and safely.

Suddenly, the engines came to life. Slowly we crept forth in motion and departed from the terminal. The plane began to bounce as we coasted to our starting point known as the runway. There was a long pause. I forgot to breathe as we held short, waiting for our flight clearance. Soon with appropriate confirmations, the engines began to wind up their excited cry, yearning and pleading with the pilot to release the brakes. Without warning, the brakes were released, and the plane shot out from her starting point. Quickly, she began gaining speed with every passing second until at last, with one final leap and bound, she magically and effortlessly sprung into the air, climbing and coming to life as if this was what she lived to do. There was no turning back. The Minnesota soil grew further and further away. Soon we were one with the sky.

I was lucky. The guy I sat next to was a business man that traveled extensively. I told him where I was going, and he helped narrate the flight for me, and answer all of my questions. Luckily for him, there were only a few...thousand.

I've long since forgotten the man's name. I wouldn't be able to pick him out of a crowd- but I'll never forget what an educational conversation he engaged me in the whole way to boot camp as I ate my last supper. Yep. *The last supper.* Plane food - back when they still served it.

Then he told me of one of *his* most unforgettable flights. He spoke of a time when he was flying in a little puddle-jumper, two-engine plane. He and the small crew were flying through a vicious storm. The turbulence jostled and threw them from side to side. They were all getting sick and frightened. Then, without warning, lightning struck and took out one of the engines. The electricity died and they began quickly plummeting to Earth. He said in that moment, he knew he was going to die. The funny thing was, though, his life did not flash before his eyes as it does in the movies. Instead, he thought about all of the little tasks he had not had a chance to finish.

He hadn't finished cleaning off his desk before he left. Someone was going to have to come into work the next day and clean off his desk for him when he died. He thought of all of his unfinished business transactions. They wouldn't know where to find a lot of information. *Was this man consumed with his business?* I'm not sure.

As it turned out, the power was regained, and the pilots were able to make a safe, however shaky one-engine landing. Obviously, or I wouldn't have been talking to this man. Still, it lead me to wonder what would flash through my head right before I died. Not the best thought to have on your first airplane ride.

CHAPTER 3

Boot Camp: Great Lakes, IL

Approximate distance from Deer River: 550 miles

A few hours later, I safely arrived at boot camp, and well, if I could sum it up in about two words I would have to say…it sucked. I guess that is kind of a communal opinion. No one who has gone through boot camp has ever said they enjoyed it. If they did, well, they lied.

It was never an unobtainable hard - not physically anyway, perhaps just mentally. It continuously and unendingly eroded on my very soul. I was naturally a people-pleaser. It pained me to have someone relentlessly barking in my face, reminding me that everything that I was doing, and any effort I submitted was wrong. It didn't matter if we followed their directions to a 'T' - they would find anything and everything wrong. It was all part of the plan.

Very quickly, we learned survival techniques that made our stay in Great Lakes slightly less painful. We would not sleep in our sheets, so as not to disturb them. Every angle, every fold was measured precisely with a ruler according to standards. So we slept on top of them, using our scratchy wool blanket to keep warm. Then we could just tuck and tweak it meticulously in the morning and re-fold our wool blanket. This proved to be a wonderful timesaver, as I only had a full 2 minutes from the time of reveille (the pre-recorded morning wake-up bugle over a loud speaker) to get up, get dressed, make my bed, and stand at attention awaiting my RDC (Recruit Division Commander) to inform us of the next mission afoot.

We only disturbed two sets of dungarees: the ones that we were wearing, and the ones that were in the laundry. The other three sets were neatly folded, measured, "squared away" and strategically placed in the precise location in our lockers where they would remain for the duration of boot camp as locker decoration. Every single item had a defined location, and a measured angle of placement. Even our bras and underwear (which were white, cotton granny-panties that I literally had to fold over my lower stomach so they wouldn't stick up out of the back of my pants) also had to be folded and stored a specific way, and in a specific location.

When we would leave our barracks in what we believed was perfect and in tip top shape, there were times we'd return to find our RDCs had had a "field day." Bunks would be in upheaval. Underwear would be strewn about the floor. Books and shower shoes were everywhere as our entire locker had been emptied, and occasionally tipped completely over. Towels and clothes would be thrown out the window in complete mayhem. Random bunk beds were lying on their sides. It was a devastating sight and our hearts sunk upon arrival to find our 'home' looking like this. Just when we thought things were at last looking up, we realized how much we were only beginning.

I had spent my entire senior year in high school 'training' for boot camp (running, doing sit-ups and push-ups, etc.). When I began training, I could not do a single push-up correctly. (The kind that you don't look like you're break-dancing "the worm" on the floor.) By the time I left for boot camp, I was able to crank out about 50 in two minutes - I was determined to be a rescue swimmer - and those were the kinds of standards we had to meet, male and female alike.

You can imagine my surprise when I discovered how many girls could not do a single push-up! *Seriously, did they not realize they'd have to do them?* Every military movie shows at least one boot camp scene of overweight, acne-ridden recruits struggling to do push-ups as some wide-brimmed, hat-wearing, muscular man is crouched over them wailing at the top of his lungs.

So while these few girls struggled to get into the push-up position correctly, the rest of us waited, and waited, and waited some more, until our arms and chests would sting and our backs began to weaken and sway to the ground until our RDC was satisfied.

In all actuality, I felt that I fell *out* of shape in boot camp. However, it didn't matter if I went into Navy boot camp in the best shape of my life - it still hurt. "They" found a way to make it hurt. That was their job. I found comfort in repeating to myself, "They cannot kill us. They cannot kill us…" It would have been a liability, and made the government look bad.

As the Marines love to say, pain is weakness leaving the body. I found this mantra to be true. They pushed us to the painful limit. They wanted us to realize that giving up was not an option. I learned to look for my extra wind. It was always there. And to know that what doesn't kill you only makes you stronger. Except for sharks. Sharks can kill you.

I was in division #324. I will never forget that number. It was drilled into my head enough all day and all night. It was an entire female division of about 90-some women. Same amount of kids that were in my high school graduating class, 90-something. Of course this number went down as the weeks went on. Girls were being sent home for random things every day. Testing positive on drug tests from pot they smoked the day before they left. "Surprise" pregnancies. Physical ailments they tried to hide. Mental ailments they tried to hide. Many learned the hard way that it was important not to smoke pot, and have unpro-tected sex the day before they left for boot camp. They also learned that if they tried to hide the fact that they were bipolar with a wooden leg - the truth usually revealed itself.

Some girls were caught having sex in the laundry room with our 'brother' division members as they just found it impossible to remain celibate for the nine weeks of boot camp. Some pretended they were insane. Some of them actually were insane. Some just preferred to take scissors with them everywhere they went for protection. Others liked to do crafts.

We were told that they were going to have criminal records for the rest of their lives because they had already signed their contract. We were told they wouldn't even get a job at McDonalds because they have some kind of deal with the government and won't hire anyone who breached their enlistment contract. The truth is, we were "told" a lot of things.

Just as the movies show, they shaved the guys' hair and chopped the girls' to their shoulders. I thought I had it taken care of before I left, but apparently I didn't chop it short or crooked enough - so they proceeded to chop it even shorter for me. It was rumored that the barbers they used in boot camp were actually prison barbers who were paid in Skittles. The more girls they made cry, the more

Skittles they would get. It was always best to go to skinny barbers for this reason.

Afterward, I looked in the mirror, and I had a huge chunk that they had just decided to leave uncut. I deduced that this was part of the "get her to cry" plan. So that night, I crept into the bathroom while everyone was sleeping; I took my own scissors and chopped that chunk off. Along with several more chunks. It made a world of difference - my head no longer appeared to be lop-sided. *Let's see who's crying now!*

Sometime right after we got our haircut, and were all checked in, we got our first phone call. How I desperately wanted to talk to someone from home. I just wanted my mom. I knew she was sick with worry. I called the clinic where she worked, and she wasn't at her desk. I asked them to page her quickly. Thank goodness the nurses at the Clinic knew me, and how desperate my mom was to hear from me (an advantage of a small town). Luckily, she was there in about a minute. Now, this phone call was originally limited to about two minutes, and when I only had one minute left to talk to someone I loved for the next nine weeks, we said a lot of "I love yous" and "be strongs" and "don't worrys." We did not want it to end, but we did not know what to talk about because we did not want to get into any stories and be cut-off. And then, when we were least expecting it, the phone is silent in the middle of a sentence.

A couple of weeks later we were permitted another phone call. This one was about 5 minutes long. I was able to get a hold of my little sisters who chatted away about everything that was going on back home. There I sat with tears pouring down my face, just nodding and listening to their sweet voices. The same ones that used to drive me crazy just weeks before. Now I was so happy to talk to them, and also so sad not to be able to talk to my mom.

Finally, in sheer desperation about a week later, I lied. I made up a story to my RDC. I said there were problems with my bank statement that I received in the mail, and I needed to get a hold of my mom to tell her what to do about it. I felt as guilty as a Scandinavian Catholic, as there are few times in life I tell a flat-out lie, but I just *had* to talk to my mom. Even more so, I knew she needed to talk to me.

So, again, I called her at work. And again, one of the nurses ran off to find her. I had interrupted everyone's work so that she could talk to me, from a place that felt like the other side of the world. I have no idea what we talked about that day, but I do know that it gave me enough strength to get through the next few weeks that followed.

Welcome to the Navy

In boot camp, if we had somewhere to go, we were marching. It was our only form of transportation. And God, how we marched. We marched until our feet blistered, and our arches fell. We marched despite whatever the weather may be. In winter, they marched in the frigid temperatures of Northern Chicago. Because it was in the dead of summer when we were there, we marched in weather that was hotter than the blazes of hell, wearing long-sleeve, button-down shirts, and our heavy, leather boots - no matter the season. As we marched, the hot sweat would drip down our brow and stain our shirts with perspiration. The white t-shirts soon grew brown in the neckline and armpits. We marched on scorching blacktop where the sun beat down all day. We prayed to God for the wind to just blow just any short burst, because when it did, it caressed our burnt skin and danced across our body, leaving the most euphoric relief - if only for a second.

The government had ownership over our body. It was no longer our own property. We were lined up and given vaccinations, much like cattle on a beef farm herded through cattle chutes for branding. They were given to us via air gun and we were warned not to jump less it would cut chunks out of our skin. There really was no way of telling what they were injecting us with. I'm sure they told us, but it could have very well been Silly Putty for all we knew. We were not to concern ourselves with these details. As one would expect, the shots hurt. They were blasting Silly Putty through our skin with the same amount of air pressure used to cut cement. But thankfully, as the RDCs are extremely thoughtful and caring of our wellbeing, they made us do lots of push-ups later to work the poison into our body nicely.

As tradition would have it, we were able to visit the gas chamber one lucky day. That was the day I had the clearest sinuses that I have ever had in my life. As we were rolled into the chamber with our gasmasks on, I was comfortable. Other than the rubber backing on the gasmask pinching my hair, I was doing well. Then they told us to take it off. And then the RDC (still comfortably in his mask) went around asking us to say our name and birthday.

I knew the RDC would not allow anyone to leave without putting on a coughing and gagging show, so the kids that tried to be slick and hold their breath ever so cautiously only made things much longer and painful for themselves. I learned quickly what was expected, to blend in and survive. And it sucked. And burned. And drained every face fluid I had. As I ran outside into the grass to join the rest of the recruits, all I wanted to do was wipe the snot off of my chin, but every part of me had been contaminated with the gas, so I knew it would only burn worse upon contact. So there I sat in the grass with snot and tears running down my face. And I could not do anything about it.

I found that once-a-week shaving on Sundays just didn't cut it for my dark hair. So I'd have my nightly rituals. At night, when everyone would be in bed, I would get up and go into the bathroom to shave my legs and armpits. I learned how to shave without water.

I would also go into the bathroom and write letters or in my journal if I needed the light. It was the only alone time I had, and I used it as much as possible. Of course this may be why I fell asleep marching the next morning, but I needed some time to myself to save my sanity. I'm sure many of the girls who would see me wander off into the bathroom for an hour every night assumed I had some form of IBS, but at the time, I really didn't care.

I was surprised to find out how many people lie about their ability to swim. This is not the same as covering up the fact that they love disco. They could hide Afro wigs and bell bottoms in their drawers. They could not hide the fact that they float like a cinder block. The thing is, there are three other branches of the military that they could have joined without being a swimmer. I simply could not understand why someone that could not swim would choose to join the Navy and be on a big floating city on the water for months at a time?

Additionally surprising was how many people would not own up to it right before their body made contact with the water. As if they thought today would be the day a miracle would happen, and they would just begin doing the breast-stroke across the pool. This did not happen. They sunk and a diver would come along and have to fish them out of the pool.

Breaking Down

I knew there would be yelling. I knew there would be push-ups. However, I was not prepared for the mind games that boot camp presented. Breaking us down to build us back up - their way. I knew it would happen, however, I just didn't expect it to be so darn depressing. Anyone can tell you that having a baby is hard. You believe them; however, you really don't 'get' the pushing-a-three-ton-boulder-up-a-hill-while-being-punched-in-the-face idea of hard until you have a baby yourself. But it wasn't until much later that I could see how it was all part of the process.

Sheila was my bunkmate and we instinctively looked after each other. She was also the first black person I had ever met. I had seen African Americans before on TV or when we drove down to "The Cities." I didn't have an ounce of discrimination, because I had no reason to. I never had to fight the white/black wars. If anything, Sheila was a novelty. I marveled at her gorgeous cocoa-colored skin. I wanted to touch it-to feel if it really was different.

We became best friends during those transforming nine weeks. And I did eventually touch her skin. But it wasn't as awkward as it sounds. I was holding her ankles during sit-ups, helping her up from the ground, or slapping her face when she made me angry. That last part never really happened. She was lucky. Of course, her skin didn't feel any different, and after a short time I didn't even notice that it was a different color.

Although she came from the South and I was as northern as they came - we were the same. Except for two things. She spoke funny. Not as funny as the girl from Missouri - but still, it was funny.

The second difference was that her hair was very unlike my own. I came to learn that on the day our RDC broke Sheila. She had beautiful, classy looking braids in her hair that grew slightly below collar length. Collar length was the limit. One day, the RDC came by and said she had better have them pinned up at all times. For the most part she did, but after marching in the grueling heat all day long, a couple would slip out. I don't know if the RDC was in a bad mood that particular day or not, but he suddenly ordered her to take them all out.

Reluctantly doing as she was instructed, Sheila began struggling to unbraid these perfect strands of shiny, coal-colored hair. Soon the tears began quietly seeping down her cheeks. Strand by strand, her hair began to fall into a pile on the floor, leaving just about 2 inches of untamed, frizzy hair. At first I panicked, wondering why her hair was falling out. Soon, two other black girls came by to help her begin the tedious task of unbraiding them all. They didn't seem worried about her hair falling out, so I took their lead and joined the process, learning as we went along.

Tears continued to stream down Sheila's face as she watched her beautiful strands fall. It was heart-wrenching. Her beauty and femininity was being slowly stripped away. I guess that was the point. There was no pride here - not unless it was Navy pride.

I wiped away her tears, and promised that when this was all over, we'd get it fixed together. When we finished, her hair was coarse and unmanageable. It stuck up in every direction and was completely unruly.

And she was beautiful.

Little Things

If there was anything I learned in boot camp, it was to appreciate the little things. I missed out on dessert one time. It ruined my whole day. From that point on I swore to always eat my dessert first. On most occasions, we only had about a two to ten-minute window to wolf down our entire tray of food - depending on where we were at in the line. After boot camp, I never looked at chocolate the same way again. I vowed to never pass up an opportunity to eat it and have remained true to my word.

If I got one letter in the mail, it made my whole day. It didn't matter who it was from - it was something from the outside world. Even if it was a bill, it had been written by someone who cared enough to think of you that day when no one there did. At least that was my theory. Getting a letter is like winning the lottery. Everyone gathers around at the end of the day to see who the lucky winners are going to be.

I had asked everyone I knew if they would write to me while I was away. Friends, family, church, Big John, Little John, the crazy cat-hoarder lady with the porcelain doll collection… I welcomed random letters from friends like they were little treasures. I still have them to this day. However, I will never forget how my mother wrote to me every single day. These letters became my touch of reality, and my happy thought. I also wrote many, and received many letters from my beloved high school sweetheart, Dillon, who was off on the other side of the country, fighting his own battles, just trying to survive Marine boot camp in sunny San Diego.

One day I received a letter from my mom saying that Dillon was having a hard time initially, and that his (DI) Drill Instructor (equivalent to Navy RDCs) had pulled him aside to figure out what was going on. He confessed that he hadn't heard from me in a while (it took forever for me to write initially once I got to boot camp with all of the crazy processing), and he was worried that something had happened. Maybe they had a nice streak in them or something because shockingly, the DI allowed Dillon to make a phone call. Of course, he couldn't call me, but he was able to call my mom and make sure I was okay.

My mom wrote to me, telling me about their conversation that night. It was wonderful to hear how much he missed me, and cared about what I was going through, but at the same time made me worry about him all the greater. It was just sheer grueling for both of us to be going through this at the same time, needing support, and unable to contact each other. What a stupid idea this all was.

During the day I was usually preoccupied, however, nights were always the most difficult. I spent many lonely nights fantasizing of my Pass and Review (graduation) Day, and at last seeing and spending time with my family. I would be a real sailor at last. I'd get to wear a real uniform instead of these blasted dungarees that were from the fall of 1972 collection. I would get to see my family. I would get to eat chocolate. Creamy milk chocolate…

More than anything, every night as I drifted off, I dreamed of the day my love and I would be reunited. I thought often of our future together. I wondered if he was thinking of me in that same moment - looking at the same moon.

I survived in my fantasy world that existed in my head. And my fantasies didn't stop at just love. Oh no, I spent much of the time I was marching (which were often endless hours of the day) in a mechanical daze. Many of my fantasies included listening to music, eating Snickers, and walking barefoot in the grass. Such simple pleasures that were nonexistent in this sea of blue dungarees and boon-dock wearing recruits.

We were cut off from reality. We had no idea what the latest songs or movies were, or what was going on in the news back home. It was an eerie sensation to be in a world so disconnected.

I found comfort in going to church every Sunday. It was the only place where I felt like I was treated like a human. It's the only place I heard music. Sometimes I was even given cookies. Cookie days were the best days. I came to look forward to that cookie all week long. Sometimes the church cookie was in my fantasies. Mostly though, I gained strength there to take me through to the next week.

Volunteering

The day we were all at 'Forward GQ (General Quarters) listening to the RDC speak early on in our training was the day I learned to never again volunteer myself. He began going down a list of certain jobs they needed to fill. Well, I seem to recall specific instructions from someone back home (for all I remember it could've been my local baker) who told me to never volunteer myself for *anything* in boot camp. (Everyone gives you their two cents before you leave.) So when all of these girls began volunteering themselves for these collateral duties, I became very confused. *Didn't they know what they were getting themselves into? Too bad no one told them not to volunteer themselves.* I was so relieved I knew the secret. However, I did tell the girl next to me. I really can't keep a good secret.

After a while though, this list of duties began to drag on and on. People were eagerly volunteering themselves left and right. The RDCs seemed to be genuinely pleased by this. Not sneakily happy either. They actually appeared quite happy for the nice girls volunteering. Soon I began to wonder if I was doing the right thing by keeping my mouth closed and hand down. Maybe I looked unmotivated or lazy. That was absolutely the last thing I wanted to look like. Soon, I couldn't handle the peer pressure anymore and when the RDC read off the next job title, my hand shot up as if it had a mind of its own.

"Maki wants Ship's Staff. Good. What's next?"

Wait a minute. What the heck is Ship's Staff? What had I just done?

Unwelcomed Guests

Soon enough, I found out all about Ship's Staff. We were in charge of maintaining and cleaning the entire 'ship' (or barracks) where we resided. These were the other spaces that weren't specifically assigned to any division (i.e. stairwells, hallways, etc). While I could have thought of dozens of better ways to spend my time, it allowed me to get out of the normal duties everyone else had and kind of broke the monotony of everyday boot camp life.

There was one slight drawback however; being on Ship's Staff you stood Quarter Deck watches. This really wasn't a big deal, and actually presented slightly more action than a regular barracks watch; however, it was more of a "high-profile" job - you could say. You were working around many RDCs, so laying low wasn't much of an option during a Quarter Deck watch. They could randomly come up to you at any time and inspect your uniform, or quiz you on your General Orders. There were sometimes you would find yourself in trouble for things that just may have been beyond your control.

In all situations in life, there are certain people we may encounter that are more - shall we say - difficult to please and/or get along with others. You know the type. They are the kinds of people that no matter what you do for them, they will never be satisfied. Many times we find ourselves bending over backwards to please them any way possible, only to be let down again by their constant disapproval.

Enter RDC Senior Chief Smith. He was a gruff man, with big, muscular arms and walked around as if it hurt to carry them because they were so big. In fact, I think it made him angry. He was also strangely charming - strangely as in you didn't know what it was about him, you really wanted to hate him - but instead you found yourself wanting to please him. Every now and then, there were glimpses of a real human in there. However, he was the most difficult person in the world to make and/or keep happy. All of the recruits feared him, but constantly sought his approval. I swore he was out to get me.

One day I was happily going about my business on one of my routine Quarter Deck watches. [Insert happy humming.] I was ahead of schedule and feeling confident as I had finished all of my duties and would be going off watch soon without a single incident or event to report. (i.e. I did not get yelled at!) So when I checked in with Senior Chief and told him I would be leaving soon and all was done - I was not anticipating what was to follow.

He walked out of his office and began inspecting everything within sight.

This went on for about five minutes as I stood at attention. So far he seemed satisfied and I was relieved when suddenly his course voice broke the silence as he paused in front of a blank wall.

"Seaman Recruit Maki, I thought you told me you had cleaned my Quarter Deck."

"Yes, Senior. I did."

He turned and stared at the blank wall in front of him. "Then what the hell is this?"

I thought to myself, *this guy is going crazy. What in the world is he talking about? He is staring at a blank wall. I don't know what he is expecting me to say right now.*

"Recruit, are you listening to me?" He barked sharply at my silence.

"Yes Sir, I don't know Sir." As soon as I said it, I knew it was wrong and I cringed at my words. *Why was that so hard to remember?*

"Don't call me Sir, dammit! I'm not an officer! I work for a living! Recruit, get over here and tell me what this is!"

Reluctantly and confused as a deaf circus performer, I left my post and scurried over to where he was staring - expecting the worst. I squinted my eyes. Then, in a small corner of the wall I made out the tiniest image of a little black house spider. *What the?* Slowly I stated, "Um, it's a spider, Senior Chief."

"WHAT THE HELL IS A SPIDER DOING ON MY QUARTER DECK SEAMAN RECURIT MAKI?"

What do I say to that? "Ah… he appears to be making a web, Senior Chief."

"SEAMAN RECRUIT MAKI, ARE SPIDERS AUTHORIZED ON MY QUARTER DECK? DID YOU GIVE THIS SPIDER PERMISSION TO COME ABOARD MY SHIP?"

"Ah, no Senior Chief. I did not." *This guy is losing it.*

"Then clearly, he is not authorized to be here. See that you remove this spider from my quarter deck immediately. Carry on." And with that he did an about-face and disappeared back into his office.

I was left unsure of what had just happened. It was a very surreal moment. But as any good sailor would, I did as I was instructed, and removed the spider from the quarter deck. *Stupid spider.*

Yes, Senior Chief Smith was notorious for getting his point across by using forms of humiliation. One day I was 'allegedly' talking in the galley line. In reality, I was simply responding to someone else asking me a question. After all, I wasn't going to be rude. Still, no sooner had I spoken the words, when I could feel his presence behind me like a shadow, with hovering angry energy of doom.

Slowly, and fearfully I turned around, my head hung low, to face his wrath. I allowed my eyes to meet his cold glare.

"You and you," he growled and pointed to me and the skinny boy in front of me that hadn't been talking. "Be in my barracks at 1300," he commanded and was gone before anything else could be spoken.

Holy crap. What had I gotten myself into now? And the boy in front of me! He hadn't even said a single word. He was innocent! And I got him into trouble. *Oh, this was bad. This was very, very bad.* What was I going to do? I was making an innocent man suffer for my incurable talking problem? (Even though I was the answer-er, not the asker - so technically, it wasn't me. Technically.)

I couldn't eat, which was an oddity in itself, since eating was the one thing I completely looked forward to doing every day. When the dreaded hour at last approached, I reluctantly made my way to the boys' barracks, which Senior Chief Smith commanded. When I got there, I saw the skinny boy was already in there. I stood at attention outside of the office, which was horrible since the entire male division was at Forward G.Q., all sitting there cross-legged staring at me. I couldn't have been more self-conscious if I was naked at a communion on Sunday morning.

After what seemed like eons, Senior emerged from the office. Before he could say anything, I blurted out, "Senior, Seaman Recruit So-and-so-skinny-guy wasn't talking. It was only me." *Whew. At least I had a clear conscious - despite whatever punishment I was to get.* Senior Chief Smith came out of his office and stood in front of me. *Don't make eye contact, don't make eye contact,* I told myself as I continued to hold my hundred-yard stare.

I could feel his stare burning down onto my head. I held my breath as his chest was six inches from my face. I was frozen in terror, and as he looked me up and down, my mind was a whirlwind of the worst possible ideas for what was going to happen next. Then, his lips parted and he hissed the most simple, yet painful words I've ever heard. "Both of you - dress left. Dress right. Hold it."

As commanded, Skinny Guy and I extended our arms out to our sides, parallel to the floor. And then we held it, in front of 90-some guys from Senior Chief's male division. And it wasn't bad. I didn't have too much difficulty doing this. *Shoot, if he thought this was punishment...*

He then turned and walked passed us, and proceeded to teach the division a lesson out of their workbooks. So Skinny Guy and I stood there, in front of the male division, like pathetic idiots, and listened, as they all would occasionally steal a glance up at us. I was unsure if they were sympathetic at our humiliation tactic, or were trying to contain their amusement. And just when I started to care about looking like an idiot, the pain decided to kick in. Seconds turned into minutes, and our arms began to burn and weaken. After what felt like hours, but in reality was probably only ten minutes, our arms began to shake. Oh, how they burned as they shook uncontrollably.

Finally, as we stood there pathetically shaking our weakened arms, we felt the senior chief had taken pity on us. He paused his lesson long enough to look over at us and order, "Arms down."

Heaven have mercy, it was the most euphoric feeling to relieve our arms at last. For about ten seconds I thought he really wasn't too bad of a guy. All those rumors of what a hard-ass he was. That wasn't too unbearable after all. Then, after about fifteen seconds had passed, he simply commanded, "Push-up position. Get there."

Was he joking? I don't think I said that aloud, but my face must have said it all, because with my hesitation the senior chief yelled, "GET THERE!"

I dropped to the floor quicker than a prom dress. My arms were already weak and it did not take long before they began to shake again. I locked my elbows into place as I soon realized our punishment was not over yet. *He can't kill me, he can't kill me.* I kept repeating in my head. Five minutes had passed. My pelvis began swaying to the floor.

I looked over at Skinny Guy. He didn't look like he was suffering. For some reason this motivated me. I refused to give up before him. *Well if Skinny Guy can do it, I can surely do it!* I put myself in another place and just felt the pain. I acknowledged it, but did not quit. It was in that moment I learned really how far you can push yourself. I just kept repeating to myself, "This too shall pass, this too shall pass..."

I'm not sure how much time had passed, but at last, because nothing lasts forever, the Senior Chief called us to attention. We popped tall and stood at attention.

"You're not going to talk in line again are you Seaman Recruit Maki?"

"No, Senior Chief."

"Dismissed, both of you."

We quickly scurried out of there, and I kept my promise.

Sometimes you don't realize how good it feels to not be in pain, until you are in pain.

A couple of hours every Sunday afternoon were awarded to us to use as our own "free" time with various options of how to make use of it. During this time, we could write home, get caught up on exciting stuff like our studies of US Navy customs or history, or memorizing our General Orders.

We could even use Sundays to get caught up on our ironing. Good stuff. We were not allowed to take naps - even though that is all we wanted to do - however, we soon learned little tricks of the trade. One in particular was how we would pretend to be fixing the sheets underneath our lower bunk, and actually take a nap under our bed on the floor. That way if an RDC walked in and began yelling (to which we would quickly wake up), we could recover ourselves nicely.

How could someone sleep on a cement floor under a bunk bed without a pillow or covers? Quite peacefully, actually. The same way one could fall asleep sitting straight up in a chair during classroom trainings, or at the breakfast table - face in eggs. I saw it all and did it all. The one that blows my mind to this day is the time that I fell asleep marching. Yes, marching. My head began to nod off and I missed a step. Fortunately, as I was falling to the ground and out of rank, I was slapped back into reality by a loud whistle. Being in the middle rows protected me from the ass-whipping I would have no doubt experienced had I been caught sleeping. While marching. The sleep deprivation experienced in boot camp is unlike anything I had ever experienced before.

On one particular Sunday, a couple of the girls spontaneously put together a little singing routine to the old classic Tina Turner version of "Rolling on the River." It took us all a moment to make sense of this strangely pleasant noise coming from their lips. *Is that... music?* It had been so long. Their goofy dance moves and over-singing soon had all of us in stitches. Suddenly, out of nowhere, it occurred to me that this foreign expression that randomly appeared on my face was a smile. My lips cracked at the new formation. I hadn't smiled in about three weeks. It was a very strange and sad realization. I had forgotten what it was like to have a sense of humor. I used to be funny. I used to goof around with my friends all of the time. I had just been in survival mode these past weeks. I had lost myself.

I decided to turn the radio in my head back on. Oh yeah. I have a radio in my head. Sometimes it plays two songs at once.

I began to hum or sing to myself whenever I was out of earshot of an RDC. I played little games, and somewhat became my own best friend just to keep myself company when we weren't allowed to talk to others. And yes, I questioned if I was going crazy on a few occasions. However, I told myself it was simply a survival mechanism. I learned that everyone has to become their own friend when they move away from home, and experience just what stale loneliness is.

Turning Point

At the end of week 7, there is one summarizing event where in a matter of 12 hours, sailors-to-be are tested on everything that has been taught up to that point called Battle Stations. It's the end-all, be-all. Fish or cut bait. Cut the loose ties. You get the drift. Upon completion of this whopper-size accomplishment, a recruit will have the ceremonious crossover from a "Recruit" ball cap to earning their "Navy" ball cap. A sign of respect around those parts. Aside from graduation, this is the next prevalent event for a young sailor-to-be during the boot camp progression.

The entire evolution begins right around the time one is about to fall asleep - that phase where one is just coming into a delusional crossover into the dreamworld phase. About an hour after taps a siren will sound, "All hands! Man your battle stations!" indicating that the simulated shipboard attack is about to happen.

The recruits are sprung into action, and never stop moving from that moment forward. The entire night is spent testing everything learned about survival swimming, first aid and safety procedures, fire-fighting, rifle shooting, and damage control, to name a few. All of this is performed to the highest standard under intense conditions - always with an emphasis on teamwork. Over the next 12 hours in a massive hands-on exercise, we feigned a wartime scenario, testing endurance, fortitude, and stamina. This test was one that carried over into many of life's situations - digging deeper, finding the extra "umph" inside to push through sheer exhaustion.

The next morning we were delightfully rewarded with pizza and pop - a "real people food" – a break from all of the dull flavored cafeteria food. It never tasted so wonderful.

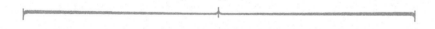

Graduation

Finally, after nine excruciating weeks, which felt like decades in a prison, our day had finally come. It was a moment of truth. It was our day of release out into the world after our sentence had been dutifully filled. We were like a bride awaiting her wedding day, a mother anticipating the birth of her child, or maybe more of a primitive convict anxiously awaiting his voyage back into civilized society.

Never before in my life did the sun shine so bright (it nearly stung my eyes), or the birds sing so beautifully. *Did they always have birds here in Great Lakes?*

I didn't recall ever hearing them make a peep before this day. After nine weeks of dreaming and in-depth fantasizing of how this day would go, it had, at last, arrived to me overnight.

I woke up that morning feeling like it was Christmas, and I was five years old again. We all were giddy with excitement. We were graduating today, and would be official United States Sailors. We were leaving this place once and for all! In a matter of hours, we would be at last reuniting with our families and loved ones. In a matter of a few more hours we would be eating chocolate, smoking cigarettes, and some of the girls would be having the sweetest sex of their lives.

Some were singing, and all were jabbering about future plans. There was an electric buzz in the air as we painted our faces with make-up, curled our hair, and began to pack our belongings together. It felt like we were a group of girlfriends getting ready together for the prom, or a night on the town. For the first time in 2 ½ months, we recognized ourselves in the mirror. We looked around, and saw each other as beautiful women instead of cloned puppets, which had been just marching through the motions for so long.

Then at the last moment we donned our Dress White uniform, slowly, and carefully, not to mess up our hair or get any make-up on the crisp whiteness of the brand new threads. I diligently placed my cover on my head to complete the uniform. And as I looked in the mirror, for the first time I saw the picture of a United States Sailor looking back at me. The uniform didn't come at an easy price, but for that reason, it was worn with incredible pride.

With a bounce in our step, we marched off to the graduating hangar where we had rehearsed so many times before. The audience began to scream, cry, and cheer upon their first glance of us. It had been a long nine weeks away, and now we had come back as changed people. Nothing could bring us down today.

We marched into the building, and fell into formation while the Navy Band played its patriotic songs. To my right, the bleachers were a blur of cheering families. Although I couldn't see them, I knew mine was out in that crowd somewhere and it gave me a shiver of excitement to know I'd be face-to-face with them in just a short while.

The performing units twirled their rifles and put on the show of their lives - the one they had been rehearsing for weeks now - as they marched in. Soon *The Star Spangled Banner* began to play. For a moment, it was a completely new song - one that I had never heard before. Our flag was led in by the color guard. And as I looked at it, I suddenly realized that it was a flag that I didn't recognize. Sure, it was a song I had heard and a flag that I had seen before every sporting event in high school, but all of a sudden, I was looking at it in a new light. From that moment on, I knew I was changed.

I stood at an uncomfortable parade rest. "Don't lock your knees, don't lock your knees." I repeated to myself as a few random sailors would pass out. As my feet began to ache and my shoulders became sore for holding a position for long, I took a moment just to pause and absorb what was going on around me. I was completely surrounded by my fellow sailors. Men and women in their whitest dress white uniforms. Most of them straight out of high school, from all around the country, with only one thing uniting them - the desire to serve. For whatever reason initially brought us into the Navy - be it an adventure and travel, in need of direction in life, money, or even to escape a gang, the underlying requirement was that we were there to serve and defend our country. We had more pride in the United States of America at that moment than some may have their whole life. Her freedom was ours to defend against enemies foreign and domestic. Our lives were not our own, but were owned by every person in the country. We were united here for a cause that was bigger than us, or bigger than anything we understood.

We were not doing anything new, as this graduation ceremony was performed nearly every week of the year. It is also performed weekly in all of the other branches of service. Thousands of soldiers, sailors, airmen, and Marines were graduated weekly and had been for hundreds of years. Nearly five decades ago, my grandfathers had felt this moment, numerous great uncles, and two of my great aunts! What pioneers they must have been for their time.

As the Navy Band played on, we were released to find our families. I took a second to just breathe in the moment as the arena was filled with families full of tears and pride, for our past nine-week journey had been theirs as well. My sisters, mom, and dad had all driven out and we were able to spend an entire weekend together. I don't remember much about where we went, but I do remember just being together. I slept a lot, walked barefoot in the grass, and ate all the chocolate that my mom had brought for me.

CHAPTER 4

Deer River - a Background

Before I tell you anything else, I think you need to first fully understand the uniqueness of the itty-bitty logging town, where I grew up, called Deer River, Minnesota. Deer River, population 903, is a small, bustling town that thrives off of its fabulously successful fishing and hunting seasons. Tourism brings in people in from all over the country. There are more churches than gas stations, but an equal ratio of churches to bars and liquor stores (as does every hard-working Midwestern town). It is a very close-knit town where the citizens look out for each other, almost too well sometimes. When anyone is in a crisis - whether it be needing a surgery, had a home fire, or a loss of any sort, the whole town unites and does a fund-raiser spaghetti dinner at the local VFW, takes up a collection at the local Cenex (gas) station to get them back on their feet - or just cooks them a great hot dish. In Elementary school, we all brought pennies to school until a young girl had enough money to receive an organ transplant. When it was a success, we celebrated the life-saving accomplishment together! A few years later our town raised enough money for another child to receive a liver transplant. And when that surgery was not successful, we grieved together as a community. Everyone just takes care of each other.

When they say "it takes a village to raise a child," this is the type of village they were talking about. Everyone knows everyone, and everyone is always up in your business. This made it extremely difficult to get away with anything as a child. Or a teenager. Especially when the cops are good family friends. It was an exceptionally safe town, where the biggest crime was vandalism and bad fashion, but I never would have given it a second thought to walk down the street by myself after midnight - you know, if I suddenly had the urge to go for a midnight stroll singing "Buffalo Girls" and dragging my stick along a picket fence. If there was anything to be concerned about, it wasn't getting mugged or abducted, but Old Man Jenkins yelling at you because you're making his dog howl.

On the other hand, perhaps some would be concerned with becoming a tasty, tasty dinner to a bear or wolf. Nah, I'm just kidding. As my dad always said, they are more afraid of you than you are of them. Unless, of course, you are in a chicken suit slathered in fish guts. Then you should be afraid. Mostly because that is a weird thing to do, but then again, so is singing "Buffalo Girls" at midnight on a street corner.

Deer River was the type of town where I could walk into the drugstore, hardware store, auto shop, or gas station, slap something on the counter and say with a smile, "charge it to my dad" and walk out. Of course they knew who my dad was, where we lived, the business he owned, and that the bill would be paid - after my dad rightfully yelled at me for charging $20 of Jolly Ranchers to his account.

My mom worked at "The Clinic" (the only clinic in town) - so no chance of medical confidentiality for me. For a *random* example - there was no way I would ever be able to get birth control pills without my mom knowing. And let's just say if I did *hypothetically* manage to sneak in and out of there unnoticed by her - later every other nurse innocently enough would be letting her know that I just had stopped in that day and talk about what a fabulous, amazing, beautiful, charming young lady I was becoming.

The doctor that my mom worked with for 20 years was the same doctor who delivered me, and virtually every kid in that town. His name was Dr. Goodall and he treated everyone from babies to grandparents. He was an OBGYN/bone-setter/skin rash identifier/allergist/"Dr-I-have-this-growth" all rolled into one. He was revered as a god, but remained humble to his bones. There wasn't a person alive that this man wouldn't help if they were in need. He fixed my bones, stitched my wounds, and gave me Grape-nuts cereal because it was my favorite and too expensive for us to keep in the house. I was never afraid to go to the hospital, as he and all of the wonderful nurses were like a second family. It was a second home to me.

There were only two schools in town - an elementary school that ranged from kindergarten to 6th grade, and the High School which went from 7th to 12th grade. High school football players were local celebrities, letter jackets were worn with pride, and when someone referred to having a pow-wow, it was in fact, an actual pow -wow, as we were honored to be called The Deer River War-riors as we were taught Minnesota's Native American history.

The football coach was also our science teacher, who was married to a lady that worked at the clinic with my mom, whose daughter was one of my best friends, and on, and on. It was the same school my dad, uncles, aunts and cous-ins had all gone to. You were known by your family name and your reputation preceded you. I came from a long line of Finlanders that had an unnatural fear of large grasshoppers and other creatures that jumped. (Refer to St. Urho- it's a *real* thing.) The teachers all had you pegged before you even walked into a class - especially if you had an older sibling or cousin to pave the way. Thankfully, I was the oldest Maki sister and did not have to follow in my sister's footsteps (af-ter all, the next one in line was the crazy one - whose fear of crickets and cotton balls was both alarming and entertaining.)

We were taught a mandatory gun safety class in 6th grade and the first day of deer hunting season is still considered a holiday. The schools are closed, as they would have been otherwise empty. We hunted for food, not for sport. We respected guns and knew they were not toys from the time we could walk. We had chores to survive, not as a punishment. We built fires to stay warm - not to play with or cause trouble. We dressed for warmth, not for fashion. We plugged in our cars every night in the winter - not because they were electric - but to keep the oil warm so it would start in the morning. Life continued to function during a blizzard, when we received a few feet of snow, or as the temps dropped below negative 30 or more. We would just put on our 'packs' (boots), and our 'chop-pers' (leather and wool gloves), and jump in rusted out four-wheel drive pick-ups - because the world did not wait for the snow to stop, *don't ya know*.

Our local newspaper, *The Western Itasca Review,* kept the town posted as to what every adult, every student, every church, and every organization was doing. The list of those who made the honor-role was published in the paper quarterly. Weekly we rejoiced over the town's births and mourned over the obituary sec-tion. And if you were arrested for smashing someone's mailbox with your pet rock "Stanley," well that would be in the paper too. (Just in case the town's peo-ple hadn't already heard it from their neighbors.) People were always watching. It was very important to keep yourself in check. This included what you wore, who you hung out with, and where your car was at 2:00am last Saturday.

The local cops were only kept busy by giving speeding tickets and busting underage drinking at parties. So any time someone threw a party in high school, the goal was to find the most remote area, 20 miles out of town in hopes that they would remain undiscovered. These usually occurred in fields, gravel pits, or just plain out in the woods, virtually in the middle of nowhere. When teenagers were busted by the cops (which it seemed like *every* time they would find us - er - them) their biggest worry would be getting lost in the woods, eaten alive by mosquitoes - or worse! It was not as easy of a decision to make - get eaten by a wolf - or go to jail. We lost many good, drunken teens to wolves in them days.

Coming from a small town, there was not a lot to do for entertainment. Other than throwing parties or going to the movies in Grand Rapids, which was the next town over (at least *they* had a movie theater). One of the biggest kicks we got as kids was to go to the dump - which literally was an open hole that people 'dumped' their trash in. (Of course this changed later on when environmental regulations came into effect.) We would watch (from the safety of our cars) as the black bears rifled through the trash. As long as you did not feed them, you were *fairly* safe and they would provide hours of entertainment. It was like Animal Planet for free - before there was an Animal Planet. Or cable TV.

The bears, wolves, deer, and the rest of nature were just part of our everyday life. My dad taught me to drive (when I was 13 or so) on the country roads right down the middle so that you had extra swerving time should a deer jump out in front of you. There were two types of drivers in Deer River, those that had hit deer with their car, and those that would.

As for the bears and wolves, they didn't make their presence known as well as the deer did, but they were always roaming around in the woods (reference the dump story). One could hear the wolves howling in the woods on ominous winter nights while lying quietly in bed - especially after they made a kill. It was both haunting and amazing.

One day, my poor grandma was taking a nap on our living room sofa while we were all at school and work. She awoke to a massive black bear standing on his hind legs, peering deviously into the living room bay window at her. No doubt the bear was sizing my grandmother up, slightly intimidated by her Scandinavian biceps, wondering if it would be worth the risk to swipe a jar of honey that sat on the floor next to the sofa. (We always kept our jar of honey on the floor next to the sofa.) So as if it were routine, we called the Forest Service and they came out and set up a sizeable live trap in our driveway. However, the awkward entity must have sat there for several weeks without a single event. (Not counting the afternoon I coaxed my sisters in there, promising it to be a secret cave full of magical stones and green elves.) But the most excitement it received was the day I backed my car into it.

You see, on occasion, I may have had a *slight* problem remembering to look behind me when I backed-up a time or two. A temporary lapse in memory - if you will. In addition to that, I may have deposited a teensy dent on either side of our garage door (maybe even twice). And despite the fact that I was voted "craziest driver" in our high school hall of fame, I did turn out to be quite a responsible driver much later - *especially* when I am going forward. I digress - but this will come into play later.

I grew up on my family's 40-acre farm set outside of Deer River in the deep northern woods. People may think of Deer River as isolated. Considering that our house was actually 14 miles outside of Deer River up in Suomi (Finnish for "Finland"). It redefined the term "middle of nowhere."

Suomi was a community made up of several homesteads that had been established in the late 1800s, mainly by Finlanders. At one time Suomi consisted of a gas station, post office, a one-room school house, and a church. The church, which is known as *Suomi Lutheran Church,* remains and is made up of the warmest, eccentric group of Scandinavians one would ever meet. It is full of names like Anttila, Huju, Rikalas, Wehvilainen, Juntunen, Saari, Aho, Salo and Mackley. These people would give you the shirt off their back if you so needed, but often (especially the men) would remain somewhat standoffish from showing their affection. They were a tough, hardworking, made-from-scratch Midwestern breed that had seen much in their day. They hauled wood every winter to stay warm, shoveled snow, and canned fruits from their gardens every year. They knew life was about survival - and if they didn't take care of things, there wasn't going to be anyone coming behind them to do it for them.

The people of Suomi also remained extremely traditional and did not like to incorporate much change. A long time ago, a new pastor had come and preached his first sermon. He happened to go ten minutes over the one-hour mark of the usual services. The following week, he was warmly greeted by a brand-new clock hanging at the back of the church - within perfect view for the pastor to see throughout the service, thus to ensure punctuality at all times. Midwesterners are generally quite punctual. It would be rude to keep someone waiting.

While the faces of the church change throughout the years, the sense of community and acceptance remains the same - as if to always welcome its guests and members home with outstretched arms. The walls emanate a low, nourishing whisper, speaking, "Come to me. Come, lay before me your burdens, and you shall be freed." There is something indescribably transforming about going to this church. Like having a mother's home-cooked meatloaf for the first time after moving away. (Unless it was my mother's meatloaf.) In an instant, one is filled with strength and a sense of renewal upon entering these doors. I find myself drifting back to this place many times throughout the years as times have been difficult. I found out later that another one of my friends who used to go to church here as a child would return here for some mental tranquility after fight-ing in the Iraq/Afghanistan War. The church's healing powers are great and have served to nurture many generations in its 100 years of life.

Our house that we grew up in was very small, built by the hands of my great-grandfather. My dad later constructed our two-story garage with the help of a few of his friends. The garage was a huge 3-car garage and actually towered over the house. Yes, in Minnesota the garages are often bigger than the homes. (In his defense, he did own an excavating business.) It wasn't until after I moved away that I realized most people's garages were not generally bigger than their homes. There once was a smaller garage on the property, but my mom acci-dentally burnt it down. She had been burning the garbage on a windy day and somehow a spark got away from her. We burned all of our paper garbage. I also thought that's what everyone did. Turns out they recycle. It's probably safer that way. This was a good example of such.

Our home was a shabby house built of wood, but full of history as it sat sit-uated on a hill overlooking the glassy, serene Maki Lake. Maki Lake was named after my great-grandfather Oscar Haapamaki. My grandfather later shortened the last name to Maki.

The lake was set so deep in the valley of the hills that its rich complexion seldom was rippled by the wind. Rolling hay fields that bloomed of snow-white daisies in the spring surrounded the lake. The outer perimeter of the property was sheltered by government land that was densely thickened with evergreens and birch. The woods spilled of wildlife and ached for thinning in the autumn, for which the local hunters were always eager to volunteer. The scenery was extraordinary and incomparable. One truly had to see it, smell it, and feel it beneath your bare feet to fully appreciate it. Growing up, my two sisters and I had no idea just how spoiled by nature we really were.

You see, Deer River isn't just a town on a map somewhere in the middle of nowhere. (Although one may think so if they are just passing through.) Deer River is the definition of a small town anywhere in the United States. It's a place where people matter and are remembered. It opens up its arms to its people and creates a shelter around them. I grew up always feeling safe (with the exception of the wolves and Old Man Jenkins, of course.) It was a feeling I took for granted - and didn't realize just how precious it was - how fortunate that all of my needs were met here. Well, every need except the deep longing to see what the rest of the world was like. I wanted to learn all about it. I had seen a tiny glimpse of the beauty the world had to offer - and I could not wait to see more.

CHAPTER 5

Approximate distance from Deer River: 1420 miles.

After the liberty weekend with our family was over, (to which I was in a sleep-deprived haze, because I don't remember much about that weekend) a group of us on orders all flew down to Pensacola, Florida, in our best dress whites uniform. It was somewhere between arriving at the airport and waiting for our shuttle bus to base that I experienced another little freak-out moment.

I ran to the nearest payphone and called my mom collect - slightly excited that I had rights to use a phone again. Yay for personal freedoms! It was in that moment (strangely enough) that panic set in. I began to shake as the magnitude of the trip became a reality. I quickly informed my mother that she must drive down here to Florida from Minnesota and get me. While I had spent my entire senior year preparing for boot camp, I guess I never really thought too extensively about what comes *after* boot camp. While I knew this was the ultimate goal, everything ahead of me suddenly seemed so vast and unattainable. How was I ever going to survive all of the schools, tests, and trials that lay ahead of me?

Eventually, my mother talked reason into me, as she always does, and explained to me why it wouldn't be the best idea to go AWOL. (Absent Without Leave - a big no-no in the military. They will lock you in the brig and only feed you bread and water. Oh yes, and you will be kicked out and not be able to get a job even at McDonalds.) Reluctantly, I decided to stay and just get on the shuttle bus to go to the base. I was convinced I still had a choice. I literally had to take it one step at a time to not get overwhelmed by what was to come.

Finally, our driver arrived outside of the Pensacola terminal and ushered us all to the dingy, white van that smelled of basement musk with hard leather seats that were sticky to the touch.

I stepped out of the airport into the September Florida air for the first time. For anyone who has not grown up in Florida, the first time you step on Florida ground is something to remember. The sweltering, humid air smacks you in the face. The humidity instantly fills up your lungs making it hard to catch a refreshing breath of air. Every pore on your body fills up with sweat and instantaneously you're soaked with more perspiration than a narcoleptic pilot.

Now, you must understand that I love summer weather more than anything - it's something we lived for - for all of three months out of the year in Minnesota. However, the only time I had ever felt air this sickeningly hot before was in a sauna - and that was always quickly refreshed by a quick dip in a 30-40 degree, half-iced lake. *People live in this weather every day?* I was in disbelief. For survival reasons only, I decided then and there that I must learn to love hot weather.

We drove to the base and my eyes were glued to the window the whole time, taking in this foreign land known simply as… "Florida." The houses were all adobe-colored with stucco roofs. Grass was yellowed, but flowers were gigantic, in every vibrant color, and in every yard. There were so many species I had never even seen before. Spectacular palm trees were in abundance every direction making it feel like a tropical island. Flip-flops were the only visible foot covering of people walking on the sidewalks. People walked around in bikinis on the side of the road. Everyone wore bikinis - whether they were 300 lbs or 80 years old. It didn't matter. People didn't have driveways - they parked their cars right on their front yard. And what was with the pink flamingos in every yard? I instantly felt like I was on vacation in some foreign land. I pretended for that moment that I was in a sweet escape being ushered to my five-star hotel in the back of a limo. Except that I wasn't. It was a land in which the drivers were rude and aggressive. It was clearly an eat or be eaten freeway. I'd never seen anything like it all my 18 years.

We drove onto the NATTC Pensacola base (Naval Aviation Training Technical Center) and over to the semi-secluded NACCS side (Naval Aircrew Candidate School). At last, the shuttle van came to a halt and we were all let out in front of a building with a wraparound porch and giant white pillars framing the entryway. The biggest eye-catcher though was the huge set of Aircrew wings that were largely and strategically attached to the front of the building directly over the entrance. No one who entered or walked by the building would miss them. They were iconic symbols to remind us every day what we were really here for.

Those that already wore their own pair were viewed as celebrities around these parts.

There were three girls, including myself, and about seven guys that all arrived together. It was then as we had unpacked all of our green canvas seabags from the van and turned to face the "wings of gold" that the driver said to us, "Gentlemen, and ladies, welcome to your new home."

The Ocean

When I finally settled, I decided to explore my new surroundings. Pensacola was the most beautiful base I had ever seen. Granted, it was only the second one I had seen, but it blew Great Lakes out of the water. I couldn't get enough of the palm trees and magnolia trees that lined the walk-ways. The southern parameter of the base was lined with a sea-wall of cemented stone, holding up the base from entering none other than the Gulf of Mexico itself. On either end of the seawall, there was an actual sandy beach!

It was my first time seeing the ocean in person and I was instantly hooked - it was my heroin. Of course I've never done heroin. Maybe I wouldn't like it at all. Okay, it was my ice cream. I couldn't get enough of it. It was just like in the movies - only much more vast and thunderous. The color of baby-blue was gentle and infinite as it met the sky on the horizon. The sand was like a white, sticky sugar besieged sporadically by darkened seaweeds that had washed ashore. Sand crabs scurried along a short distance before quickly vanishing into their sinister little holes. The waves crashed up onto the beach one after another and then would fade into the sand, leaving behind dancing sparkles. I suddenly couldn't help but feel a bit more wee and humble.

I longed to touch the water, as it beckoned to me, but that was an impossible task to execute without getting my immaculate shoes and socks wet. Here I was, trying to keep my whites clean, and my shoes snooty and polished at the beach. It was a lost cause that I quickly forfeited. My socks became drenched with the next unexpected wave - but I was at least able to touch the sea this time.

I was amazed at its warmth. It felt like bath water. Granted, it was the end of summer in Florida in the Gulf, but you couldn't get water like this in any of the 10,000 lakes in Minnesota. It was fascinating. And then, I couldn't help myself. I had to see if the stories were true. I quickly glanced around to ensure the coast was clear. Bringing my hand to my lips, I tasted the water that was dripping off my fingers. *Oh my gosh- it was actually salty!* It was salty like the kind of normal salt you'd have at the table - not like the kind of salt you sprinkle to melt icy sidewalks. (That kind is gross - don't try to eat it) I was thoroughly impressed and awestruck at the same time. I took a deep breath of the warm, misty sea air and gazed at the peaceful setting sun. In that single moment, time froze and I was completely by myself. But somehow I did not feel alone. It was then that I asked the heavens above for the strength and courage that I knew I was going to desperately need. I prayed for help and fortitude. For some reason, I felt so close to the skies; it was as if I could reach up and touch it. Then, I at last felt comfort, and it became clear to me that everything was just as it should be.

Squirrel

As I was walking back to my barracks from the beach, I happen to accidentally glance across the street at the OCS (Officer Candidate School). This is the school where enlisted sailors that have earned a degree and have been accepted into the officer program come back to an extensive 'boot-camp' like training (reference *An Officer and a Gentlemen*). Now, having been warned not to make eye contact with them across the street, I did my best to quickly turn my head to look downward and in front of me, but when I heard all of the yelling in the front yard, it was all I could do to peek out of the corner of my eye with curiosity. There, on the green, I saw quite the fiasco. While a Marine drill sergeant proceeded to yell two inches from an officer candidate's face, another man beside him was extensively doing push-ups, as sweat dripped off his face and his bald head began to steam. While the rest of the candidates remained in ranks, a young man repeatedly saluted an apathetic squirrel that was out gathering its morning breakfast of acorns. Not only was the young officer candidate continuously saluting the squirrel, he was yelling at the top of his lungs "Good morning Mr.

Squirrel!" over and over again. It was a surreal scene – I wouldn't have believed it if I hadn't seen it. And it was all just too much to take in. I bit my lip so as not to giggle.

Suddenly, from across the street I heard, "AIRMAN! YOU'D BETTER KEEP WALKING AND KEEP THOSE EYES OF YOURS TO YOURSELF OR I'LL COME OVER THERE AND DRAG YOU BACK TO MY HOUSE!" The drill sergeant roared. *Oh my god! He's shouting at me!* Instantly, my stomach sank, sobering me up. I quickened my pace to a near run. My heart was pounding as I rounded the corner and took the front steps of our porch two at a time. Quickly, I asked permission to come aboard and ran to my room – never to glance back.

Training

Aircrew Candidate School was basically all physical training. It is a weeding-out process where only the most determined and strong-willed survive. The purpose was to provide one with enough training that they would survive physically should their plane ever go down over enemy lines or enough skills in the water that they could swim miles for help or for days if necessary. We would have grueling workouts all morning long including beach runs - which if you've never run on a beach, thank your lucky stars. I could only compare it to stabbing your own hand. Painful and dumb. Running distances for most people can be challenging enough. Well, think of trying to run with someone holding onto your ankles. With each step you sink deeper and exert more energy, but in actuality you are going nowhere.

We would also perform our daily calisthenics, and obstacle courses, etc. Then we'd have a quick lunch, finishing just in time to meet at the pool for an afternoon punishment.

The pool, however, soon grew to be my favorite part. I had grown up on a lake so I was a seasoned swimmer. We were tested on our strokes, our endurance, as well as trained for survival situations. We swam in flight gear which often included a flight suit, boots, and a helmet.

The helmet floated, but it would also fall over our eyes. When our head is the only part emerged from the water and the dripping helmet falls over our eyes, it can cause quite a drowning sensation. My struggle was always to find boots that would come as close as possible to fitting, since whatever space was left in them after my foot filled them would be filled with water, acting as a perfect anchor. After searching through all of the soggy boots that lined the yellow wooden rack, a men's size 10 was the smallest I could ever find. There was only one pair of these coveted boots, so they were a hot commodity among the women. I can only imagine what the young sailor who used to wear and sweat in these boots day after day would think if he only knew how happy his little boots made young women sailors going through Aircrew Candidate School.

When we first classed up, there were the three females (including myself) and ten males. Within the first week one girl fell out because she didn't pass one of the first physical tests. The other girl and I continued on. She was quite a character to say the least. She was extremely rough around the edges, telling it like it is, and not caring who she pissed off along the way. It was even speculated that she was "heterosexually challenged." But we did live in the "kinder, gentler Navy" in which we "did not ask, and did not tell" thanks to former President Clinton. Whatever it may be, she wasn't the least bit feminine at all, though it was both amusing and annoying to her how much I was. In fact, we were pretty much polar opposites in most ways.

Had we been any other place in the world, I'm sure we would have never even spoken to each other. But under these conditions, we were not only forced to be roommates, we depended on each other to ease the pain of loneliness. In the beginning we did everything together but mostly because we didn't know anyone else. We would shop for supplies together and eat our meals together, not because we were compatible, but because some company was better than no company in a time that was so lonely. We would sit in silence a great deal of the time like an old married couple that stayed together for sheer fear of being alone.

She was hardcore. If I didn't iron every military crease, wear shirt-stays every day, or polish my boots before bed, she would call me out on it and make certain that I corrected it promptly. Keeping her happy was exhausting. One time in particular, I had come home quickly to change for dinner on an inspection day.

Seeing that we had already taken out the garbage (which had to be completely empty on inspection day) I quickly tossed my used gum in the toilet, with every intention of flushing it down. Well, I seemed to have gotten sidetracked as usual and for some mystical reason that still puzzles me to this day, the gum was never flushed. (I lie awake in bed at night sometimes, haunted by images of chewed up gum in a toilet.)

Upon my return an hour later I was greeted at the door by my roommate, Ms. Rules Nazi, with hand on her hips and her eyes glaring right through me. You would have thought I was sitting naked on her pillow playing the banjo all night by the way she was looking at me.

"What if we would have *failed* inspection?" *Well, what if? I'm sure there are worse things in life.* (See, with my impure thoughts like these, it was no wonder we didn't get along.) "I can't believe you'd be so *selfish* to leave your gum in the toilet! Maybe next time you can try thinking about me instead of being wrapped up in your la la land that you live in."

I quickly apologized and promised to never chew gum again, but she had already stormed off, leaving a wake of steam in her path. I couldn't fault her for being angry, nor did I get mad at her. I mean, I did want to punch her face, but it was all she knew how to be. With a roommate like Ms. Rules, there was *never* a break from the military. I could never relax.

Day after day, I came home completely and utterly exhausted. Never before had I done so much physical training at one time. My muscles were torn and ached. My bones were beaten. I went to bed, falling asleep instantly, and sleeping hard, but not without thoughts of the days' events constantly running through my mind. It was in one of these moments of sheer exhaustion that I did something I had never done before in my life. I woke up in the middle of the night to find myself standing near the desk on the other side of the room. Rules politely woke me up, asking me what in the hell I was doing.

"I ah, I don't know. I think I was sleeping."

"Oh my god!" She gasped as if I had just committed a heinous crime. You were... *sleep-walking!*" The way she uttered the actual word, you would have thought she was speaking of the most appalling thing known to man. Sleep walking *is* against the rules in the Navy. Meaning, if you know it's a current condition you have, it is grounds for discharge (at least that was again *the rumor*). I suppose it stems back from the fact that you cannot be on a ship and be sleepwalking, or you will walk right off of the side of it into the ocean. Granted, this is a very hypothetical, extreme notion. But nonetheless, rules were rules, and I just had Ms. Rules Nazi witness one of them being broken.

"Are you going to say something to the instructors?" I asked, a bit worried and still quite confused.

"Well, that depends." She said in her matter-of-fact tone. "If this should happen again, I just may have to. Now just go back to bed for now."

"Ah, okay." I didn't know what to say. I was at her mercy. And it was rather ridiculous. I guess she had a point, but it was still a stupid one.

Chester

Our class was combined with a group of Marines that were training for aircrew billets in the Marine Corps (such as Crew-Chief and Door Gunner). It was both interesting and intimidating being with Marines. They definitely were a different breed - though to no fault of their own, as that is how their boot camp trained them to be. They whole-heartedly believed they were different [*and better*] from the rest. Frequently, we would meet the Marine who completely believed he was superior to everyone around him. Most of the time though, they were an extremely dedicated group of individuals. I respected the Marines, and generally received the same in return. After all, I *was* dating a soon-to-be Marine.

Of all of the people I met in Aircrew School, not a single one stands out more in my mind than Chester. This guy was a six-foot-something-tall, Frankenstein-looking Marine. Everyone looked up to him. Well, physically, anyway. He was lofty, intimidating, and had a distinctly chiseled face. His hair and complexion were dark and his head was shaved in the typical Marine flattop crew-cut. I once asked him what was with all the scars on the back of his head. He simply shrugged his shoulders and logically replied that they were from pool sticks during various bar fights.

He was from Louisiana and was about as back-woods as they come. I learned a lot from Chester. He had taught me that people in Louisiana eat buckets full of cooked crawdads, but not before they first suck the brains out of them! They actually have *parties* to do this kind of thing. That had to have been the most absurd thing I'd ever heard. I guess it's somewhat similar to my dad having a corn feed party in Minnesota when he grew too much corn in the garden. Of course this was accompanied by a keg of beer and later became an annual event that lasted well past us owning a garden...

Every Thursday night in Pensacola, Hooters had all you can eat buffalo wings and pitchers of beer for a steal. And every Thursday night, Chester would eat all of the buffalo wings he could, and drink all of the beer necessary to accompany them. This always led to an interesting Friday morning, as we were routinely given our PRT's (Physical Readiness Tests) Friday mornings. While we were all running our little hearts out along the seawall, trying to beat our previous week's score, Chester was bent over the wall disposing of last night's nutritious repast. When he was done, he'd get back into his run. Somehow through it all, he still amazingly enough always finished on time. We would come to accept this as part of our weekly routine.

Chester talked with an exaggerated, slow Southern accent. He came across as an extremely dense guy, but as comical as they come. No one ever messed with Chester - I think mainly because of his size - but we all knew he was a 'unique' one. I simply thought he was awesome - so different from anyone I'd ever known. We didn't have any Chesters in Deer River.

He took me under his wing right away. I was his little side-kick during those four weeks of Aircrew school. To a new eye, I'm sure we made a strange pair. He would always affectionately say, "Maki, you're such a crack baby." I'm not sure why, but I felt it was spoken endearingly. People didn't mess with me when I was around Chester.

Part of Chester's appeal is that he had a best friend we called Lumanar. They were such great fun to hang around when they were together. Chester loved getting into trouble and Lumanar was afraid of nothing. Lumanar was well-built, shorter (but not too short), and vividly muscular. He was by far the best in our class at everything (running, swimming, you name it). He was well on his way to winning the physical fitness ribbon and breaking many of the records. He was great fun to be around and not too bad to look at either. That is if you are single - which I was not.

The Break-up

Dillon occupied my thoughts on a daily basis. I was still so broken up that I would not be able to make his Marine boot camp graduation. I thought how wonderful it would be to surprise him - me in my Navy dress whites, he in his Marine dress uniform. We would be such the pair and would have so many stories to tell each other. Unfortunately, I was stuck in my first week of Aircrew Candidate School with a curfew of 2200 on weekend nights. I hadn't even earned my civilian clothes privileges yet. Just as it is a privilege to wear our uniform, it is a privilege to wear civilian clothes again.

I was dreadfully lonely for him - especially at night when the training was done and all was still. It was then that I had time to think. So you can imagine my surprise one night as I was lying in my bed reading a magazine, decompressing, when suddenly there was a knock at my bedroom door. I opened it to find one of the girls, Janessa, standing there telling me some boy was on the payphone for me in the lounge. *Some guy? Oh my god - could it really be?* I ran down to the lodge and grabbed the phone. "Hello?"

"Hey, Babe. How are you doing?" It was the sweetest voice I could have ever heard at that moment in time.

"Oh my god! How are you?" I was flooded with emotion and began to cry. So did he. It was such a release of all of the stress and longing we had saved up for the past 13 weeks.

"Baby, I miss you so much." He said. He told me how he'd called my mom to get my number. He went on to tell me about his graduation… his family was so proud, but it wasn't the same without me there… He said he wanted to see me so soon…

I told him how much I missed him and how my training was going. I wanted to see him too - but I didn't know when we could since I knew they'd never give me leave in the middle of training… we'd have to figure out a plan. It was all the sweetest conversation I'd had in months. God, how I'd missed him. I missed hearing his voice. I missed being a girlfriend and spending time with a boyfriend. I just missed reality in general. We talked for as long as we could and ended with a promise of us being together soon - and hopefully forever - sometime after. I went to bed with a smile on my face and my heart full of love.

As the days continued on, so did my training, and so did his leave. He flew back with his family to Minnesota from his boot camp out in California. We talked every evening and every chance in-between that we could. He begged to see me. I told him that we would as soon as we could and it would be wonderful.

Of course the only phone I had was a payphone in our public lounge which usually was full of people. Many of whom were waiting around for the next available phone, or on the other payphone right next to me. This made much of our conversations limited in both length and content, especially since I'm a very private person when it comes to emotions. The last thing I needed were the guys to see me in a vulnerable state. That would only set me up for hours of hecklings slung my way. I learned quickly that if they overheard any kind of 'sweet talk,' they would be oohing for the next 5 minutes. It truly felt like grade school sometimes.

Dillon didn't always understand this. To him, I appeared somewhat withdrawn. Still, I knew he had to have understood the circumstances were not always ideal and this was only the beginning of the long-distance relationship trials to which we had committed ourselves.

Night after night we would coordinate our phone meetings. Night after night we would spend summing up our days for each other. Me in my training, he on his leave back home. I couldn't help being jealous that he was back home, seeing all of our families and old friends. We hadn't been granted our leave yet, as our school began three days after our boot camp graduation.

Now that it was September, most of our closest friends had gone off to college. So Dillon spent a lot of his time hanging out with those that were still left in town, including the class that was a grade lower than us who were now seniors - most of them girls. While it initially seemed peculiar to me that he was spending his time with a couple of these girls since we had never really been friends with them, I had nothing but trust for him, as he had never given me a reason not to.

I also knew in order to make this work, trust was the key. There could never be room for jealousy.

Somewhere along the way, his demeanor began to change slightly, and our conversations began to grow shorter and less intense. He began to hang around one girl in particular, and despite the fact that my sisters and friends told me they saw them together on a few different occasions, I still was not worried.

"Oh yeah," I replied. "They've become good friends now… in the past week and a half since all of his other friends are gone." I knew we had been together for two and a half years, and that he had told me over and over how much he wanted to marry me.

"Okay, Julia. I just thought it was a little weird, that's all," they would say.

"Oh, please, you know him." I replied. "He can be just one of the girls sometimes. He's the most devoted man I know."

Every night on the phone when I'd ask him about it, he would reassure me that they were just friends. How could I possibly consider anything else? Besides, he told me that I was the only one for him; we had a history. And we promised each other that should our feelings for each other ever change, we would tell the other one immediately. What more could I ask?

It wasn't until my mom called me just a few days later and with a nervous tone in her voice, did I even consider the idea that something may not be right.

"Julia," she began. "I saw him with *her* last night at the football game."

"I know Mom, they are *just* friends." I began to grow annoyed that I was having to constantly reassure everyone else of what he'd been telling me.

"No, I saw them together in his truck."

"What do you mean?" I asked, confused, assuming he was just giving her a ride.

"I mean, they were sitting together in the parking lot, talking or… whatever, and she was sitting on the middle seat… right next to him."

My heart dropped. That was my seat! Didn't she see my prom garter that hung around his mirror? Why would he let her… There had to be an explanation. I just needed to talk to him. Maybe he didn't want to hurt her feelings…

"And Julia," my mom continued. "He had his arm around her. I'm so sorry honey, but I thought you needed to know. I don't want him to keep doing this to you behind your back."

My whole world flipped upside down in that moment. Everything that I thought was real and true - was not. *How could someone I loved like that lie to me over and over? And for what? Why was he insisting everything was fine, if it clearly wasn't?* I gave him so much of my life for the past two and a half years. We had plans. And now, because he can't be alone on his own for a couple of weeks, he has to get with the first girl that shows interest in him? I had never felt more betrayed. I was such a fool.

"No, thank you for telling me. I've got to go now." I managed to say to my mom. I hung up the phone and quickly dialed his number, my hands shaking.

"Hey Babe." Was the first thing he said when he recognized my voice. "What's wrong?"

I had no desire for small talk. "My mom told me she saw you two together at the football game." I hesitated. There was no reply. "Why are you lying to me?"

"Oh." He paused for a long time. I'm not sure which route he wanted to take. Finally, he attempted to come clean. "We just… understand each other." He began, not denying anything, but trying to reason with me. "She's been there for me when I've needed her. And she really is a nice girl."

I was crushed. *What the hell was he trying to convince me for? Was he implying that I wasn't there for him?* "I couldn't care less how nice you think she is. Nice girls don't *steal* other people's boyfriends while they are away serving their country! What the hell? I've been there for you every possible way I can. I'm away from all of my friends and family too. I'm going through the same thing that you are - so don't give me that crap." *Did he want sympathy from me? Is that what she gave him? I was trying to survive all the same crap.*

"I am such a fool." I continued. "All this time I've been defending you, telling everyone that has told me this that they are mistaken. I can't believe this. I am such a fool."

"Look, I didn't mean for you to find out this way…" he began.

"I don't even know who you are anymore."

"Julia, just listen..."

"Please don't call me anymore." I slowly put down the phone and made it almost all the way down to my room before I burst into tears. It was there that I lie on top of my bed, sobbing the horrible, loud, ugly cry.

Rules was in there. She didn't say anything. After a while, she came over and began to pat my back. In pieces, I cried to her and told her everything. I told her how foolish I felt. *How could he? And her! Ugh. I can't even speak of what I thought of her. What kind of a girl...?* Rules just listened to me. She told me the usual - what all friends tell each other after they've been cheated on. I shouldn't be the one that feels like a fool. He was a jerk and didn't deserve me. And for the first time, I saw Rules' heart. She had become a friend.

Finally, when all of my tears were out, I was so exhausted I could do nothing but fall asleep in my clothes. During the following few weeks, I thought of him often, as all of our dreams together were slowly withered away. I promised myself I'd never cry for him or our relationship again. I also swore that I would *never* let any man do this to me again.

Needles

One of the things we had to do at Aircrew school was to ensure that we were mentally and physically in optimum health. This consisted of getting even more extensive physical tests than we had had before entering the service. On the day we were getting our cholesterol screening, we were instructed to fast (i.e. starve). I'm a big breakfast eater - can't live without it, but on that day, I did as I was told. After all, what choice did I have? Still, I liked to pretend I had options. When it was time to line up to be poked and prodded, I was already feeling less than good from not eating. When it was my turn for the blood draw, I sat down in the cold metal chair next to Chester as the corpsmen began taking two of us at a time.

Now, I'm not a big fan of needles. I've never pretended to be. I know that I shouldn't be looking at them while the corpsmen are drawing blood. However, Chester, noticing my uneasiness seemed to find this amusing. And like most military members, honed in on any sign of weakness. "Check it out, Maki, that needle is huge!" I could have killed him. "I think it's made for a Holstein!"

"Shut up, Chester." I could feel the needle penetrate through my perfectly sealed flesh. Damn it hurt. Stupid corpsmen. I could see him amused over the banter. I hated him already.

"I'm serious, Maki. That's the biggest one I've ever seen. Oh shoot," he wiggled and attempted to sound excited, but his slow, southern accent made it near impossible. "My blood's squirting all over."

Don't think about it. Think about something else. I'm on a beach lying in the sand. I attempted to distract myself and was doing a good job of it until it began to feel like the corpsman began to carve a cavern inside of my arm at that moment. I looked at the corpsman, carefully not to look at my arm. "Problems?" I asked lightly, hoping I'd get a simple 'of course not.' *Breathe. Just Breathe.*

"I can't... seem to hit... your vein here... oops."

The waves are crashing and the sun is so bright it hurts my eyes. I am on a peaceful beach. I said a peaceful beach, goddammit! It was all enough to make me want to vomit. *How could this be happening right now?* And then I began to feel "*it*" come on. The feeling was not a stranger to me, but it was by far unwelcomed. I had passed out on numerous occasions - all for a good cause. Watching a procedure being performed on my cat at the vet. Watching a needle being stuck in my mom's neck before her surgery. I mean, what rational person *wouldn't* pass out in those situations? I tried to shake it off and focus on something. Anything. I squinted my eyes. *Find a focal point.* I couldn't find one. It was already getting dark.

"Whoa, Maki, your face is turning white. You okay?"

My vision began to tunnel. The corpsman continued to dig away at the hole in my flesh. I could hear everything, but it sounded hollow and far away. "I ah, I'm not doing... too... well..." my voice trailed off and my words were blubbery. At last the corpsman, who was not so much the master of the obvious, realized that his inexperienced excavating job in my arm was affecting me quite severely. Chester was already done and band-aided up at this point. He stood up and came over to me.

I knew I was going to pass out soon if I didn't do something quickly, but I didn't want to draw attention to myself. *Maybe if I just do it quietly in my chair here, no one will notice.*

"Airman Recruit, you need to put your head down between your legs." I heard the corpsman say off in the distance.

But that would make me look like an idiot - and everyone would see how weak I was. I would never hear the end of it. Surely there was another way... And then - there was complete darkness.

Seconds later, I came to. I was lying on the floor. *Why am I on the floor?* As I looked around I saw standing over me my instructor, the corpsman, a few of the other guys that had been waiting nearby, and Chester. *Poor goofy Chester. I wonder if he'll ever find a wife. I miss my cat.* My thoughts were garbled and ran together. Just then I caught a glimpse of my arm. It was completely covered in streaks of bright red blood. Blubbery, I mumbled, "Can I get a goddam corpsman mmm knows how to... do hissss job?" My tongue felt huge. And then it was black. Again.

When I woke up the second time, they had at least wiped up my arm and taped a cotton ball to it. Everything I had feared had come true. I had shown weakness in front of my class and instructors. I didn't know if they would ever respect me again. Maybe I'd even get kicked out of the program. I also realized what an experiment Navy health care was. I lost a lot of blood that day, but thankfully I wasn't kicked out of the program.

The Wall

There were a couple of other girls ahead of us in other classes: Castro, Aylanna and Jenessa, who were on "wall-hold." What is a "wall-hold?" you may ask. Well let me take this time to introduce you to - "the wall." No, we're not talking Pink Floyd. What I am talking about is the pieces of wood that are compiled together, painted bright orange, standing six feet tall and surrounded by sugar sand in the middle of our Aircrew obstacle course. Now, this doesn't seem like it should be something feared and loathed as much as it is. After all, what's a little six feet? And to most men that will leap over this wall like little gazelles, not a darn thing. But to the majority of women (I'm stereotyping here based on experience) that will encounter it, that are not ordinarily created by God to have the natural upper body strength to propel themselves over a six-foot wall in a single leap and bound, the wall is often the one thing that stands in between them and their "Wings of Gold."

It is then, if one should not pass the final timed obstacle course, that they will be put on "wall-hold" and spend all morning - every morning - attempting to get over the wall. They will break for lunch, and then again spend the entire afternoon making deals with the devil and selling their souls to get over this blasted wall. They will return to the barracks with bodies that are blackened from bruises with the underside of their arm looking like something that is seen only in freakish medical books. Then next morning they will wake, eat breakfast, and begin the whole process all over again until at last they either give up, are forced to quit, have broken their bodies enough that they can't physically continue, *or* have mastered their technique and at last have conquered the loathsome beast.

I was advised by many of the class ahead of us that it would be best to practice on the wall as much as possible. So one night after Rules and I had a grueling day of training, we (or I think she) decided it would be best to beat ourselves up more at the wall - willingly and in our own precious and limited free time. This way we could "be prepared." We weren't going to take any chances. Reluctantly I went. Not because I wanted to, but because I knew Rules would nag me all night until I relented.

Well, let me tell you, we practiced and practiced that night until it was well past dark outside. Not one time did either of us make it over the wall. Instead we just kept slamming ourselves repeatedly into the torturous device. It was anything *but* motivating. We went to bed that night with bruised bodies and broken egos. I couldn't believe my career was going to be over so quickly - and all because of a stupid wall.

About two weeks into my aircrew training came our 'obstacle course' day. I barely slept but a few hours the night before. As we lined up behind the starting line, my stomach became nauseous and I had to pee. I knew it was just my cursed bladder trying to psych me out as usual, but I had to go so bad. When the instructor yelled 'go' and the first guy burst out from behind the line, I achingly felt a surge of nervous adrenaline shoot out from my heart and filter through my blood.

One by one they all took off until finally it was my turn. *"I've gotta pee. I've gotta pee."* I sang repeatedly in my head.

"And…GO!" shouted my instructor.

Ugh, the adrenaline pained me again like a stabbing knife to my heart as I took off into a run. Each step took an exorbitant amount of effort and I only went half the distance I felt I should have. *Damn sugar sand.* I balanced across the plank of wood, danced my feet into each required tire step, swung from each "monkey bar," and climbed the rope ladder without any more strain than necessary. Soon I could feel 'its' presence upon me. The blasted wall knew I was coming. It firmly stood its ground. I felt it laughing condescendingly as I barreled towards it.

Putting forth my greatest fight, I jumped as high and as hard as I could. By doing so, I managed to slam myself hard into the wall without gaining a bit of height that would be necessary to take me over it. Again, I jumped up, this time I was able to wrap my left arm over the top, perching my armpit on the corner, causing the weight of my body to slam my side into the wall once again. And oh how it hurt. My bones began to weaken.

Suddenly, I gained awareness of everyone around me. The Marines and Sailors of my class were all shouting at me. "Come on Maki! Get your ass over that wall! Push it! Go!" I could hear Chester and Lumanar. It was nerve-wracking and intoxicating at the same time. There is no way in hell that I had the strength to pull myself over this wall. However, I felt their eyes on me. I knew there was no choice but to go over. I just couldn't face the shame of giving up in front of everyone.

Catching a second wind, I began to swing my legs back and forth drawing off the strength of my abdomen, building height with each swing. My left arm still clung to the top. It was shaking now as my muscles were growing weaker and my blood vessels were bursting under my skin. By the fourth swing I was just barely able to catch my right toe on the top of the wall. With this, I was somehow able to work my toe and heel over the top of the wall. It wasn't pretty - but it was working. Well, once I was able to get my leg over the wall, the rest was downhill from there. Using the strength of my legs, somehow I pulled myself up and into a straddle on the top of the wall. I was up! I could hear the cheers and whooping behind me.

Had I really done it? I checked again. I sure as hell was on the wall! I had survived this day and all of the days up until now. Screw the blisters and bruises.

And screw stupid old cheating boyfriends and their "nice" new girlfriends. It was in that moment that nothing else mattered. I had made it over the wall! They could go to hell for all I cared.

"Keep going!" I heard someone shout from the ground and instantly snapped me back into reality. Oh yeah - I was still being timed. I leapt down and continued on my way, the sand pulling my legs into its depths with every step. I crawled under the trip wires; got my sweaty body completely encased in sand in places you don't want sand. I was a mess, and I barely made it to the finish line before my time was up. But it didn't matter - because in that moment, I knew if I could make it over the wall, I could make it through anything.

The reality of the situation is that I was never able to make it over on my own when I practiced a few more times days later, but every time my class was there screaming at me to get over it - I never failed. I couldn't show weakness. And I couldn't let them down. It was from that day on that I knew I was part of something bigger than myself and I found strengths I did not know I was capable of having when I knew others were relying on me.

Gulf Breezes

In addition to daily calisthenics and swims trials, we were subject to room inspections, and good ol' Navy heritage training. We had a checklist to complete to get into the next phase of training. With this next phase came later curfews, less inspections and mustering (checking-in with the quarter deck watch at weird and random times to make sure you were still alive and not in jail) and of course the longed-awaited recompense of at last wearing civilian clothes! Yay for individualism!

We were slowly on our way to becoming real, adult sailors. Actually, the phases were introduced into the Naval Training Schools shortly before I got there. (Lucky me!) The strict rules were put into place after so many incidents of sailors fresh out of boot camp were enjoying all of their long-awaited for freedoms a little too much and ending up in jail or worse. (Somewhat similar to what would happen in college dormitories if there were no rules.) Overall, it was a decent system - but oh, so painful while we were on it. As a result though, I will never take wearing clothing of my choice for granted.

You can imagine my excitement when the day finally arrived that I could wear my first civilian outfit. My mom had sent me some clothes a few days prior, and it was so exciting to have options when picking out clothes! (Girly-ness coming out) I went with a nice, but casual fitted top. It was long-sleeves (as to cover all my bruises) with just a hint of cleavage - it was so nice to not have a uniboob smooshed into a sports bra for once! I also wore a fun miniskirt that fell slightly above my knees. (Anything above the knees is considered a miniskirt in Minnesota.) Of course, to top it off, I had to put on a pair of silver high heels that I had picked up at the Navy Exchange (NEX) a few days before. My poor feet had longed to emerge from the heavy, black boon-dockers and into the light of day again. I yanked my hair out of a standard pinned-up braid (it was growing longer now that I actually had to pin it up!). I curled it, giving it some volume, and put some make-up on - like "normal" teenage girls do. Overall, it wasn't too bad - from a distance one couldn't even see all of the scrapes and cuts on my legs.

I glanced in the mirror and was shocked at my reflection. *I AM a girl!* It was the strangest thing to nearly forget what I once looked like. I left my room with that little excited feeling in my stomach - the one you get when you feel your best.

I walked past the quarter-deck and asked Emerson, the guy who was on duty, for permission to exit the ship. He was a skinny guy that stood about a foot taller than me. He had the face of the kid you grew up with next door. Brown shaved hair (as they all were in the military) and friendly blue eyes that drooped down in the corners when he smiled.

"God, Maki. You're a hot chic," he spoke as casual as if he was telling me it was hot outside. To him he wasn't hitting on me, he was just stating it matter-of-factly- as the concept somewhat surprised him.

Surprised, flattered, and embarrassed. *Try not to feel too flattered, he hasn't seen a real girl in about 4 months. Think of something witty to say...* I had nothing. I settled for a quick, awkward thanks, and walked out.

I had nowhere important to go, but it didn't matter. I bounced down the sidewalk headed to nowhere in particular. The sun was shining, it was a beautiful day. I smiled at everyone I met. I felt alive and somewhat human again like I hadn't felt in months!

As I walked along past the Marine barracks, I even heard a few catcalls. Okay, now it was hard not to let that go to my head. Soon after, I spotted two of the cutest Marines walking my way. As they began to pass right in front of me, I made up my mind to shoot them both the biggest smile. You know, to see if I had any girly-ness left in me. No sooner had I done that than a big gust of wind swooped down and encircled me, grabbing my skirt and tangling it well above my waist, exposing my rainbow colored panties with hearts all over them. Quickly I pushed it down in a Marilyn Monroe-like fashion, hoping that I recovered in time. *Maybe they didn't notice...* The Marines passed me without a word with their eyes forward, so I could only assume and hope that I had caught my skirt in time before they noticed.

Two seconds later as they were behind me, they lost their perfect marching composure and belted out in roaring laughter. Quickly to follow were even more catcalls from the barracks. It was in that moment that I learned a quick lesson in humility. Having divine intervention (or rather a little Gulf breeze) brought me back to reality as quickly as my ego had begun to expand. I also learned that when you're a grown-up, it's time to buy some grown-up underwear.

Emerson

It was the beginning of the third week when Rules injured her ankle, causing her to be put on medical hold. There are so many 'holds' in aircrew: swim hold, medical hold, PRT (Physical Readiness Test) hold, legal hold, GPA (grades) hold, helo-dunker hold, wall hold - basically any aspect of the training that we could not initially pass, we would be put on hold for, or if we needed to be held for medical or legal reasons. None of them are much of a good thing when we were there, though. It can make one feel like they are idling as everyone else is quick to zoom by. It's also a place where one will quickly grow bored and likely to get into trouble. With Rules falling out, it left me alone to face all of the faster and stronger men in my class on my own.

Some days it felt as though the rest of the class just waited, assuming I wouldn't be much further behind. There were many times I too was nearly convinced I was right behind them as well. Somehow, though, I just kept telling myself, I just have to make it through today. And the same thing again the next day.

It was hard losing Rules. I felt like I lost the last person I could (somewhat) relate to. I also lost my sit-up partner, which was an unfortunate loss. This may seem like a miniscule detail, however, losing a sit-up partner is a *huge* deal. The last thing in the world that I wanted was some random guy to hold my feet while I did as many sit-ups as fast as I could. It could be dangerous in so many ways.

If there was a class clown of Aircrew school, it would have been Emerson. He didn't take life too seriously, and was always cracking jokes. It was rare that I saw this man upset. And though he made fun of everyone - he also was constantly making fun of himself. He was cute, but like a brother cute, or maybe I just thought that because he was constantly goofing off.

One day by default, I ended up with Emerson as my foot-holding sit-up partner. Of course, when he was one-on-one, he was tense and wouldn't utter a single word to me. Awkwardness began to creep in as we silently waited for the instructions as all of the other guys around us chatted. I felt like I should have apologized to him for myself. *Sorry you got stuck with "the girl." I know it must suck for you. You'd probably do so many more sit ups if you had a different partner.*

The instructor's whistle blew and I began pounding away doing my usual sit-ups. All of a sudden, I felt the unwelcomed 'pressure.' Then the big question came - do I go for the required sit-ups and making my time needed in order to pass the test, or do I go for my dignity and just gently sit-up, knowing that I will have to make this up later should I fail. Agh! *This is a nightmare - this can't really be happening!* I decided to attempt to be discrete: however, that quickly proved to be impossible. *Maybe no one will notice*, I thought to myself. But sure enough, it came loud and with vengeance.

"Agh- Maki! You farted in my face!" Emerson (who was obviously in the line of fire) shouted loud enough for the entire class and instructors to hear. Just then another one came out. I couldn't help it. "Eeeeew!" He cried like a little girl.

My face became redder than a nun's in a dirty book store. Of course, by now everyone was beginning to pay attention as to what was going on.

Oh he was *so* not cool. *Why can't he just be a friend and pretend he didn't hear. Maybe that'd be worse?* I smiled sheepishly, and mouthed the word *sorry* under my breath. And then, another let go unexpectedly.

"Ahh! Stop it Maki - you stink!" Now, I know they didn't stink and he was just being dramatic but oh my god - I could've killed him! I have never been more embarrassed...

"Shhh!" I hissed back. I tried to give him a pleading look saying, *please shut up and I'll do anything. Just shut up.* Of course though, it was too late. By this point everyone was distracted and looking my way. I heard snickering in the distance. And I knew they were just acting like they weren't doing it too! The snickering soon became full-on laughter. It was the longest two minutes of my life. But the damage had been done. Ugh, I hated Emerson. I tried to hold my head up the rest of the day, but the truth is I just wanted to jump over the seawall and swim as fast and as far away as I could.

As Aircrew class went on, the week-days were spent exercising, swimming, testing, and training. I found myself longing for the weekend, but by the time it arrived, I didn't usually have much planned. I didn't really know any of the 'older' girls (that had been there longer than I had). I didn't have a vehicle or very much money, so I was usually stuck on base. I often found myself shopping at the NEX for things I didn't need or wandering to the club on Karaoke nights just to hear other people attempt to sing. I found it quite entertaining. I wasn't old enough to drink, and too paranoid of getting caught to try it. I would wander to the beach many days and just sit. But you could only do that for so long. While I enjoyed being alone, I found myself very lonely at times.

That bastard Emerson would try to talk to me in class at different times. I would *allow* myself to talk to him - a little, but I had already made up my mind that he was no good. I also couldn't stand his friend Weinerstein (or Whiner as we called him,) that he seemed to be attached at the hip to. Whiner was from

Minnesota, so you would think we would have had something in common. Like eating fish or being nice to strangers or something. However, he was from "The Cities" and it may as well have been a completely different state. We called guys like him "metrosexual." I had never known a guy to go tanning before; the thought was absurd. Whiner tanned *and* was proud of it too! He drove a little sports car (instead of a truck like all the men I ever knew). He even had gotten manicures in the past. But probably the most despising of all was that he had the cockiest attitude of anyone I'd ever met.

He was about average height for a guy - not too tall and not too short. He had dark hair that was always delicately gelled in place. He had piercing blue eyes and was a handsome guy - and was so sure that every woman he met wanted to sleep with him and often bragged about how many he had (sometimes at the same time), or what they'd do, and how he'd ditch them afterward. Still, they would flock to him, and it drove me insane. I wanted to shake them and warn them. I think he knew this and reciprocally didn't like me much either. He rarely would speak two words to me, and if he did, they were never anything positive. No one got under my skin more than he did.

Obstacles

Our third week consisted of the fun training. Well, fun in my eyes. We tested our skills in the Helo Dunker, which was a huge cylinder-shaped cage that had seats for 2 pilots and 4 crew members. The cage was held up several feet above a pool by cables that extended down from hoists on the ceiling. When it was our turn, we were instructed to climb in and find our assigned seat in the 'helo.' The cables were then released and we were dropped into the (freezing) water, and then slowly began to sink. When the water was about chest high, the entire cage or 'helo' tipped over to one side and we went underwater sideways, continuing to submerge. The goal is to wait until all motion stops, count to 3, and release your seatbelt and arm-over-arm make your way out the closest window or the main door depending on what the instruction was. It was also important *not* to kick as we swam through the water to make sure we did not kick another trainee in the face that could be behind us. Of course, there were instructor divers all around us, to ensure no one panicked and had to be rushed to the surface.

We were also taught how to fall the 'correct way,' and disconnect the parachute from ourselves on land (once you were on the ground, of course), and what to do if we landed in a tree, etc. The scenarios were endless and it really was overall a good time. Not as good of a time as actually landing in a tree - especially if it had monkeys in it, but still a good time, nonetheless.

Next was parachute training for water entry. Since the P-3 was primarily a submarine tracker at that time, this was a more likely scenario. For this we went down to a separate pool. One at a time, we attached ourselves to a huge parachute that swung out over the pool and released, causing us to fall into the cool blue water, followed by a huge parachute canopy and hundreds of little strings, anxiously waiting to attach themselves like jellyfish tentacles to our body. We were to exit the parachute death trap by swimming out from under it using just our arms in slow, steady, movements so as to not to entangle the strings around our body any further. It was a delightful and impossible trap that forced its victims to put up a good fight before they were reluctantly at last released. The key in surviving this obstacle was not to frantically swim like someone who was being drowned by his parachute, pulling us to the dark depths of the ocean as tiny clownfish began to gnaw away at our flesh. One just had to be calm as in, oh yeah, my plane just crashed and burned, I just may be the lone survivor, and my parachute has a death grip on me - *but every little thing is going to be okay!* This was Navy training at its finest.

The following day we attempted to master the parachute hoist, drag and pull. First was the endless classroom training. I couldn't quite understand why it was important for me to know that the drop rate of a parachute is 18 ft/second. I'm going to be falling fast. That's really all I needed to know. Besides, considering no one has ever bailed out of a P-3 in an emergency over the 50+ years they have been flying, odds are slim that it's going to be me. Still, it's good to know - and I secretly hoped that maybe I would be one of the first AWs to jump out of a P-3 and survive. Of course, I would only want to wish it if the whole crew survived too, and the plane wasn't too damaged… okay, maybe it was just all-around a bad idea and I should look into parachute jumping out of planes on purpose - when there is not an emergency going on.

The "Hoist, Drag, and Pull" device attached to our parachute and to a mechanical hoist that dragged, and pulled us up and down, through the pool until we managed to unfasten ourselves and roll out of our parachutes. The goal was to perform it quickly so we were not one of the unfortunate souls who got to ride the rig up and down the pool lanes in front of everyone, as we attempted to figure what was preventing the necessary disconnection. It had potential to be most hilarious to the by-standing classmates: however, not so much to the victim.

Another great day was when we were introduced to the Low-Pressure Chamber, and the Spin-and-Puke. As usual, it all began with the standard classroom training, which consisted of learning the technical names to the reactions we could possibly have during flight in the event of rapid or explosive decompression such as "Blue-Face-Guy," "Bloody-Eye-Syndrome," or "Sinuses-Bursting-Through-Face-Condition."

We learned what hypoxia could cause a person to do. Hypoxia, a deficiency in oxygen reaching important organs such as the brain, will cause one to do funny things, almost as if they were drunk. However, they will not realize they're doing them. (Like those annoying people that believe, and insist - that they are completely sober as they run out into the street and pee on the neighbor's cat. *"I'm not drunk - I always do this!"*)

Then we were all lucky enough to personally experience the effects of hypoxia! This was to give us a better understanding of what it would feel like, since while we're experiencing hypoxia we are usually unaware of what is happening to you. (Kind of like when an art student smokes pot and thinks that they just painted a picture rivaling a Picasso.) It also enabled us to recognize the signs in our classmates. ("Dude, that's not a Picasso.") Some reacted quite differently than others did. If one was a smoker, they generally performed much better in hypoxic situations as they were used to having less oxygenated blood throughout their body. And although it was quite serious training, it was equally amusing as we watched fellow classmates attempt the simplest of tasks, such as playing pat-ty-cake with each other to end up smacking each other in the face, or forgetting what comes after clapping their hands together.

As a visual cue, there was also a rubber-glove that was tied off with just enough air in it to cause the fingers to be erect. As the pressure in the chamber dropped, the glove began to expand nearly four or five times its original size. It was explained that this is what happens to any air bubbles inside our body which are then released in the form of gas. (Hence why airline flights are often quite odor-some.)

Following the low-pressure chamber, we were awarded a ride on the infa-mous Spin & Puke, of which the title is fairly self-explanatory. Based off of the tea-cups ride at Disney World, we rode in these spinning cylinders to test our body in the centrifugal force circumstances. Those that didn't puke got extra points. Not really. But it was a quick glimpse into your future flights and how our body would react when pulling a few 'g's (Gravitational force). Much to my own surprise, I did not puke. Though I did feel nauseous the rest of the day.

We then spent the remainder of the day testing and conducting experiments as to how our eyes reacted to the darkness. We learned ways to maintain our night vision and the tricks that the darkness could play on our eyes. Luckily, I was really good at this due to all of my midnight treks in search of Big Foot in the Great North Woods.

At last came the day I had looked forward to for some time. We were going to see a *real* Navy helicopter in action! It was the day I jumped out of a perfectly good boat and got left behind, floating in the middle of the Pensacola Bay. There we all floated a few hundred feet from each other. An entire class all lined up, spanned across the ocean, unable to defend ourselves against predators of the sea. As we waited helplessly to be hoisted up by our "D rings" (rings shaped like the letter D) on our SV2 (survival gear/life vest) up into a helicopter, I covertly decided that it was my duty to be on shark watch and diligently scanned the surface around us for shark fins.

Rumor was that they loved this warm bay. I never quite figured out if it all was true or if they were just tall tales passed down to freak out the newbies by the classes ahead of us. Still, I wasn't about to take any chances. The first thought that jumped into my mind was the commercial in which the shark was looking up from under the water at the guy in an inner-tube, displaying how he appeared to look just like a mouth-watering doughnut from the underside. *Don't be a shark doughnut*, I thought to myself. As I waited, I did my best to stretch my legs out so I didn't appear to be a scrumptious treat and at the same time made sure not to kick around more than necessary, as I did not want to appear to be a baby seal.

Holst (another classmate - more on him later) was just down the way from me. "Maki, what the fudge muffins are you doing?" (He didn't really say fudge muffins.)

"Oh nothing!" I yelled back. I think he was expecting more of an explanation at that moment, but I just wasn't in the mood to try to justify my actions. I knew he'd never understand that I was simply trying not to look like a doughnut. Stupid rumors.

Still, I couldn't help but smile happily to myself as I thought of the alternative - I could be sitting in a college classroom right now listening to some boring lecture. "What a great day to be in the Navy!" Again, I got the raised eye-brow stare. Did I just say that out loud? Embarrassed, I realized how much I sounded like a recruiting commercial.

Soon, we could hear the rhythmic pounding of the helicopter blade as it peeked over the horizon and made its way over to us. The powerful war machine paused and lowered its altitude as it arrived over the first student in the line. All of a sudden, real Navy fleet operators opened the door and began to lower the static line into the sea. I felt like I was in junior high, watching all of the cool seniors walk down the hall as if they owned it.

The helicopter acted like a tornado the closer it got to the surface of the water, thrusting and spraying the saltwater wildly. I anxiously watched with awe as my classmates slowly were raised out of the ocean up to the metal beast and lowered back into the water. It was all too incredible.

At last, it was my turn. The helicopter jostled over to my direction, then began hovering and rocking in mid-air as it sucked and twisted the sea into cyclone-like courses all around me. My eyes stung from the saltwater as I blinked hard, trying to see through the cascading water. The cable was lowered and I held back touching it as instructed until it had made contact with the ocean as to ground it and discharge any built up static-electricity.

With a nervous knot in my stomach, I swam blindly over to the metal piece and fumbled around with it until I managed to wiggle it and securely snap it onto my D-ring. Ignoring my nerves, I crossed my right arm in front of me and then, slowly raised my left arm with a thumbs up - just like I was in some heroic movie. *Whoo-hoo!* I don't know what came over me. I watched the ocean become further and further away as the helicopter grew nearer. Almost there... I was on top of the world! I must have been about 30 feet high, dangling from a thin wire that was secured to a flying piece of metal at the other end. For a fleeting moment, I got a little shiver of fear and excitement as I saw how high I was. What a trip!

And then, without warning, the cable stopped rising. I began to lower slowly to the bay as the helicopter and aircrew moved onto the next guy. *Awww.* Disappointment set in and I felt like a little kid when the county fair ride comes to an end.

I since was told that if you bring a candy bar out there with you that they'll raise you all the way up to get it. Not sure if it's true or not, but it couldn't hurt. Just like feeding peanuts to the monkeys at the zoo. But at least the crewmen don't throw poop at you if you don't bring food.

After four challenging weeks, our graduation day at last made its longed-for appearance. It was a simple ceremony conducted by our instructors who had pushed us to our limit all day. Every day. There on the porch outside of our aircrew barracks and underneath the infamous pair of "Wings of Gold." We all stood proudly in ranks, dressed sharply in our working whites. In the sweltering Floridian autumn weather, we were given a short speech that boosted our egos, took a class picture, and were given certificates of completion - symbolic of a tiny piece of the entire puzzle.

The school in retrospect was short - only four weeks. Nevertheless, the day we graduated, we felt we had earned every minute of those four weeks. I had never put my body through such physical exertion before in my life and pushed it to the absolute limits. And in the end - I made it. I didn't really know for a while in there if I was going to. I knew if I could make it through this… there was no turning back now. I would not let these 4 weeks, and the nine weeks of hell in boot camp be for nothing. Failure was not an option.

CHAPTER 6

Still in Pensacola, FL.

October 1997

Approximate distance from Deer River: 1421 miles

It was at this time the sailors were separated from the Marines as we all continued the technical side of our training. This part pained me. I wasn't good at saying goodbyes, nor the thought of never seeing these people again that I saw day in and day out. They played such a huge role in my support system, and then they were just gone.

With all of my earthly possessions on my back and in my arms, I set out walking across the base, carefully staying on the sidewalks until I arrived on the other side: The Naval Aviation Technical Training side (aka NATTC). This school provided the technical training in our designated field or "rate." My technical school, or "A-School," as we called it, was to train me as an Aviation Warfare Operator (AW).

The barracks were new, built within that year, and still very nice. From the bird's-eye view, they were shaped like capital "H's," with stairwells on each end. They stood three floors high, and upon entry the smell of freshly polished wax flooded your nostrils. This was because someone was either stripping and/ or waxing the floors at all times. If one does not have paint to chip or decks to buff, the Navy will ensure there is another floor to strip and buff all over again.

Two barracks would face each other, forming an open square with two volleyball courts in-between. There were eight different barracks; all labeled phonetically Alpha through Hotel. The females were in "Alpha," males in "Bravo," "Charlie," and "Delta." Echo was the plushy barracks, reserved for fleet returnees. By plush, I mean they didn't have to share a bathroom with four other people. In the military, it is a privilege to be able to take a shower and not have to worry about catching a foot fungus. You had to earn this privilege with rank and time-in-service. "Foxtrot" had the strange "performing unit" sailors, while

"Golf" was more male barracks and "Hotel" was reserved for the Marines. There was always something exciting going on over there. Lawn parties, yelling, explosions.

On my first day of class, Petty Officer Bert was my instructor. He stood in front of the classroom that morning, in his crisp, working-white sailor uniform and his bushy mustache looking like a caterpillar on his upper lip. He had a chest that was decorated full of colorful ribbons, each of them with their own story to tell. He didn't rise much more than a mere five foot six inches from the ground (and I think I'm being generous here) as he stood behind the podium in the corner of the classroom, observing us, hawk-like, as we filtered into the barren white-walled room.

Finally, after everyone was seated and silence had fallen upon the classroom, Petty Officer Bert began to leisurely draw on the dry erase board with a green marker in his hand. He drew a not-so-perfect square. With a slow, Southern drawl, he pointed to the middle of the square, tapping it as he stated, "This is the box."

It was a true statement. The class, however, was perplexed. Then he took his marker and pointed to the right of the square.

"This is outside of the box." Again, an obvious statement. "This is where you need to be," he declared as he left messy dots all over the board. No one spoke as we sat in those cold, metal, schoolhouse chairs. We had just begun our classroom training and were already bewildered. Louder this time, he continued, "In order to get through these next months..." he paused to carefully choose his words and slowly began to walk around the room, scuffing his shiny black shoes on the tiles as he walked. "YOU need to think outside of the box." Another long pause as he made eye contact with each of us. "And someday, when you least expect it, it may all just click together, Skippy." He smiled a half smile and his bushy mustache rose on one side. Then he slapped his fist into his hand and continued. "Until then, the more you try to make sense of it... the more jacked you will be." I didn't realize at the time, but no truer words had ever been spoken -

even though I had no clue what they meant.

Our first class was Oceanography. Now granted, I had just barely met the ocean. We were still getting to know each other. Suddenly, I was learning intimate characteristics of the ocean that I never even knew existed. It's like we skipped right to the third date and hopped in the sack.

We were taught about the different water columns and how sound travels through different types of water and what kinds they all were. It was fascinating and odd. I never thought sound travel was so complex. Time travel...sure. But not sound travel.

We learned how the temperature, salinity, and pressure (TSP or the "teaspoon factor") all play a role in how sound travels through the ocean. We were shown bathymetric charts and sound velocity profiles, and taught formulas for configuring it all. We learned of the different types of sound waves, various kinds of obstructions and what they can do to sound, and for someone like myself, well, it was a lot to take in. At this point, I had no idea what I had gotten myself into, and I wasn't sure how long I would be able to last. It was a lot for an ocean virgin to take in.

As soon as we were put on our first break, we all raced out of the classroom, wishing like mad we could just keep going and never return. We scampered down the hall, some filtering into the heads (sailor talk for restrooms), while others continued to the open lounge that was full of candy, snack, and soda machines (gee-dunk). As I was walking, Emerson came up behind me. "Holy shit, Maki. Are you getting any of this?"

Relief flooded back into my pale face as I realized that maybe I wasn't the only one and I began to put my thoughts of planning to go AWOL again on the back burner. Maybe, just maybe, there might be a little bit of hope. "Yeah… not so much," I replied back to him.

"Man, we are so screwed." A higher pitched male voice popped up behind us. I spun around to find myself staring into Holst's eyes, which were about the same height as mine (which at 5'4" isn't very tall for a guy). He wore a ludicrous smile that made it impossible not to smile back. "So who wants to go drinking tonight?" he asked, still smiling.

"Dude, I don't know." Emerson replied wearily, half ignoring Holst's last comment. "I'm going to have to study my ass off to make it through this class."

"Holst, you're such a dumbass." Whiner chimed in speaking to Holst. "You know you're going to be screwed if they catch you."

"Come on, man, they're not going to catch me," Holst replied, still smiling. His brown eyes sparkled with the mischief of a college boy on a panty raid.

And so began our school days. While we were busy learning about submarine characteristics and "magic assholes," which is what the Navy schools call formulas. (Magic assholes are still the only way I understand algebra - hence the reason I am not allowed to teach children math to this day). Holst came in nearly every morning reeking of alcohol. Of course he wasn't the only one, just the most recurring one. Initially, I had no good reason to like him. He was a slacker that didn't seem to care if he made it through school or not. He made crude jokes and made fun of pretty much everyone. But for some reason, somehow over time, he began to grow on me. He was likeable. We would challenge each other by trying to find lyrics from old 70s music and writing them all over our name tags on our desk. He told wild tales of his crazy drinking nights and his wild rendezvous with taller women. Soon he met this girl who became his alleged 'girlfriend' - though none of us ever confirmed that she actually existed. If in fact she actually did exist, she was quite perfect for him as she was a self-diagnosed nymphomaniac. Every morning he came in more and more tired, but with a satisfied, love-sick, I-just-had-crazed-sex-all-night look. All of the guys in class were completely and utterly jealous of Holst's action, so naturally, they made even more fun of him every chance they got.

Whiner would often take our break times to brag of his tales of his crazy past, and his current girlfriend who was (theoretically) still his high school sweetheart. Ugh, did I mention how crazy he drove me on a daily basis? Sexist bastard.

Slowly, Emerson and I began to talk more and more. He was so easy to talk to and so goofy to hang around. He was real and kind-hearted. I could completely be myself around him and not have to worry - unless Whiner was around. Then I had to be on the defense or I would catch hell about anything and everything. When he wasn't being a dickhead with Whiner, Emerson was a complete dork, as I affectionately called him, and we soon became inseparable.

I became one of the guys so to speak - which in a sense was my whole goal all along to fit in. But sometimes I didn't. They made no bones about holding much back - and I did my best to never act too shocked - as that was the effect they were often aiming for. The Fleet Returnees (guys that had been out in the Fleet and were returning to go through this school) gave us all an education in itself. They spoke of faraway places - like Thailand and the Philippines and the crazy happenings that went on there if you were a Navy sailor. I would leave the classroom at the end of the day trying not to throw up, and vowing to go on a mission trip over there someday to save these girls. I would teach them when to appropriately slap men and that bananas should be used for consumption only.

I was taught fabulous terms like "choking the chicken" and "spanking the monkey." Apparently this was a normal thing for guys. Not only did they do it - they weren't shy about it, nor attempted to keep it a secret that they did! Everything that I ever thought about boys was completely turned around in about six months of an education that went beyond my expectations.

The Truck

Pensacola, as beautiful beachy and touristy city that it was, also was flooded with pawn shops, tattoo joints, bond brokers, strip clubs, and car dealerships, all surrounding the entrance to the Naval base. They were bait sitting there with enticing signs, luring the young and naïve sailors by presenting them with shiny ways to spend their guaranteed bi-monthly paycheck. The dealerships were the all-time worst. They posted amazing promises in their windows of too-good-to-be-true sales, only to get a sailor to sign a contract with an outrageous interest rate for a piece of junk car.

No one fell harder for this little scam than poor old Emerson. Being that it was the first time on his own, away from his family in Michigan, he wanted to establish himself and do it on his own - to prove to his family, as well as himself, that he could.

So after a small dispute with his parents who were offering too many helpful, but unwanted suggestions, he went off and spoke to one of those dealers with a snake-like tongue. Somehow, despite the fact that his parents, who both worked for GMC up in Detroit and he had the family discount waiting for him, he was convinced by the dealer that a Nissan would be the way to go. And due to the fact that he hadn't a lick of credit yet, being the spring chicken that he was, he was blessed with the gift of a 28% interest rate for his little, used, silver truck. So yes, Emerson got a vehicle on his own. He made all of the payments like a responsible customer. Everyone else was envious that he had a set of wheels to get around (except for Whiner… he had his Thunderbird from back home). The only problem was that Emerson was going to be paying for his little truck for the next 20 years. And it didn't even have a *bumper*.

Freedom

Emerson and I did everything together. Now that he had his fancy shiny truck, we would go to the movies, or shopping for civilian clothes. He was always brutally honest with his opinion, and I liked that…. most of the time. His bumper-less truck brought us to obtain freedom and regrettable tattoos. Well, he got one and I just watched. (I had already gotten one when I was 16 from a guy with a nail through his nose, naturally.) We would drive around with the windows down with the music blaring, pretending we were gangsters - except that neither one of us could rap. Not even a little. And on my favorite days, we would go out to eat exotic southern foods I had never had before, such as bourbon chicken, hush puppies, and fried okra from the mall food court. It was amazing! We saw each other through the trials and tribulations that being in Navy A-school will throw at you. He had become my best friend.

And while I was enjoying the freedom of being on my own for the first time in my life, I felt like I was drowning in school. It did not come easy for me like it did for some people. Still, I was bound and determined to do well, or at least just pass. I simply *had* to pass - there just weren't any other suitable options. I would study after hours at the school house that smelled of microwave popcorn. Then I would go home to my barracks and study some more. But despite being tied to the school, I felt like I was living large. I felt more freedom than I had in months, literally. I didn't have to be back into my barracks until midnight on school nights, and on the weekends I could stay out the whole night long. And since I had gone into the Navy right out of high school, well, this was the first time in my life that I was allowed to do that.

The Kiss

One day, as I was walking home I ran into Chester and Lumanar, who were going through a couple weeks of tech training before they were off to their next duty station.

"Maki!" Chester shouted and quickly ran over to me, careful to round the corners of the sidewalk without stepping in the grass. You'd think it was made of acid the way they drilled it into our heads not to touch it. He gave me a squeeze - not realizing how strong he was and that it actually sucked my breath out of my lungs. "What's going on, little one?" He smelled of beer and greasy foods, just as I had remembered him. Lumanar looked as hot as ever, with his fancy smile and bulging Marine biceps.

"Nothing much - what are you guys up to?" I replied, trying not to sound too desperate.

"We're just headed out to the beach for a bonfire. Ya wanna come?" He asked slowly, with his Southern drawl ever pronounced.

"Sure! Can I go change really quick?"

"Okay, but hurry up - no time to git all pur-dee. We're just all gonna hang, ya got it?" He spoke so slow I felt as though I could have already been changed before he finished his sentence.

"Okay Chester!" I raced to my room and took all of three minutes to get ready. Half of that time was going up the stairs. I really despise having others wait for me, but I was just so excited to be *doing* something. Of course, I didn't have much selection, being that my main source of clothes were a few items that I bought at the Navy Exchange (our only on-base department store),and from a shopping trip out in town with Emerson. Still, they were better than dungarees. I threw on some nice jeans and a stylish top. I firmly believed it was important to always overdress than be the one underdressed. I quickly touched up my make-up as well. Since I was over at the schoolhouse now, I could actually wear make-up and fix my hair somewhat without worrying about going to the pool or sweating it off in the dirt. I slowly began to feel like a human again.

"Whoo-hoo!" Chester called out as he saw me heading toward them. "Ain't you just a little tootsie roll!" (I had never been called a tootsie roll before, and I wasn't quite sure if that was good or bad.)

"Wow." Lumanar exclaimed as he opened up Chester's rusty Ford pick-up truck for me to climb in. I smiled and climbed in-between the two as they piled in. Chester had to duck his head slightly as he drove his slightly-too-small Ranger. I couldn't believe it. *Was Lumanar, the star of our class, really into me?* I couldn't help but smile as we bumpily drove off base to the beach, our arms brushing each other's with each bump.

A few beers later with a small buzz, and damp with sea water on our clothes, we returned to base - cautiously passing through the gate guard. Somehow, it ALWAYS came down to trying to get past the gate guard at the end of a great night. It was like sneaking into your home way after curfew and after running into your mom, doing your best to act as normal as possible so she will just let you past and you can safely go to bed. It is at that time your bed feels like such an achievement if you can make it to it. It's the gold medal after a running a marathon.

———

As we arrived back at our barracks, a little less than in our clearest state of minds, Lumanar and I began to say our heartfelt goodbyes as Chester stumbled off to the woods on the edge of the parking lot to go kick some squirrel's ass that had been pissing him off all night.

"You know my room is just right there," he said all smoothly as he pointed to the corner of the building on the *ground* level. "Just thought I'd let you know… And I never lock my window." My first thoughts were, *why on earth would anyone on the first level not lock their window? Anyone could just climb in there at any time… Oh, wait. I get it.* I was a little slower than usual in my cognitive abilities at that hour and number of drinks.

Now of course you know I was a good girl and would NEVER think of doing anything beyond making-out in a boy's room at 2 o'clock in the morning. However, I sure wasn't ready for the night to end with my new dream boy that I had been lusting over every day for a month now, who was actually into me that night!

"Oh my goodness, I couldn't do that!" I replied.

Where I'm from, it's always customary to say no at least 2 or 3 times before accepting anything - even if it's desperately what you want.

Lumanar interrupted my thoughts, "Maki, life is short. You never want to pass up an adventure." *Oh he was good.* He knew the way to my heart. He also INSISTED that it would be okay. There was no way I could possibly get caught. No one came around this side. For some reason, I began to have the sneaky suspicion that this wasn't the first time he had done this.

Oh well, what the hell, I thought. I was always up for an adventure. Perhaps it was the beer talking, but somewhere in there I told him that I would take a stroll around the building and meet him at his window in about 5 minutes. Yes, I said stroll.

So I took my little 5 minute *stroll* around the barracks buildings (I really had no concept of time at that point). I did my best to look casual. Well, about as casual as it looks for a 19-year-old female strolling around Marine barracks at 2 in the morning. Doing my best attempt to be covert and stealthy, I continuously would check over my shoulders to ensure I wasn't being followed, bad James Bond villain.

As I rounded the corner of the sidewalk that was directly in front of Lumanar's window, I did a quick and final check and darted off the sidewalk to it. For some reason, in that moment, all I could think about was how I was going to be in trouble if someone should catch me walking on the grass. Like a swift Army Ranger, I was in that window in a single leap and bound. And once I was in, it didn't take a moment before I realized that I really didn't have a plan at all. His roommate was asleep across the room, his burly body curled up in a petite, single mattress bed with a single scratchy gray wool blanket covering half of him. Lumanar sat on his bed. He flipped on some old South Park episode and patted the bed next to him, signaling for me to sit by him. He was dreamy, so I willingly obeyed. All I could think about was trying to avoid being awkward. So I did what I always do when I get nervous. I began to ramble.

I rambled on and on in that wee hour of the morning. I felt if he was going to be my dream man, he had to know the entire history of my family. I wanted to know his contemplation on the meaning of life - where he was going with his and what his short and long term goals were. At times, it may have appeared more of an interview than a spontaneous rendezvous.

Then suddenly, without warning, he grabbed the back of my head and pulled my face to his. "Maki, stop talking," were his simple, yet life-altering words that he uttered. Again, I obeyed. And then, the moment that I had been lusting for so long now. He kissed me. Hard.

His beautifully chiseled face pressed up against mine, and all I could do was just hold my breath. And then, expecting fireworks and butterflies, I was startled when not even a match would light that fire. His tongue was sharp and it felt like he was using it as a weapon. In and out like a lizard. *What the heck was happening?* His breath tasted like a musty basement that was the gift of his chewing tobacco. It was in those never-ending moments that I learned the significant importance that chemistry brings to a relationship. *What had happened? Was I shallow? I couldn't help it - I had to make this man stop!* All I knew was that it was over before it had begun.

I sat back up on the bed, awkward, and rambled some more for the next few minutes. I didn't want him to think it was him - but I had to get out of there. I thought how delicate the situation really was. Had I told him that he was the worst kisser on the face of the Earth, that it felt like nothing short of licking an ash tray and then repeatedly trying to break a hole through it with my tongue, or that I would rather kiss a stray dog with a foaming mouth than him, well, that may have left scars on him that would take years of women-using to recover from. So, when the time seemed right, and I didn't feel like I was bolting out of there like a bat out of hell, I swiftly said my goodbyes, and falsely promised to see him soon. Pretty sure I never saw him again. He really was a *nice* guy. And beautiful. But I suppose beauty only goes so far.

I was really beginning to feel as though I'd never find a guy that was right for me. I thought I had once found the man I would marry - all to be left for someone else when I least expected it. I still had no idea why. And now Lumanar? He was the best looking and the best at everything in class - and yet, I felt nothing. It wasn't that I needed a guy to be fulfilled - I just was beginning to feel like perhaps there was something wrong with me. And being away from my family and all my friends didn't help the situation at all. I was so very much alone, struggling to keep up in school. I went to bed that night as I had in the past wondering if the Navy had been the right choice for me.

Performing Units

It was shortly after A-school started that we had a couple of young sailors, all spiffy in their dress whites, come into our classroom one day and introduce themselves to us. They stated that they were the ones that lived in the Foxtrot barracks [the weird ones] and that they belonged to the base's Performing Units. As soon as I heard "performing," my ears perked right up and I began to pay close attention to their little spiel. They went on about how they traveled all over the area performing in parades and doing Color Guards for sporting events and many other things. *Ooh, travel…* I thought. They did marching routines and rifle twirling. Being the little "joiner" that I am, I was instantly intrigued! The only downfall was that they practiced every night for two hours. I worried about being able to keep up with that as well as my homework that was already giving me a run for my money. But I only worried for a second. At my next break, I signed up and began my move over there that very night.

Up to the third floor of the Foxtrot barracks I went. Luckily, everything that I owned fit in about 2 bags, so moving wasn't too difficult. And holy cow, when I got there, what a completely different world it was. It was like a secret society. It was a military within a military. People fell into ranks and had to go before a Board in order to advance. And there was always a fair amount of hazing going on - mostly the harmless, just make-fun-of-you-in-front-of-everyone type of hazing; the stuff that built character. People were told to "post" and would stand at attention until told to move. There was a pecking order among these little sailors that everyone followed.

Another huge perk was that since there were only a couple of females and plenty of room up there - I had my own room (for the time being anyway - it was always made clear to me that should another female join, she would be *my* roommate.) It was amazing. My own room. I hadn't had my own room in what felt like eons. Yay, to temporarily bypassing any foot fungus worries! I promptly threw gum in the toilet... and I did not flush.

Adam

With the Performing Units came new opportunities, new things to see and do, and a whole new collection of friends. Finally I was beginning to feel like I had found a group of people I fit in with. Chelsea, Razzano, and Wilde were all part of my new group of 'performing' friends. We called some by their first name, others by their last. I think we just chose which we liked and which suited them best. The place was crawling with eccentric personalities. Every day it was entertainment to just sit and watch the 'normal' festivities take place.

All of this as it was, I couldn't help but notice one of the guys in our group. He was tall and thin, blond-hair and the bluest of blue eyes I'd ever seen - ocean, sky, whatever you'd like to compare them to - they were beautiful blue and always sparkling. It's true, they sparkled. He had the younger, baby-like face of innocence, but very handsome features at the same time. He looked like your all-American California-type blond hair blue-eyed guy - except that he was from the Carolinas. All of that aside, it was his joyful and energetic personality that drew me to him like a moth to a flame. Being with him was easy. When we were together, we were always laughing. I hadn't been this happy since I had joined the Navy.

Being around him made me feel like a kid again. I could be myself and he was just as crazy back. But not in a weird, creepy kind of crazy - more like an up-for-anything, spontaneous type of crazy. He loved to hunt and fish, which classified him as very manly in my book (in northern Minnesota, nearly every man I knew hunted or fished. I didn't realize there were other optional hobbies for men). On top of that, while he was going through his A-School to be an AT

(Avionics Technician - not the easiest of rates), he was also on the Performing Units with the rest of us, AND was training like a madman to try out for the Navy SEALs.

Now granted, every third guy that was going through the tech schools down there was "trying out to be a SEAL." It wasn't something that most instructors took very seriously, as they were a dime a dozen and usually didn't get too far. However, Adam was different. He would get up before he had to meet his class and worked out on his own - running several miles, before his class met up to do THEIR morning workout - as theirs wasn't strenuous enough for him. But probably the best of all was that he wasn't full of himself, though he had every reason to be. I was instantly hooked on this dreamy man. He was perfect and he made me want to be a better person.

He kept me on my toes and kept me laughing. He was motivated, always wanting to try new things and explore new places. He took me for my first time actually swimming in the ocean (Helo Operations not included). Over Thanksgiving weekend under a full moon one evening, I learned how much fun it was to swim in real ocean waves. We dove in to them and allowed them to pull us out to the sandbar then push us back to the beach. My body tumbled and was pulled, and I was at the mercy of the mighty ocean's strength. The sand sparkled under the moonlight and the sand crabs scurried about. I must credit Florida, for as hot and humid as the days get, the nights are nothing short of beautiful and full of possibilities.

We would fish and we would hunt for sand crabs. We watched magnificent black herds of stingray swim parallel to the beach and tried to keep up with them. We sang songs in the truck at the top of our lungs, went to movies, and tried new restaurants. He introduced me to southern foods and traditions. Waffle House was a favorite of ours and it was mandatory that if there was a jukebox, we would graciously use it and try to outdo each other with who picked the best song.

One cool autumn night he took me camping on the beach where we froze and shared our first kiss. We became inseparable - all at the same time trying to convince everyone else as well as ourselves that we were no more than great friends - as relationships were not allowed up there since it was co-ed. And as much as I fought it and tried to resist, I accidently fell in love with Adam.

Mardi Gras. New Orleans, LA.
Approximate distance from Deer River: 1390 miles

Being a member of the Performing Units turned out to be one of the best gigs down in Pensacola. It introduced me to a world of new friends outside of my schoolhouse. It got me away from the daily grind of school, barracks, and homework. Besides raising and lowering the flag everyday on base - which was both fun and stressful. (*Crap - it's 2 minutes until sunset - where are my dress black socks? Here, just use these Christmas socks - they have black in them - just try not to let them show when you march!*) It was also an opportunity to get involved in the local community. We performed at various local events: a Veterans Day parade, the color guard for a Pensacola Pirates hockey game, and even a Beehive Convention at the local Holiday Inn. Yes, that's a real thing that apparently needed a real Color Guard. Bees are very important. But none of these events could have prepared me for our biggest performance all year.

Have you ever heard the song, "Mama Told Me Not to Come" by *Three Dog Night*? That song, originally written for Woodstock, pretty much sums up the enormous, party-like-it's-1999 festivities that go on annually in a little town called New Orleans, Louisiana. (Ironically it was 1998. Ooh-so close!) You may have heard of it. It's where they hold a tiny celebration called Mardi Gras. And to quote from the song "I seen so many crazy things, I ain't never seen before." It is funny to me, but that song always pops in my head when I think back to Mardi Gras.

We went there by bus - a school bus full of young sailors only months or weeks out of boot camp. Many were sailors that had limited opportunities to get off base. It was like we were a bunch of preschoolers that had been dropped off in a candy factory. There were dazzling lights, succulent food, and all the beer and women a sailor could dream of. I still have yet to see a bigger party in my life.

Of course, I must add we were there for work. That night, we just happened to represent the Navy in one of the most famous of the several parades - The Endymion Parade. This is one of the largest parades in one of the craziest and wild celebrations that our country has. People actually bring their grills, paint their territory on the side of the road, and camp out for days in advance to get a good seat. The crowd that this parade alone brings in is astronomical. The parade route is several miles through the heart of the city, lasting for hours with the Super Dome at the finishing point.

We marched in this parade for nearly four hours straight. And we didn't get to be the happy people waving and blowing kisses to the crowd. We were marching, performing, and twirling rifles with bayonets on the end of them. By the time we had finished, our legs were numb and swollen, and our arms were stiff. We had been bitch-slapped so many times in the face by random strands of beads flying through the air that we had developed an unnatural urge to strangle people with the beaded necklaces. Our ears continued to ring throughout the night from the bands, music, and sheer screaming from the crowds.

At one point during our marching performance, one of the guys was set to receive a rifle from the row in front of him as he tossed his rifle to the guy behind him and so on. Something slipped somewhere and he wound up with a 6-inch slice in his hand from the bayonet. He was quickly ushered out of the parade and brought to the hospital. How our director ever found him and got him out of the crowd was beyond me. This occurred sometime in the early evening. It wasn't until nearing 10am the next morning he was returned to the barracks with 20-some stitches lining his palm. He wasn't even seen by the doctors until somewhere around 6am, as there were so many other people in much worse shape from the celebration mishaps that they kept trumping his hand that held a soaked-through towel, with blood pooling on the floor in front of him. However that did not stand a chance next to gunshot wounds, stabbings, falling from balconies, and those with internal injuries that had been trampled by the colossal crowds of people.

So at the parade's conclusion in the infamous Super Dome of New Orleans, awaited the "VIP" crowd of onlookers wearing floor-length gowns, and garnished with sparkling jewels from head to toe. Masks, decorations, and costumes of emerald, gold, and purple were everywhere the eye could see. There was an elected King and Queen. It was an elaborate masquerade if I'd ever seen one! (I had actually never seen one.) The whole night was just lit with color and spiced with the most soulful jazz music I'd ever heard.

After our march, we quickly changed on the bus out of our once crisp uniforms that were now laced with beer and champagne from the crowds, the stench of dirty, populated streets, and of our own blood, sweat and tears. We threw on some civilian clothes and proceeded to embark on our great adventure in this dangerous sea of drunks and shirtless women, otherwise known as *Bourbon Street*.

The famous French Quarter was our starting point. The intricate architecture of the antique buildings captivated me. As I admired the twisted black iron balconies and Victorian-style details, I barely noticed the two half-naked women that were making-out on it as admiring men from below did their best to throw their approving beads up to them - as if they had just passed the test.

Suddenly a camera was shoved in my face by the guy next to me. "Maki, take my picture," instructed David as he stepped back, and affectionately put his arms around two blonds - one on each side. I attempted to squeeze the shutter button on the cheap disposable camera, and suddenly, as if it had been a practiced routine, the two girls in unison proceeded to lift up their shirts, exposing their bra-less bosoms. I snapped the picture before I fully realized what was going on. *Wow. They totally just lifted their shirts up. Right here, in public. And I just got a picture of it for David, my classmate's personal collection. Didn't their mothers tell them never put anything on film that you wouldn't want your grandma to see - because eventually it always catches up with you?* My mother explicitly spelled that out to me.

So in that moment, I made the conscious decision that though I planned to experience Mardi Gras to the fullest, I would not "*show my tits*"! No matter how many times I was asked that night. Honestly, it was also an easy decision knowing that I would see all of these guys (my classmates) every day for the next few months. Finally, and most importantly - though not defined - Adam and I both knew that we had something, as we continued to spend every chance we could together, but had to do our best to make it look like it was a coincidence that we both always ended up in the same places.

So that night, I became the official photographer of the group, with Adam at my side, acting like he was doing his own thing, but teasing me for the job I had taken on. And he was such a gentleman too - never did he insist on getting in on any of these pictures with 'voluptuous' women on either side of him. I'm sure he didn't mind them though. He never had any desire to drink either - it just wasn't his thing. I found his willpower both astonishing and refreshing.

Next on the agenda - get into one of these swanky infamous jazz clubs you hear so much about when you speak of the Big Easy. The problem was that we were all 18- and-olds, and you had to be 21 just to get inside most of them. However, word on the street was that if you had a drink in your hand, they wouldn't bother to ID you as you walked in. And the only place you could get a drink without initially being IDed was down at the other end of the street - where for some reason the lighting was much dimmer and crowds were somewhat more... sparse. It was known as the 'gay' side of town. Hmmm. (Remember this was 1998 - before Hurricane Katrina - and a tad more segregated than it is today). So we headed down to what we believed was our first official gay bar.

Outside of the bar was an abnormally large woman dressed in what appeared to be a black "flapper" from the 1920s complete with fringed hem and all, holding a sign. It wasn't until I was up close could I read the sign. "Seeing is Believing." I wasn't quite sure what that meant. I was thinking like a Ripley's Believe it or Not Museum?? So I asked. "Excuse me ma'am, what does your sign mean?" As I began this conversation, a few others moseyed on into the bar in an attempt to order drinks.

As the woman opened her mouth, a very strange sound came out. It was an extremely low voice - not what I was expecting from a woman this curvy. A heavy smoker perhaps? "Well, what do you think it means?" She wore a half-cynical smile on her face.

The cheesy smile sent a chill up my spine, immediately I was annoyed. Was I being ridiculed, or quizzed? Was this an obvious answer that everyone knows except for me? I could not tell. Ugh.

"I'm... not sure," I answered cautiously, "or I wouldn't be asking." Just then Adam and a couple other friends "shushed" me and pulled me out of earshot.

"She's a he!" My friend Chelsea yelled at me.

"What?!" I paused for just a moment to wrap my brain around this one. Yeah, I had seen *Geraldo* before. I knew where she was going with this. Still, I couldn't help but be a little shocked. I mean, who isn't when they meet their first transvestite? "Oh my god. You mean..." I trailed off as I came to the realization she was a he-she. Or a she-he?

Just then somewhere in the background the song Lola came on. Or maybe that was in my imagination. *Well I'm not dumb but I can't understand, why she walked like a woman and talked like a man...*

"Uh huh!" Chelsea nodded loudly.

The rest of our entourage emerged from the club, everyone's arms loaded with what appeared to be glasses that were nearly two feet long, filled with crimson-stained ice. I took a sip of it through the gigantic straw and as cold as it was, it burned all the way down my throat. What the heck is this?

"They call it a hurricane," David said, smiling, pleased with himself for scoring some crazy drinks. But the great thing was despite the fact we were essentially a bunch of teenagers, no one cared!

Que Sera, Sera! Especially if you told them you were in the Navy. "Old enough to die for your country, you damn sure are old enough to have a drink," was the general consensus. And it wasn't like we went around blabbing to everyone that we were in the Navy. We stuck out like a sore thumb. Well, the buzzed-cut guys did. You could spot them coming from miles away. We girls, not so much.

The night continued and got hazier and the crowds grew larger. Policemen on horseback trotted in a single rank up and down the strip to attempt to continue to break up the crowds. When this happened, you either got out of the way, or you got trampled. I even had a few moments where I felt I was being swallowed up by the shoulder-to-shoulder crowd. Luckily, I was surrounded by taller men, who would grab me and help pull me out of the consuming mess. I wouldn't recommend going to this place on your own. Not that I couldn't if I wanted to; however, sometimes it's nice to have back-up.

Now, don't get me wrong, Mardi Gras was the craziest party I'd ever been to in my short 19 years. (Of course I had not yet been to a Navy party). However, it was more than just a drunk-fest, full of flashing exhibitionists. Mardi Gras celebrations led up to Fat Tuesday (the day before Ash Wednesday), which begins the 40 days of Lent until Easter. The tradition behind it is to eat, drink, and be merry, for tomorrow you die and repent. Mardi Gras is about the biggest celebration of life our country has to offer. Taking place in The Big Easy, it is all about being what you are and letting your instincts rule.

Really, there are no rules - as long as everyone is good to each other. Strangers become best friends for the night. The whole city becomes united in their celebrations. They gather together to cast off the monotony of day to day life and to celebrate. Individuals get to dress up and be whoever they want for a night. They catch plastic beads thrown off the back of a truck and compete for getting the biggest or most elaborate set of beads and compare lavish stories at the end of the day. Mardi Gras is a celebration of the history of an entire culture that embraces traditional jazz music, classic Cajun cooking, and centuries old voodoo magic. It's about the entire community letting loose, and savoring just being alive! Laissez les bon temps rouler! (Let the good times roll!)

Thankfully, we all made it back to our barracks by Sunday night.

Bittersweet

It was only a few short weeks later that our training was finally complete. And by the grace of God, or Petty Officer Bert's extreme patience, I somehow managed to pass the class. Much of it still didn't make sense, but parts were beginning to stick. I definitely found a passion in deciphering acoustic grams. Now that's not something I had ever thought I would say! But submarine signatures excited me and the big puzzle that we had to solve for this job became enticing. While most of my friends, Janessa, Whiner, and Emerson, all decided to go down the non-acoustic route and operate the radar, I found sound travel exciting. And so I chose to become an acoustic operator.

On March 2, 1998, our class full of characters stood in front of the classroom to receive our certificates of completion for our Naval Aviation Technical Training Center's Anti-Submarine Warfare Systems Operator course. Another check in the box and a step closer to receiving our wings and beginning our career in the Navy. Next stop - SERE school. I was not exactly excited about this one. Well, maybe just a little...

And so I said goodbye to Pensacola forever as well as all of my Marine friends - and basically anyone who wasn't going on as an AW - including Adam. But we promised we would make this work. "It never makes sense to me that people break up because they can't see each other - wouldn't that just cause them to never see each other?" That was his logic. I would see him after SERE school again when I came back down to Jacksonville. When I thought of him, I couldn't help but smile. He was my happy thought that would get me through the next 6 weeks or so. It was going to be okay. It had to be.

CHAPTER 7

I can neither confirm nor deny that any of the following events in this chapter really did occur or not. Granted, one can do a Google search of SERE school and come up with all of these stories and many, many more about what goes down in these trainings. One could watch *GI Jane* or other movies out there for a completely other point of view. There are all kinds of rumors and/or reports, each somewhat similar in theme - but different to suit the individual that is relaying the story. Additionally, I would never want someone who plans on going to SERE school in the future to assume this would be their particular experience, as everyone has a completely different perspective, and one would get so much more out of the experience if they went into it with no expectations or preconceived notions.

I will let the reader be the judge on whether the following really did occur or if it is all simply a story I have concocted in my own head for your reading pleasure...

⊣ Background ⊢

At precisely 8 o'clock every morning on any military installation, the National Anthem can be heard sounding powerfully throughout the air. In this ceremonial event, the American flag is carried, attached and raised to the top of its respective pole. Everyone outside is expected to pause for a moment and observe this act of tradition. This includes those that are walking, running, and even driving. And for those that are running slightly behind schedule, this can become a mundane task, as it takes place Every... Single... Morning. You will often see these people quickly dart into the building, pretending they just "made it" or cannot actually hear the music.

However, for anyone who has ever spent time in a third-world country, any time in combat, an extended time away from America, or has ever gone through an event where you realize the significance of this daily ritual, that routine moment of every day that the sun rises takes on a whole new meaning. Anyone who has ever lived a day without freedom, or has had it stolen away from them understands this. Anyone who has come to this country in the hopes of 'The American Dream' can understand this. Or anyone who has witnessed the horrors upon another soil, where the dirt and the air that one breathes does not belong to them, but a government that rules with an iron fist. They have about as much control over their own destiny as a worm lying bloated on a sidewalk after a rain. Their future does not belong to them and they are not allowed the dreams we Americans possess and take for granted. Anyone who has witnessed a community of sheep - that stone their own brother if they are ordered to. It's all they know.

These people share a common bond. It's the undying love for their country. They know the importance of preserving that freedom, how fragile it really is and how easily it can be taken away in a split second. These are the ones that you will see standing at complete and utmost attention anytime a flag is proudly raised. They are the ones that will respectfully remove their hats in church or when they eat. They are the ones that cannot listen to the National Anthem without getting goose bumps or a lump in their throat every single time they hear it.

⊣ My SERE School Story ⊢

Somewhere in the Mountains of Maine
April 1998
Approximate distance from Deer River: 1400 miles

Survival Evasion Resistance and Escape (SERE) School was located in the desolate mountains of Northern Maine. There are others, but this one was mine. I went through this training in April of 1998, the spring after one of The North East's infamous ice-storms. This one in particular happened to coat the entire forest and power lines with several inches of ice and left half the state without power for a week or more. And although it was April, there was still a significant amount of snow in the mountains. As a result, our class additionally received our Cold Weather Training Certification.

The school began with classroom training. During this time, we were taught basic methods of survival, including how to snare small, cute little animals, which bugs were most nutritious, which plants were edible and which would turn your tongue green and cause you to crap out your large intestines. Of course being that it was April on the snow covered mountains, none of these plants or bugs existed. We were taught the skills we needed to survive should we ever 'go down' (crash) and become captured over enemy lines. Naturally, there is a substantial gap between listening to them in a classroom setting and applying them to real-life situations.

On the day that our classroom training was complete, we rode the old and rickety military bus that looked like an old converted school bus surely not suitable for school children anymore, up the mountain side. I passed the time by staring out the window in a child-like wonder of what awaited me. I sat alone, feeling unsocial, and just observed the passing towns, wondering what the townspeople were doing on this sunny near-spring day.

Children were playing kickball in a snowy park near the side of the winding road that had few travelers. One of the kids stopped for a moment, glancing up at us and as our eyes met for that brief moment, it felt as if he was looking right through me, no doubt wondering what we were doing. Or perhaps he already knew, as this bus passed this way up the mountainside every three weeks or so and then back down again a week later, carrying with it changed people.

How I wish it were a time when I was playing kickball instead of the fate that lie before me. At this moment, I knew the next week was going to be grim, and my bones were weighted with a feeling of dread. I longed for my freedom as I already was taken as prisoner, off to fulfill my sentence.

When we arrived, the temperature at the higher altitude had already dropped and we were swiftly greeted by our first challenge. Lug all 100 pounds of our gear up a desolate gravel road that was too windy, muddy, and steep for the bus to make it any further. Once everyone had gathered their goods, they began the painful hike. I wasn't sure if the weeding-out process had already begun, but I knew one thing for sure - if I could not make it up this mountain side, there was no way I'd survive for a week on this unforgiving mountain. Luckily, when you're working hard, you're staying warm, and I was sweating like a whore at Sunday Mass in that 20-degree mountain-chilled wind, by the time I reached my destination. I did my best to ignore the sharp aches that already had arrived in my back and legs.

I'm not sure how much time had passed by the time we all arrived on the top of the hill, but I do know that the sun was well passed above our heads and onto its downward slope. The day was late and we still had much to do.

The class was divided into three groups of nine or so. Each group was assigned a tent. This 'tent' was actually a round orange-and-white-striped parachute strung tightly around a few stakes (aka tree branches) tall enough that one had to bend over at the waist when standing in it. We had a gray canvas tarp on the ground, which was generous of the instructors to let us have, as it helped keep our sleeping bags somewhat dryer than having them rest on the bare, still-frozen ground.

We unloaded our gear, set up our sleeping bags, and somewhat attempted to settle in. I ended up making my bed right next to a nice Marine who seemed to kind of take me under his wing. "Sticks" was very kind-hearted and seemed to look at me like his little sister. I recall waking up in the middle of the night to find Sticks tucking me in with another blanket as the temperature had dipped to sub-zero freezing. There was something very charming about seeing a tough Marine delicately tucking his neighbor in with such secretive concern. As I normally prided myself on my independence and felt asking for help would show weakness, I had to secretly admit that it was kind of nice too; to be somewhat taken care of when we were sleeping under a parachute on a mountaintop somewhere in Northern Maine. So I pretended to stay asleep, touched by his compassion, but careful not to let on my awareness as to embarrass him. That's just how Marines roll. They are taught from the beginning to look out for each other at all times.

In addition to Sticks, I roomed with eight other men in that makeshift tent. Needless to say that whether it was the unavoidable rock edge that jutted into my side as I slept, or the chorus of chainsaw-like snores, or the foul stench of eight men who hadn't showered for days living in close quarters will emit, there wasn't a whole lot of quality sleeping involved during my lovely stay. The next morning, everyone (myself and the guys) all awoke to find ourselves cuddled up to their neighbor as the temperature had dropped so low.

We quickly learned it was all about survival. I once had a Navy Seal admit to me that during their training, while they were hosed-down in the freezing ocean surf in the middle of the night, they would secretly pray that the guy behind them would pee on them - just for the added warmth for a few seconds. They just understood the unspoken rule of never mentioning it again.

Our daily lessons consisted of reading compasses, navigating with just landmarks and maps of the terrain, and learning how to catch rainwater with condoms because *every* good sailor should carry condoms in their flight suit - you know, for storing water, covering the muzzle of your rifle as to keep water and debris out, trips to Thailand, etc. I know, I know. Navy guys don't carry rifles.

In addition to making our little animal snares, we also learned how to make rabbit stew, so we'd know what to do with the rabbits once we caught them. With live rabbits. From start to finish. Like they were alive, and then they were in the stew. We learned what happened in the middle of that. And it did not consist of running to the grocery store.

It all began as we were called into the main lodge, which was also a makeshift classroom. Basically, it was shaped like a stage with rows of benches to sit on and listen to the presentation. For some reason, I ended up right smack in dead center in the first row. I hardly ever do that.

As our instructor began our lesson about how to snare, skin, and disassemble a rabbit for our rabbit stew, he walked over to the side of the stage and reached into a wire cage that contained four or five rabbits. As he was doing this, I began to realize that this was going to be an actual live demonstration of this. It's one thing to see it in a book. It's another thing to see meat in your grocer's freezer section. It's an entirely new thing to have an adorable little white fluffy bunny innocently wiggling his nose in my instructor's hands, completely oblivious to his horrific fate quickly approaching.

Now, understand, I am not a vegetarian by any means. I grew up with my grandfather owning a beef farm that butchered our own cattle annually. I am 100% for the humane treatment of animals. I feel much better about eating an animal that I know has led a good, healthy life, was well taken care of, and that has died an instant, humane death and with the dignity that I believe small farms provide. I never will be okay with the mass-production slaughter houses that treat their animals inhumanely. The thought alone makes me shudder to my bones.

My family is a family full of hunters. My dad always encouraged me to hunt. While I will fish, I am not a hunter. I just never had it in me. Of course, if my family were starving and I needed to hunt for survival, I absolutely would. Thankfully, that is not currently a worry.

So occasionally I have been known to have a weak stomach. I cannot stand needles or violence, and I'm not a fan of blood and guts. I can push through that in an emergency situation - but I don't put more of it in my life than I have to.

As I realized what was about to take place right smack dab in front of me, I did my best to *quietly* move over to the side of the room and a few rows back. However, a move like this does not go unspotted when you are one of three girls in the entire room. I swear they are constantly watching your reaction. So when I heard a few of the guys begin to snicker and say, "Aw, come on Maki - don't want to see the poor bunny rabbit die?" *Um, no, not really.*

"Just don't worry about me. Pay attention to the teacher." I was definitely annoyed. *What a bunch of asses.* They severely infuriated me at times.

The next 30 seconds were a blur. The instructor, not missing a beat, continued to speak as he grabbed the rabbit by its hind legs and hung it upside down from his hand as the animal struggled, no doubt confused. In not even a full second, he swung his entire arm that clenched the rabbit's hind legs down, back and up in a full-armed circle, gaining momentum as the head of the rabbit came crashing down in contact with a huge flatly-sawed stump. There was a mortifying cracking sound and at once the rabbit was dead and hung limp, as blood shot forth from the instantaneous arrival and sprayed all over the faces of the mouthy guys that were sitting in the first couple of rows.

Everyone froze for the next ten seconds or so, paralyzed as they processed what had just happened. I was horrified at the sight, but at the same time felt incredibly justified with my decision to move.

"And that - is why I moved." I broke the silence - trying to sound normal, but inside I was welling up with emotion and I didn't understand it.

"Okay now," the instructor began, seeming unphased about the blood that was dripping down his leg, or the splatters that were speckled upon the front two rows of students. "Let's divide into groups. I want one group to come here and start skinning this rabbit - one group to begin to get the next one ready - and one group to go outside and start setting up everything for the stew." It didn't take me a second to know where I was going - stew prep - as I tried not to look at the lifeless animal, still dangling from the instructor's fist.

Suddenly, out of nowhere, I felt the overwhelming need to get away from there all together. I ran outside to the nasty port-a-potty that they had at the base camp. Once inside, I shut and locked the door just as a flood of tears began pouring down my face. I didn't know why. I knew in that moment I just felt completely and utterly overwhelmed. This wasn't fun anymore being up here. Not that I ever expected it to be - but I just wanted it to be over already. I was so sick of feeling as if I needed to prove something to everyone - including the instructors - and of course, myself. The thought of witnessing an innocent life die so horrifically made me cry harder. I pictured the poor rabbit, so sweet in his arms. I thought of our pet rabbits that we had growing up. I thought of the other four rabbits in the cage and what was probably happening to them at this very second. I was sobbing uncontrollably now - but I couldn't hold it in anymore. It wasn't just about the rabbits anymore.

I was cold, hungry, lonely, and just wanted the comforts of home. I wanted so badly to talk to my mom. But mostly I missed Adam. I wanted to be with him - far away from this place. Four more days. I just needed to get through four more days. Four of the hardest days imaginable were ahead of me. Maybe I just wasn't cut out for this after all. I had come too far to give up now, but that's all I wanted to do. Five minutes passed. Then ten.

Finally, I decided I had cried enough. I grabbed a wad of toilet paper and wiped my face off. I attempted to fan it to relieve some of the redness I knew was there. I gave it thirty more seconds to clear up my eyes and opened the port-a-potty door.

Everyone was off completing their assignments - no one noticed my absence or if they did, they didn't say anything to me. I walked up to my group, grabbed a knife and began peeling the vegetables for the soup.

The next morning, which was a Monday, we were released from the base camp and the Evasion portion of our training began. Armed with what we could carry - a sleeping bag, gloves, hat, canvas tarp, rain coat, water canteen, compass and map, and a pack of lifesavers in which I was extremely careful to ration one for breakfast, one for lunch, and another for dinner each day. I had to make my single pack last. That was basically all I had to eat for the next four days. They pumped tons of water in us, so that we wouldn't dehydrate. As a result my stomach constantly felt bloated. I began to hate water.

Of course, we always had the option of snaring little animals and eating bugs, however, when there are a few feet of snow on the ground and all the animals are hibernating, our options were limited. It's amazing though - after the first day, our hunger pains just kind of - went away. I was so incredibly hungry that I just wasn't hungry anymore.

From our groups of nine, they narrowed us down to pairs for this part of the evolution. Each pair was taken from the highest ranking paired up with the lowest ranking. This was how I ended up with an anti-social, follow-the-rules, each-man-for-their-own Lieutenant Junior Grade (JG). I mean, I'm sure he was a decent enough guy and all, but in a survival situation, I didn't quite have that bond-thingy going on. He was quick to answer all of my questions with one-word answers. When you have nothing better to do than navigate around a mountain side all day, it's nice to have a little conversation, however, I've learned that not everyone felt the same.

So we spent the day hiking along through densely wooded terrains to some random location that the instructors had chosen. When we got there, there were instructions for another point to navigate to. We were practicing our map and compass reading skills. Reading a map on a mountainside is not exactly the same as reading a city map with roads and identifying labeled locations. This was all done with latitude and longitude, trees and rivers to guide you - before days of

GPS. This is why it was so vital to learn to read a map correctly.

JG and I hiked up mountain sides and down mountain sides. We saw Mother Nature at its most glorious. The snow that blanketed this wilderness was untouched and sparkled in the sunlight like millions of diamonds. The snowbirds let out their calls and pecked at the dry tree bark, desperately seeking any form of nourishment. Despite the time of year and many creatures that had settled for their long winter naps, the dense forest was full of life and critters scattering about as they heard us near. Evidence of the ice storm earlier in the year was all around us in uprooted trees and branches freshly broken off in every direction. As we trudged further into the thicket, we even came across an enormous moose - though it was no longer alive. It lay in the snow frozen and perfectly preserved in its final resting place, but ever still so majestic. The bull's legs alone would have come past my shoulders had he been standing. It was one of the most magnificent creatures I'd ever seen.

Despite the direness of the situation, it was difficult to not be amazed at the beauty that was bestowed upon us in those few days. We were given the opportunity to see some of the most amazing uninhabited country that most never had. It was also hard not to feel close to God, or whoever one's maker was.

I thought back to a conversation I had once overheard between my mom and dad. My dad had just lost one of his best friends, Bud, in a horrible car accident. I was in second grade and went to school with Bud's only son. It was a terrible time for everyone, but especially his closest family, as the pain was too apparent to hide. Bud, like my dad and his other rough-around-the-edges friends, wasn't exactly the church-going type of guy. So when he died, my mother asked my father, "Do you think he believed in God?"

My father, who was also a logger with Bud replied simply, "How can anyone work in such beauty and wonder surrounding them every day and *not* believe?" It was a very basic thought, but held so much truth to me over the years. I don't necessarily see God in a church - but perhaps in the people that make up the church. God is something that surrounds me (as the Native Americans up there also believe), and is in everything living. So in these days that were filled with fear and anxiety, I also felt closer than I ever had to our Creator. The feeling encompassed me.

My legs burned and my body became weaker as the day grew long. I kept the radio in my head going the entire time - except when I was counting my paces for measurement of our distances. The strenuous walk kept me warm to the core, but my fingers remained icicles in my gloves as circulatory system deemed them not worthy enough to keep warm and decided to focus on the more vital organs. During breaks in the walk, I would remove my gloves and restore warmth to my hands by pressing them in-between my thighs, in hopes of warding off frost bite.

As nightfall drew in, we decided to set up our tents while there was still a smidgeon of daylight left. Now I hope you can see by now that I never expect special treatment when it comes to my job. However, I also do not like to be singled out as different either, and when the JG discarded the idea of combining our canvases together to keep it warmer because he felt it'd be an "uncomfortable situation," my jaw dropped in disbelief. *Are you kidding me??* I was extremely dismayed, shocked, and offended! *Wasn't this as hardcore of a survival situation as we were going to get? And he refused to sleep near me because what? He thought I was going to make a move on him or something?? Seriously?* Instead, I fantasized about throat-punching him.

Yes, because that's the first thing I think of doing when I am literally starved, exhausted beyond belief, and frozen to the bone - and most of all, I hadn't showered or brushed my teeth in four days at that point! (Detect sarcasm here.) I had never been this dirty before in my life. (Truth.) I could have been in a room full of poisonous snakes and rotting pig carcasses with a stench that burned your nostril hair off, and the thought of sex would have been more appealing than it was at this very moment. (More truth.)

So, as to not make the JG uncomfortable due to my lack of a penis, I used my canvas to cover a piece of twine I had strung between two flimsy twigs staked into the ground. It created a mini-triangle that was just tall enough that the peak of it did not come in contact with my nose when I laid inside of it. I had to first get into my sleeping bag standing up and then crawl like an inch worm into the mini tent - that basically just kept the wind and any rain or snow off of me, should there be any.

That night was one of the worst nights of my life. All night long, I could hear "The Enemy" off in the distance as they carried on yelling and screaming in an unrecognizable language. We all knew sometime in the next days that we were going to be captured. We just did not know when or how. It was a horrible fate to just have to sit and wonder when it would happen.

I realize this must seem strange. Of course, we knew these were trained instructors that were playing these roles. However, we had also heard the stories of what they were allowed to do to us and it wasn't a fate anyone would ever covet. Still, we knew it was coming and I think that was the thing that was so hard about it. It's kind of like that fear that one has when playing an intense game of Hide and Seek. You are hiding from someone you know isn't going to kill you or cause severe harm to you. It is a game. Still, when they do find you and you know you're about to get captured, more often than not most people will scream or shout in fear and struggle like mad to get away. It still is a terrible feeling in your sinking gut. But the anticipation and wondering if you are going to get caught as someone creeps up behind you - and the not knowing how it is going to happen - is the scariest of it all. In these surroundings, I soon was convinced that is was more than just a cat and mouse game - we were living this.

A few hours into the night, still awake, I suddenly heard the sound of footsteps not far from my head. Another set shuffled in the other direction with only a tiny piece of canvas separating me and whatever it was out there. Every muscle in my body locked up. I could not breathe. All I could do was lie there, clenching the opening of my sleeping bag. *Oh God. Was this it? Was this them coming to take us? How was it going to happen? And if it wasn't them, who or what was it?*

It felt like hours before the shuffling in our campsite finally seemed to disappear, fading away into the distance. I remained in silence, still paralyzed. During the day we were busy concentrating on navigating and hiking through the thicket - we didn't have time to think about it. But now, I just lay there - with nothing else to do but listen and wonder what was happening. I began to shake with coldness and fear. I was in the pitch black night, miles upon miles away from any form of civilization. I was scared and alone. Alone like I had never been before, with only myself to rely on to make it through this. If at any time I didn't survive, I would forfeit it all and forever lose any dream I had of flying in the Navy. It wouldn't just make the hard work from the past week be in vain, but all of my Aircrew and A-school training I had been going through for the past eight months be for nothing. I had no choice in the matter. I just couldn't give up. But I really wasn't sure of how much more of this I could take.

My breaths became short and panicky as I felt I could not get enough oxygen. My chest felt like a ton of bricks. My eyes flooded with tears and my nose began to run. The tip of it was an ice cube. *Calm. Calm yourself* - I kept saying over and over in my head. It wasn't working. I held my breath and closed my eyes. I began to dig deeper inside my aching guts to try to find a way to deal with the fear and panic.

And then, since I didn't know what else to do, I began to pray. I prayed for strength like I had never prayed before. I asked God for help. *Help me God... Please help me God... Please be with me God... Please help me get through this. I don't know how. I don't know what to do.* I prayed this prayer over and over as the minutes turned to hours.

When you're alone on a mountain on a bitter winter night in complete darkness, there is lots of time to talk to God. And for one of the first times in my life, I suddenly knew God was right there with me - I soon felt a warm comforting feeling engulfing me - quieting the inner screaming, warming the numbness, and keeping me safe. I slowly let my breath out and relaxed all of my muscles that had been so tense. *Was I dying?* I felt at last oddly at peace. Somehow I just knew in that moment that I was going to be okay. I prayed for the night to end. And eventually it did end, as all things do.

The next morning I was startled awake to screaming and shouting off in the distance, but close enough to hear and cause my stomach to jump into my throat. I sprung from my make-shift tent, still entwined in my sleeping bag, causing it to collapse into a heap, tripping, and nearly falling over my string ties. I spun around a complete circle, taking in the situation, doing my best not to panic. The air was crisp and cool as it held a low fog, blurring the objects surrounding our campsite. I could make out the JG springing to his feet on the other side of the clearing. We made eye contact and both shared the same look of confusion and fear.

He mouthed to me, "get your stuff," pointing at my gear and waving his arm toward himself. A sense of urgency came over us - even though we had no idea what we were doing. We could hear yelling - some was English and we recognized some of the voices - others were foreign. It was several groups of people that were getting captured by "The Enemy."

My hands trembled as the JG and I threw our gear into our bags, and delicately began to trek off into the woods in the opposite direction. We walked as swiftly as we could through the snowdrifts for at least an hour before we stopped for a quick break, deciding to consult the map and concoct some sort of a plan. As the day grew on, my memory became hazier and hazier. I knew it was Tuesday. I knew we made it to a point of contact where they gave us a cup of broth. It was basically salty water with probably a little chicken grease in it, but it was the first bit of nourishment I had had in nearly 2 days - well, not counting my trusty single Lifesaver rationed at every mealtime.

My hands trembled and with every step, my feet reminded me that each one sported a nice size blister on the back of my heel that continued to grow at a steady pace as my too-big boots - which were the smallest of the men's sizes I could find - rubbed my heel raw with every step. Because of the lack of food, sleep, heat, and just sheer exhaustion, I don't even remember sleeping that next night. I know I did somewhere, somehow, but I have no recollection of it. Into Wednesday we continued to hike from sun up with no real destination in mind other than a few land marks or "safe houses" with the reward of chicken broth waiting gallantly for us - all so they could see how well we navigated and used our survival skills. Because they were always watching us - you could always feel the eyes of The Enemy on you - watching your every move - deciding what they wanted to do with you next. And it was sometime around noon on that Wednesday (judging from the sun directly overhead) that I at last lost my freedom.

What happened next was very much a whirlwind. Suddenly, we were surrounded by a group of armed malicious bandits in camouflage with their faces covered. We were pulled out of the woods and to a gravel road where a huge covered truck awaited us. But before we went anywhere, we were made to stand in a line (others had been captured at this point as well and there were probably around eight or ten of us in this line).

The Enemy began shouting at us. Mostly in words we did not recognize, but enough broken English that we could figure out the message they were trying to convey. Their favorite word was Pig Dog. That was what we were referred to from this point on.

A single man with a rifle strapped around his chest continued to yell obscenities at us as he walked up and down the line, pausing to rip an article of clothing off of the guy next to me, then jerked him around, forcing him to get on the ground. I didn't have time to think about what was happening. *Just do what they say.*

He came in front of me, yelling something. I didn't understand or move fast enough. And then it came, the biggest open-handed crack across my face. It stung my frozen cheeks. My jaw filled with pain as my head flung in the direction the hand shoved it. My first dose of pain inflicted intentionally and instantly my eyes began to well up as a reflex. I was stunned. And my feelings were hurt. *Why would this person - another human being - hit me like that?* I didn't do anything to them. I took it personally.

My hands were bound behind my back and a musty, black hood that smelled of body odor and mold was forced over my entire head - blacking out my world. I could only hear now, and see a little bit of daylight at my own feet. I was shoved violently into the back of the canvas covered truck. I was thrown against another body as I lost my footing and collapsed on this unknown person. Before I had time to react, I was pulled up to a sitting position as more shouts went on and a huge thick boot began kicking my legs. My shins stung and began to swell until at last I figured out that they wanted me to cross them.

It felt like I was in a dream. *This is just training. It will eventually end. They are just acting.* But pretty soon, I forgot that it was just an act. The surroundings, the languages. I was tired, and starving. My weak body led to my weakening mind.

It took everything I had in me not to panic in this moment. I could not see. I could not move. I was sandwiched in-between other bigger guys like a pack of sardines, and I could not do anything about it. In a moment I was stripped of every right I had as a human. I was lower than an animal in captivity at this point. The only way I could keep from panicking was to keep breathing and to imagine myself in another place.

Because I couldn't see anything, I imagined I was lying on a sandy beach, soaking in the sun. We bounced along uncontrollably in the back of the truck as it rounded corners and slammed over rocks. I attempted to convince myself that it was my choice that I could no longer see and at any time, if I really wanted to, I would be able to open my eyes and see. But I couldn't.

Suddenly, I felt a very light touch on my left forearm. The person sitting next to me reached out with their bound hands and rubbed my arm ever so slightly with their finger. I had no idea who that person was, but their touch reminded me that I wasn't alone. That it would be okay.

Eventually the truck stopped. I would've rather it keep driving all day than pause at this dreaded location we feared, as the climax of our training was about to begin. Suddenly, I was grabbed under my bound arms and carelessly pulled across and out of the truck. My feet hit the ground with a slam that jarred my entire body and I struggled to gain balance, completely disorientated. I was dragged over to a designated spot and dumped, then kicked and yelled at when I did not rise to my feet quick enough. I could hear all kinds of yelling, back and forth between The Enemy to us, and to each other.

My bag was ripped off my head, and my wrists were cut free. The back of the knife gouged into my skin, pinching it between the ropes. Nothing was done carefully or with concern. Cautiously, I glanced around to find myself in a row with everyone else that was captured. Several of The Enemies were working all around us. There were a few random buildings off in the distance and a few more covered trucks near us. It was where they had set up camp. An entire world was alive up here on a mountain in Maine. It was a world that existed completely separate from any world I had ever known. Here, we were as removed from civilization as I ever knew possible.

More yelling ensued. One of The Enemies marched up and down our rank, as he did, he forcefully threw a loose rope around our neck with a circular piece of wood attached to the end of it, probably about the diameter of a baseball - only flat like a dog collar and tag. On that flat piece of wood was a number, pressed in black. They shouted in broken language to us that this was our new form of identification and we must always address ourselves as "War Criminal number so and so." Failure to comply with their rules resulted in pain. So from that point on, I became War Criminal number one-five. It was a number that I will never forget.

Quickly we were divided into groups of men and women. Well, men and me. They were escorted one way as I was brought the other, by men carrying M-16s snuggly strapped around their shoulder. I was tossed into a small trailer and told to crawl through a small dog-hole-like entrance. On my hands and knees, I obeyed. When I crawled through the hole into another room, I was greeted by an apathetic-looking woman who sat at a desk full of papers. She didn't even look up as she gave me orders to rise to my feet immediately. Again, I obeyed. I was putty in their hands. It was like boot camp but so much worse. There were no rules here. They were only here to teach you a lesson - and you were going to learn it no matter what it took.

"Strip." Was the one word that the woman stated, still reading from the piles of papers that surrounded her.

Strip. The word echoed in my head. With dread, and a feeling that I was surrendering any last bit of dignity over to The Enemy, I began to slowly peel off my week-old unwashed clothes. My nose was too cold to smell anything, but I knew I smelled foul. When I was done, I stood there, naked, shivering, and completely exposed - both physically and vulnerably. I knew in the back of my mind she was checking for signs of frostbite or distress. Still, it was every bit as degrading as it was intended to be.

The woman came over, looked me up and down and commanded, "Turn." She had some strange, unrecognizable accent. I obeyed. "Now poot deese on." She handed me a pair of men's underwear. I put them on, and of course they were huge. However, they felt amazing. They were clean. It was a wonderful gift. I did not let on how happy she had just made me. "Poot dis... back on." She pointed to my bra, and I did as instructed. I was quickly given a short medical exam - listening to my heart, breathing, the works.

I was given a clean white T-shirt and instructed to put it on and get the rest of my outer clothes on. I did and then crawled back through the doggie-door into the next room where I was not so kindly greeted by the man holding the rifle. He gestured and yelled at me to get up and file out. Outside, I met up with the rest of the guys as they were slowly filtering from the little shed that they, too, had been "examined" in.

Once we all were in ranks (a long straight line in front of one another), our heads were yet again forcefully covered with the canvas bag and we were instructed to place our hands on the person's shoulders that was in front of us and attempted to march blindly this way. I'm not sure how long it was we marched. I just know it wasn't easy to coordinate and omit stepping on the guy's ankles in front of me as my ankles were simultaneously being stepped on by the guy behind me. It was the true definition of a goat rope.

Eventually we were brought into another building and individually separated from the group. There was much clanging and banging of metal bars. It smelled of a musty cellar. I was shoved forward and my bag was removed from my head by one of the armed guards. Using only my eyes, as I was scared to move a hair, I glanced over and saw a cement floor, and a solid, cemented back wall. The two sides must have been made out of some type of dark, aged wood. In the dim light of the cell, I could clearly see that I would be unable to even fully stretch my arms out from side to side without the walls preventing them from doing so. From the back cement wall to the door I stood in front of, I calculated it was probably an arm's length and a half. There on the back wall was a tiny slab of wood no more than 2 inches high from the floor. "Sit, Pig-dog." The guard demanded with a growl, "there." He gestured to the slab of wood. I sat. "Back against the wall. Feet together. And arms out, resting on knees. Palms up," he commanded. I managed to conform into the awkward position. I knew I couldn't last like this for a long period of time without my muscles burning and falling over only to be punished again in some way. But I did stay that way.

"Welcome home." The guard sneered with a half-cocked malicious smile as he turned, slamming the metal door with a clang. Another clang echoed as the metal bar fell in front of it, locking me into the cell. And it was silent.

A lump began to grow in my throat. *Don't get upset now*, I told myself. *Put yourself in another place. Think of another place.* I closed my eyes. Suddenly another slam and bang and my door was thrust open with the guard standing there. "Get on your feet when I enter, War Criminal!" And he instantaneously reinforced his anger by slapping my face, so hard that it stung and instantly filled my eyes with water. "No sleep! Understand Pig-dog?" I nodded haphazardly, still dazed from the pain in my face. "In the pose-ish!" He barked and I obeyed.

The door slammed and clanged again as metal crashed into itself once again. It was then, as I looked forward, that I saw the hole, with an eyeball staring right back at me. I quickly looked away. It felt like an eternity of feeling uncomfortable as I knew it was just staring at me. I tried not to shudder. At last the eyeball disappeared and only when I heard the feet shuffle away, did I make eye contact with the peep hole.

I allowed my mind to go numb. I tuned out as much as humanly possible. My body was physically there, doing as instructed as mechanically as I could function, by my mind was long gone. It could not stay, or it would not survive.

And then, the most deafening noise I'd ever heard began. I looked up and saw speakers above my cell. There was a woman with an Asian-type language singing a screeching, song that sounded like it was from the World War II era.

This form of non-entertainment went on and on for endless hours. There were whiney songs in foreign languages, something that sounded similar to a Tokyo Rose broadcast, a woman reciting the Boots, Boots, Boots chant. It went on and on, over and over again. It was enough to drive anyone insane. That was the point. But the kicker of them all was a recording of a horrific 911 call of a little girl who's daddy had beat up (or worse, killed) her mommy. It was all very sick and twisted as the screeching record player played on continuously into the night. [*Boots—boots—boots—boots—movin' up and down again...*]

In the corner of our dingy cell, there was an old rusted coffee can. This was our toilet. However, we had to ask permission to "urinate" before we used it. As in "War Criminal number 1-5 requests permission to urinate." (God forbid we had to ask permission to *defecate*.) And the entire room full of our imprisoned peers heard it all. I knew they were there in cells next to mine as I could hear them requesting to urinate or the guards coming in to slap them around and give them a hard time because they were not sitting properly or did not address the guards in the correct manner. It was humiliating, but yet we were all in the same boat.

Every hour or so they would give me a new canteen full of water and slip it under my cell door. I was then required to leave my old one in its place. My old one had better be empty, or they would come in and pour the remainder on my head. I drank so much water, my stomach ached and bloated even more. After a while I just began pouring the water directly into the coffee can. It was too much and I was so tired of having to use the coffee can every half hour. [*Don't— don't—don't—don't—look at what's in front of you...*]

The hours passed, drawing on as slow as a rainy weekend. I could hear foot-steps coming forth. All at once, the cell door was flung open and a dark figure hastily threw another sack over my head. By now, I seemed to be getting used to these sacks. However, not being able to move my hands from their position really was a disadvantage to say the least. Even for something as simple as how my nose began to run because of the cold. No amount of sniffing could contain it. As I walked along blindly, snot began to drip down my upper lip creating the most horrific itch along the way. I felt disgusting. My last little bit of dignity was hanging on by its pinky finger to the edge of the cliff. I had already lost my femininity, as I was dressed in men's clothing down to my underwear, no make-up and hadn't shaved or bathed in a week. I was hairy. I stunk. My hair and skin was greasy. And now I was only a number.

I had nothing left but one thing. It was the one thing that kept me sane - my fellow sailors. When I would fall, get smacked around, or was forced to announce my request to urinate, I had the empathy of my peers. We would try to help each other when no one was looking, or whisper, "you're okay," to each other. Our hearts ached with every slap another received, more than it did when we were getting slapped ourselves.

We did our best to act as if we could not tell what was going on when another was being humiliated, as if we could help save face for them. Every chance we got to have contact with one another, such as when we were led around by placing our hands on the person in front of us, we would secretly squeeze the shoulder of the person in front of us. If we could actually see each other, we would exchange an all-knowing and all-understanding look, or even purposely brush arms as we passed by. It was what held us together.

Then we were separated again. One at a time, we were thrown into a room and the door was slammed shut. There was so much yelling and banging. Others were thrown into a wooden box that couldn't have been more than two and a half feet tall and about the same in width and length. It was so small that some of the guys barely fit into it. Somehow the guards mangled us individually into it.

For the first time in my career, being short had its advantage. I had no problem getting into the box. The lid was slammed shut and a heavy weight was put on top of it. It was designed to create panic in those that are even the slightest bit claustrophobic. I continued to breathe. It dawned on me that I was okay in the box. They couldn't hit me while I was in the box. I actually made the box my safe place in my mind so I would vanish the idea of how trapped and helpless I really was at this point. Every now and then, the Enemy would come by and slam one of their night sticks onto the lid of the box, creating a horrible jolting shock to the system as it was impossible to know when it was coming. They just wanted to make sure that I knew they were still there. *Ha ha*, I thought to myself. *You're not bothering me a bit*. And War Criminal Number 1-5 wins this round. I had to keep track of the littlest victories.

Abruptly, the lid disappeared and I felt myself being lifted ruggedly out of the box and dragged to another location. There was much that happened in those several hours. There were smoke rooms, and there was water-boarding. [*Men— men—men—men—men go mad with watchin' 'em...*]

If SERE school was comparable to a ghastly horror movie, interrogation had to be the slow, gruesome death of the leading role. Any last bit of self-worth that your mind may have still contained was slowly and steadily squeezed out of your head. I was thrown into a dimly lit room that resembled a typical, but eerie office. There was a desk on one side, and a podium on the other with a chalkboard on the back wall. And from there on, the details of interrogation are somewhat hazy. I do recall them asking me my name. They asked about my job, who I was with, and any information they could get from me. They said if I didn't tell, they would do something to my family in Minnesota. That was a shocking statement. How did they know about my family?

They said they called my dad and he said to tell them what they needed to know. Tell them or they would kill him. I couldn't make sense of anything. I forgot what I could say and what I couldn't say. I knew I was going to get beat no matter what I said. So I just kept saying "I don't know." They had this special technique of grabbing my shirt right above my pectoral muscles with a hand on each side, twisting to get a grip. Keeping my heels to the wall, but pulling my upper body forward, they would then slam me with the force of a grown man into the solid wall behind me. By doing this, it does not cause any major damage to your body, but thrusts the wind out of you in such a panicky, painful way, that it just made me go weak and brought tears to my eyes. I didn't know what else to do but endure it - ride it out, knowing at some point they had to stop.

My skin pinched in their grip and I could feel the bruises form instanta- neously. I was slammed into the wall over and over and my face was slapped continually. I just kept saying "I don't know, I don't know." I began to get de- lirious and soon, they were holding me up as my legs had buckled. Tears were pouring down my face. I didn't understand how a human being could do this to another human being. *Did they not have any compassion? Did they not care about how badly they were hurting everyone? I would never do this to one of them.* Hell, I let spiders go outside rather than smack them. And then I realized, I did sign up to kill people during a war. I knew I was blowing up submarines, but there were *people* inside of these submarines. They were not just huge chunks of scrap metal floating in the ocean. They were The Enemies' friends. Their brothers and fathers. I was no better than my enemy. I believed that what I was fighting for was right and just - and so did they. They felt they were justified. I killed people too.

I didn't know how much time had passed. I only knew they couldn't kill me today, so I just removed my mind from that place and just prayed for it to end. Over and over. I coughed and gasped in attempts to catch my breath. I couldn't stand. My head ached and was ringing from the shouting. And after what felt like hours, when they did not get what they wanted, they at last let go of my limp body and I fell into the interrogator. Of course he did not catch me, and I fell to the floor, collapsing like a ragdoll. I didn't have the strength to stand on my own. [*If—your—eyes—drop—they will get atop o'you...*]

My cell door was flung open. I rose immediately. In the hands of The Ene- my is the most savory smelling roasted chicken that I'd ever seen. There were mashed potatoes that never looked fluffier and some vegetables on the side - which despite my abhorrence for vegetables, in that moment looked more de- lectable and mouth-watering than anything I'd ever seen in my life. I had earlier forgotten about food. I didn't think I was hungry anymore. But as soon as the smell caught my nose, my stomach was doing violent flips. "What do you see War Criminal? Tell everyone what you see," he growled at me as to ensure everyone in their cells surrounding me would hear.

"Chicken, sir," I replied, feeling empty.

"And does it look and smell delicious, War Criminal?"

"Yes, sir, it does."

"And what else do you see on this plate?"

"I see mashed potatoes, gravy, and green beans," I stated simply.

"And do they not look like the best mashed potatoes you have ever seen?"

"Yes, sir." My mouth watered at the mere thought of tasting them.

"Ah, my friend, well enjoy it then!" He said, turning around, leaving my cell door to slam and lock behind him, taking the food along with him. Of course the other prisoners were unaware of this last silent detail. [*We—can—stick— out—'unger, thirst, an' weariness...*]

At some point, the night had passed and the daytime came dutifully in its place. So fair and foul a day I have not seen. I could tell it was sunny and beautiful despite my dire surroundings as I was led out into the open with my good old familiar friend, the bag, on my head.

When my bag was ripped off of my head, my eyes were instantly blinded by the plaguing light of day. It was the first I had seen of the sun in quite some time now and it stung, brilliantly and painfully. All around me were my fellow prisoners, all made to work odd, tedious and insignificant jobs that lasted forever - such as hauling dirt to one side of the camp, all to be told by the Enemy to take it back to the other side. There was no satisfaction of a completed task. It was never to end. Everyone was assigned to their 'working parties.' We were at last all reunited - though we could not speak, or even make much eye contact, but just to be in the presence of others of our own was therapeutic. [*'Tain't—so—bad—by—day because o' company...*]

I went about my routine of stacking pebbles as instructed. Every time I made any progress with my pebble hill, it was all to be knocked down and I was told it wasn't good enough - start again. My hands grew raw and began bleeding from continuously scraping the cold ground.

After a while I was approached by one of the guards. "You!" He pointed at me. "Take your clothes off." I stood there, stunned - unsure of what to do. Everyone within earshot paused, if only for a second before they realized they had stopped working - and quickly began again - looking away this time, but now paying the utmost attention at the scene that was being created by this guard.

"My clothes?" I slowly began.

WHACK! I moved too slow and questioned authority and my jaw had paid the price by this delay. I felt a scratch accompanying the slap - quite possibly from a ring and then the warm liquid running down my cheek.

Unphased, the Guard continued. "Remove your shirt and pants and get to work in your underwear. Women are dirty and do not deserve clothes." He snarled and walked away to tell the other female the same instructions. She glanced my way in disbelief, but slowly we obeyed. I threw my t-shirt down and removed my pants. There I stood in my men's underwear and bra in front of an entire POW camp. *No big deal*, I told myself. *They are just trying to hurt you. I show more in a swim suit. I am at a beach, playing in the rocks. I am at the beach.* The cold, April mountain air stung my skin as it blew in, making my beach fantasy a hard one to convince myself.

Whatever. I muttered to myself. As I glanced around, I could see sympathetic looks by the men surrounding me.

"Maki. Maki!" I heard my name loudly whispered and carefully turned around to discover a nearly, but most welcomingly unrecognizable face. It was stained in dirt, cuts and bruises, and had a look I'd never seen before. It only took a second to realize this was Emerson. I was so happy to see my friend, but so nervous at the same time. We would be punished if they caught us talking.

"Maki," he whispered loudly again.

"What?" I said, wishing I wasn't noticed at that moment by my best friend. I didn't want anyone I knew to see me like this. I was disgusting.

"Are you okay?" he said, with the most genuine look I'd ever seen on his face. "We're going to be okay," he said, before I could even answer. "I promise - just be strong..." As he spoke the words, the closest guard whipped his head around to see where the noises were coming from. We quickly put our heads down, and continued to work.

I knew I couldn't look at him, or talk to him, but just knowing Emerson was there was more comfort than I had known all week. We would survive this. There couldn't have been too much more they could do to us, could there? [*Try—try—try—try—to think o' something different...*]

A piercing siren echoed throughout the camp, stinging our ears and causing temporary paralysis. "Air raid! Air raid!" the guards yelled. "To the shelter!"

Everyone started running in chaos. No one really knew what this meant, but just ran after the guy in front of them. The siren was screaming at this point and everyone became a big mosh pit trying to squeeze through the tiny door of the shelter. People began falling over each other. I looked over just in time to see the other girl, Terra, was knocked back onto the ground. Others continued to push forth. And then, it only took a small gesture to break the blind trance of the stampeding crowd. One of the Marines stopped and held his arms out on both sides to stop the crowd behind him. "Wait!" he shouted. The shoving stopped - as he reached down and grabbed her hand, pulling her up and safely into the shelter.

"Someone help me grab those two injured guys." We looked over and near the door where two guys were lying on different stretchers. They were both next to the door - but may as well have been miles away as they could not move, nor help themselves to safety. A hush of shame fell on us as we realized how much we had slipped into survival mode. That we forgot about those around us for that moment of sheer chaos. Our heads hung even lower, if it was possible. [*Oh—my—God—keep—me from goin' lunatic...*]

"Lessons time!" shouted The Enemy. Again, our "work" was interrupted and we filed into the shelter one-by-one and were made to sit like cross-legged children packed on top of each other. After everyone was at last settled and hushed as we had no idea what was coming next. Every moment was full of dreaded surprises.

"Hello, Pig Dogs." There was a long silence. We had no idea what was next. Finally the guard began.

"You sit there thinking you can just kill our women and children and not have to pay," The Enemy began. "You kill my children. You rape my wives. You disrespect my god and you don't care. You call yourself American?

"Well this, my little American, this is what I think about your country." He reached over to a chair next to him where a neatly folded American flag lay. In that moment, we helplessly watched him began to rip the flag in half. As he did it, some gasped in disbelief, but unfeelingly and amused, The Enemy continued his work with a smile on his face as if to pour salt on the wound. As the flag tore, I felt despair. My eyes welled up again with tears. They took another piece of me. They disrespected everything we stood for, had learned to take pride in - and there was nothing we could do about it.

"Ha, my Pig Dogs! How does that feel? This is what you do to my people every day. You are not superior. You are not powerful. Alone, you are nothing. Your President is a fool and a liar. Your god is a liar. Where is he now?"

In that moment, he reached back on the chair again. My heart sunk as I watched him pick up the Bible. I knew what was going to happen next and I felt like I wanted to throw up.

"This is what we think of your so-called god." In that moment, he grabbed a handful of pages, and tore them from the Bible. He opened the stove next to him and began throwing pages into the fire. Piece by piece, he destroyed it until it was all ablaze. Then he finished it off by throwing the shreds of the flag that was left on top of the Bible into the fire. The material was up in smoke in less than a minute. Everything that I believed and was taught to cherish was destroyed in front of me in a matter of minutes.

"Your country does not want you to come back. Your family is ashamed of you. You have failed to protect them. You *are* failure."

[*It—is—not—fire—devils—dark or anything…*]

My fingers became calloused from hauling dirt and rocks. My joints ached along with my heart. My stomach had long given up on me and just showed its dissatisfaction with me by draining every last bit of energy I had. I stunk. My body was weak and shook. I hadn't eaten anything in four days. I didn't know how much longer I could stand it. I looked around me and saw all of my friends in the most vulnerable way I'd ever seen them. Boys that normally are full of such cockiness and arrogance were broken, withered, and pained. We had all been broken down to scraps of a human - and it had only been two days since we had been captured. We hadn't planned on failing so badly.

Some of the them that had been there for three days - the ones that were in the first group to get captured began to grow delirious, not making sense in their speaking - seeing things. Mostly from their sleep deprivation. Periodically different numbers were called over a loud speaker and sent into one of the shacks. More banging and yelling. No one knew for sure what was going on in there, but the worst was imagined. This had been going on all day. At some point, one of the guards had instructed myself and Terra to get dressed again. We willingly did, as my shoulders were beginning to blister in the heat of the high sunlight. [*Boots—boots—boots—boots—movin' up an' down again...*]

"War criminal number 1-5... get in here," was bellowed over the squawky loud-speaker. My stomach instantly dropped. I had no idea what was going to happen now. I don't know if I could take much more. I slowly rose to my feet and dusted the rocks off that were imbedded in my knees. Quietly, I knocked on the door of the building, wishing like anything that I could just disappear in that moment.

All at once, the door flung open and a hand reached out, grabbed me by my shirt, and forcefully pulled me into the building, slamming the door behind me. It was dark. I squinted and guessed there were about four guards in there at that moment. They were yelling things back and forth. Someone slapped my left cheek in its usual slapping spot. It had long grown numb to it. There was only one left handed guard that would slap my right cheek. However, for whatever reason, this short left-handed Enemy loved to deliver with a wind up, so despite its less frequent thrashings, my right cheek seemed to have swollen of equal size to match my left.

"Pig Dog, stand straight!" One guard yelled. He had an object in his hand that looked like a hardened, thick rubber hose. It was longer and thicker than a night stick. He raised it over his head and slammed it down on the table just next to me with a deafening slam, as if to show me its crushing strength. I jumped at the impact.

"Pig Dog, pull your shoulders back." Again, I did as instructed, though it took so much energy to stand straight. He responded by yet again slamming the heavy object forcefully into the table.

"Pig Dog, stick your hands out in front of you. Palms up." Slowly, and with dread, I weakly stuck my shaking hands out in front of me, terrified of what was to come.

"Now, shut your eyes," he commanded in a low whisper that took me by surprise. I shut my eyes and every muscle in my body tensed up, bracing for the god-awful impact. *Breathe. Just breathe. The pain will pass.*

A few seconds went by and it felt like an eternity. Instead, I felt nothing. Then, all of a sudden, I felt a warm hand clench firmly around my right hand, closing it, and turning it, and shaking it. Stunned, I opened my eyes - one at a time - not knowing what was going on.

"Congratulations, Airman Maki, you just graduated SERE school."

I was confused. Shocked. What kind of a trick was this?

He smiled. And for a second, he looked human. My mind became mush and my throat swelled up. I began shaking and couldn't hold my tears back any longer - even though I still did not want to cry in front of all of these people. *Was it over? Was it really over at last? But where was everyone?* All of the guards in the room began shaking my hand, congratulating me. I just stood there, stunned. I didn't know how to react. These were the people that were just beating me and my friends an hour ago. Now they acted as if everything was okay? That I should just forget about everything that had happened on this mountain over the past few days?

"Airman, come in here - have something to eat." They pulled me into the next room, handing me a piece of cornbread and milk, as if we had been friends for years. *Was this a joke? Or a test? Were they just going to take it back from me?* I was apprehensive to do anything. And then as I entered the room, I saw one of my fellow classmates. He was a Captain in the Marines. He had been called into the building just before I did. But there had been people being called in and released all day long. *What was going on? Why was this happening to us while everyone else was still out there working?*

"Have a seat," he began. "It seems that you and the Captain here did the best in your interrogations. In fact, you could have told them a little more information, and it would have been okay, Airman Maki. You probably wouldn't have been beaten as hard."

Wow. That's just so great to hear now. Not.

"So," he continued. "Since you two scored the highest, we are going to need your help for our finale ceremony."

As I attempted to take some bites of the dry cornbread, instructions were explained to us as how it was to go down. I was starving, but could not take more than a couple of bites. It was just too much for my stomach. I was ill.

"Fall into ranks!" The Enemy shouted to the working parties. I had silently resumed my position of working in the dirt. Everyone dropped what they were doing and ran over to the Guard, attempting to form some type of ranks. *Oh yeah, we were in the military. This was one of the things we did. Form ranks. Stand at attention. Parade Rest and march.* Looking at us right now, in our tatters, we looked more like homeless people than the most powerful military in the world.

The next few minutes were again quite a blur. We were in ranks and being shouted at about some arbitrary thing as usual. Suddenly, as planned, the Captain came running from out of nowhere towards us carrying the flag in his arms, flapping behind him as he ran. He was shouting, "Save the flag! Save the flag!"

Some guards were running after him a ways back, yelling something at the other guards.

Everyone turned from formation, watching, confused. "Help him! Help him save the flag!" I yelled as previously instructed to do. I ran forward, pushing people in ranks in front of me to run forward as well, towards the Captain. Still confused, but slowing beginning to oblige, everyone began to run towards him. It became a mad chaotic rush of the crowd - no one could really see what was happening. Suddenly, cutting the yells like a knife, our own National Anthem began playing over the loud speaker as the flag in the Captain's arms attached to a flag pole and began to raise. Everyone froze in their tracks, including The Enemy. They stopped, stood at attention and saluted the flag. The rest of us prisoners turned back to the flag and followed suit. We stood there for the entire two minutes that the song played. Saluting. Soon there wasn't a dry eye in the crowd as the flag and the National Anthem took on a whole new meaning from that point forward for every man and woman on that mountain.

As soon as it was over, the simple, sweetest words ever were shouted from the mouth of one of the Instructors. "Congratulations class. You have all just graduated SERE school." Soon trays of dry cornbread and milk were passed around for all.

I braced myself, holding my weight by using the wall in front of me. Minute after minute passed as I continued to let the hot water beat down on my head, and run down my body, stinging the dozens of scrapes and cuts that covered my body. I couldn't get enough of it. Slowly, I ran the hard, solid bar of soap up and down my arms, over my chest and stomach and down each leg. I was careful not to press too hard, as even that bit of pressure on my bruises caused them to ache even more. Carefully, I lowered myself and sat on the shower floor. A week ago, there was no way I would have sat on the floor of a community shower that was probably cleaned only once a week by some sailor in a hurry to get off of work.

Today, I did not give germs a second thought. I had had so many bugs crawling over me in the past week, ate so much dirt, that there was nothing that could have bothered me in that moment.

I had to sit on the floor to reach my leg in order to shave the disgusting week-long growth, as I was too weak to prop it up and stand on one leg. I was too weak to do much of anything. I needed food and sleep, but a shower trumped both of those, as I wanted first to feel like a human again and my empty stomach had grown used to the feeling. I had no food in my barracks, and was afraid of how I would look to others going out to get something to eat.

After about a half an hour and nearly falling asleep in the shower, I shut it off, grabbed a towel and stepped out onto the rug in front of the sink. Looking up, I was shocked to see the face staring back at me in the mirror. It was pale, with black circles under and around my eyes. My skin hung off my cheekbones, the left side was bruised. I looked ghastly and sick-like. I thought this was crazy - after only a week I barely recognized myself.

Quickly as I could get my body to move, I dressed in some loose-fitting clothes, grabbed some food to go at McDonalds, ate about half of my burger and passed out on the bed by 5pm - not to wake until 15 hrs later.

⊣ Afterthoughts ⊢

After that week, many things about myself had changed. I know this school was only a glimpse, as it would be impossible to ever fathom what a real prison camp could consist of. I know I would have been subjected to torture on a much greater scale that no doubt would have included multiple rapings of my body, mind, and soul. Obviously this could never be replicated. There is no way I could ever experience the real magnitude of a prison camp without actually going to one. Additionally, and most importantly, I knew this training I experienced had an end in sight. I could cling to that hope to get me through each day. In a real camp, there is no guarantee, only hope. There is no telling yourself that these people are really here to train you to be a better person. I think of how John McCain among so many others spent 5 years or more in a prison camp. That is unfathomable. I spent two days in a training camp and had a life changing experience. And there were so many others. They define what it truly means to "sacrifice so that others may live." How they never gave up their hope and fight to return home after weeks, months, and years - I'll never know.

But this is what I do know. I know now what it is like to not have a flag. I know what it feels to have your Bible burned in front of you. These things represent so much of who we are and what is precious to us. We take them for granted - thinking they've always been there and always will be. I know now that every time I hear the National Anthem, I am excited just to hear it play one more time. I will take those few minutes to truly look at that flag and think about the soldiers that have seen it rise out of the depths of despair. I will never duck inside a building so that I don't have to stand in the rain and mess up my hair to watch the flag rise to its glorious position. It is my honor to see it every day because I know now what it feels like to have it taken away.

I have yet to listen to The Star Spangled Banner and not get goose bumps or tears in my eyes from the power it possesses and everything it represents. Please don't forget.

CHAPTER 8

Jacksonville, FL.

May 1998

Approximate distance from Deer River: 1600 miles

The flight to Jacksonville was like any other one. The flight went up and the flight came back down. This is always a good thing and should never be taken for granted. This time however, I resisted the urge to call my mom and tell her to come and save me because I wasn't ready for this new change. This time I had someone waiting for me at the airport. Someone I hadn't seen in what felt like ages. Someone whom I had been dreaming about the days we could be together again during some of my dire and most humbling moments of SERE school. My happy thought. Well, him and quarter-pounder cheeseburgers.

Quickly checking my tiny hand-held mirror to ensure my lipstick wasn't smudged and I didn't have spinach in my teeth (which would've been odd - since I wasn't eating spinach), I eagerly exited the plane and began looking around for a familiar face at the gate. Everyone around me began to find their significant others that were there greeting them each upon their arrivals. They paired off, and then strolled away together, arms linked and whistling 1940s show tunes.

Where was he? A slight panic shot in my stomach. *What if he had been attacked by a shark during his morning swim?* I began mindlessly searching down the terminal, when suddenly, as I rounded the chairs directly in front of me, there he sat, all dreamy with his legs out and arms crossed against his chest. He wore a navy wool sweater with khaki shorts and Birkenstocks and appeared as though he had not a care in the world. His sleeves were pushed up in his suave manner and he looked like something out of a Lands End magazine. I sighed. He was more handsome than I could have ever remembered. *Of course* this is something he would have

125

done.

"Hey. What's going on?" Adam casually nodded to me as if I were any perfect stranger passing by.

"You dork!" I exclaimed, smiling. "What are you doing?"

As he stood up and came near me, I flung my arms around his tall, muscular body. His chest was firm and his biceps appeared much larger through his fitted sweater than I had remembered. He squeezed me back and picked me off my feet. My body was still one gigantic bruise that throbbed with pain when touched, but I ignored it. He smelled wonderful and it was the most euphoric feeling to be safe in the arms of the man I loved once again. I prayed for the moment to last forever.

"You look awful, kid," he said with concern in his voice.

"I know."

***

We joyfully spent the next four days together, both on a mini-leave before our next duty station. They were days spent full of carefree laughter, storytelling, fishing, singing, and nothing but pure, young love. I felt like a Double Mint gum commercial - we were just so ridiculously happy. And when the day finally came that we had to part, he simply kissed me and said goodbye - like quickly removing a Band-Aid. I remained in Jacksonville and he began his five-day cross-country drive alone out to San Diego, where he had been accepted into SEAL training (aka BUDS). His dream was coming true.

We talked every night on the phone. We wrote letters. He'd draw me funny pictures of frogs and scenes with stick people. We'd write about our future dreams together and the struggles we were facing with our trainings. I fell in love with him more with every day that passed. And the longing to be together grew stronger. It made us temporarily insane. We set our goals and counted down the days until we could be together again. I would have loved to do nothing but lay in the Florida sun and dream of our future together. Unfortunately, the Navy thought that was a ridiculous idea.

"The Rag"

During my lovely stay in Jacksonville, Florida, I was lucky enough to be there from the ripe months of May through beginning of November. (Please note the sarcasm here. There is *nothing* lovely about Florida in the summer.) Additionally, it just so happened to be during one of the worst summer of fires down there in decades. The swamp fires had been burning for weeks and although they were many miles away, we suffered the effects of having soot littering our air so badly at times that our instructors cancelled our morning PT (physical training) outside. (Sailors are always looking for a reason to cancel PT - but this time it was actually legit.) The cars were lined with an ashy film after sitting out all night in the parking lot. Boot prints in gray ash trailed up and down the sidewalks.

And yet we had no choice but to breathe this air, on a daily basis. We were powerless. Much like the third-world countries that drink the contaminated waters because that's all they have to drink - this air, this was the only air we had to breathe. We knew with each breath there was damage being done, but what choice did we have? Air was important.

In Jacksonville, there were three of us in a room. We also shared a communal bathroom, having only one on each floor. It was the first time the barracks did not have a watch at the door, so though there were female and male barracks - there was no one to reinforce this. So for the first time in my life, I had absolutely no rules or supervision - nor did the rest of the sailors in our classes. We were finally adults!

Living in the barracks, sharing bedrooms and bathrooms with multiple people from all over the country and walks of life was an experience in itself. It was the first time I realized you could be best friends with someone, but when you live with someone, suddenly you see an entirely different side that you may not have known before. Unwelcomed habits make their appearance and minuscule annoyances soon become astronomical.

My roommates during those six months of VP-30 training were Jenessa and Alyanna. Sometimes they got along great, and other times it was like being caught in the middle of two cats in heat on a hot spring night. Jenessa was a small-town, freckly-face country girl from Texas who was determined that if Texas ever seceded from the Union, she would immediately go AWOL to support them. She spoke funny and called every pop a Coke - even when it was a Mountain Dew. Her hair styles and colors changed with her mood. Jenessa pulled me out of my small-town shell and taught me that bigger was always better, that one could never have enough pairs of shoes, and that we didn't have to become men to do what was traditionally considered a 'man's job.' She was full of big ideas and was a friend to all in need. She often collected friends that were in turmoil and then didn't always know what to do with after she had them, much like an old lady that feeds the neighborhood strays and then cannot get rid of them. I never knew what feral animal I'd be coming home to in my barracks.

She also taught me a lot about boys - mainly how not to pick one. Unfortunately her 'picker' was broken and she tended to pick all the wrong ones. I'm not sure if she just saw the best in people and ignored the rest of the warnings, or if she just wanted to help everyone, but as I watched through the years, poor Jenessa always ended up on the raw side of the deal when it came to the men she was with.

Alyanna, on the other hand, was a firey Chicago-raised Italian with thick, curly hair that was as black as the night and covered much of her. She preferred to keep only a few good friends, but would do anything in the world for them. She had a generous heart, often lending her clothes, car, or whatever I needed without ever expecting anything in return. She taught me what it meant to 'pay it forward' before it was even a thing.

I always loved spending time with Alyanna, unless she was brushing her teeth. She took the job far too seriously and would come up gagging every time, creating a stomach-wrenching noise. If I happened to be caught at one of the sinks when she came in to brush, I would skip wearing make-up that day and bolt out of there (as casually as possible) to avoid being caught in the bathroom by the time the gag came. Much like many people can't stand the sight of puke, I just can't handle the noises that lead up to it.

Alyanna was very wise, but often failed to follow her own advice. Drama seemed to encircle her wherever she went. The majority of this came through her extremely theatrical marriage to a tall Marine, who treated her - well, for lack of more creative terms, like ass.

Their love was drawn from the same place as their hate. They loved hard and fought harder with all of the passion of a Frenchman rowing up the Loire. When the husband came to town to visit her, we could expect that late night tears would follow and we'd be left to pick up the pieces of our dear friend. It was the kind of situation where everyone knew better except for her; of course she was the only one who could do anything about it. We, as her friends, just had to simply be there for her when she needed us.

Million Dollar Question

It had been a blistering hot day. The kind that caught your breath and drove it back into your lungs like a punch to the windpipe as the air was too thick to allow a deep, relieving breath. The only place one could find relief was in a purely air conditioned room or completely engulfed in water. We chose to go to the pool.

After swimming for some time, Aylanna and I hung out by the edge of the pool, and chatted away about inconsequential subjects, and simply enjoying the fact that we had set aside some time to do so. Soon, we rested our legs up and over the edge and floated on our backs and hung from the wall. The sun warmed and swallowed up our bodies, feeling blissful and carefree. We pulled ourselves up, crouching from the wall like a grasshopper on a tree trunk, and continued to talk with our face to our feet now.

Suddenly out of nowhere, Aylanna randomly asked me, "Do you think I should shave my toes?"

As I peered down at her beautiful, Mediterranean skin, I couldn't help but notice the garden of black hair that sprung thick from each Italian toe. It had been a source of conversation for everyone around her - except no one had the courage to say it to her face. Here, I stood. The question facing me. *How could I possibly answer?* In my head, I was secretly thinking, *Yes, Aylanna, for the love of God and everything holy, you need to rid the forest that springs forth from your toes. It is against every code of wearing flip flops to be sporting toes like that in public. And please don't just continue to paint them pretty, attracting colors to draw even more attention to them!* It was like sprinkling glitter on a port-a-potty. It may sparkle, but it's still a port-a-potty- and it's still going to smell.

Still, all I could muster in that moment was, "Well, some people do... if it's something you think would make you happy, then... why not?"

What kind of easy passive, evasive, answer was that?! I was weak and I knew it. I had failed everyone around me. I had the opportunity and blew it. I just didn't have the heart to say it. *What kind of a friend does not tell a friend important stuff like that?* The moment soon passed and was never discussed again. Aylanna continued to sport Amazon-woman toes, the rest of the days we were together. Emerson never forgave me. I learned in that moment it would have been much better in the long-run to have just told the truth. Even when it risked angering a loving, slightly-crazy Italian woman.

The school work in Jacksonville continued to be a challenge and on many occasions, I couldn't help but wonder if I was going to survive. I often screamed and protested. Other times I decided to just open up my book and attempt to do my homework. Still, there were people in that class that I knew could barely figure out which end of the pen to write with, so I figured if they could make it, so could I. As bad as it sounds, they were my insurance policy. I knew as long as they were there, I would still have my place. If the day came that they were finally sent away, then I would really start worrying.

Besides that, I felt I had come too far to give up now. While I had fun in my 'off-time,' I took every extra opportunity to come in on days off before a test and study. I was not one of those people that are just naturally smart without having to study. Not about this stuff. Just about meaningless, made up things like the periodic table. There was still so much "thinking outside of the box." I just wanted to smash the box.

VP-30, or "The Rag," as it was called, was where we learned everything about the P-3 and how it functioned. We learned our safety of flight operations and the necessary mechanics of the plane. Did I mention how un-mechanical I really am? Very much. Un. Mechanical.

Additionally, we had to memorize every piece of equipment that was energized in the internal racks of the plane, and where its coinciding circuit breaker was located. This meant there were hundreds of these foreign circuit breakers on square racks that we had to memorize, where they were and their purpose. Fortunately, I was really good at memorizing random things. For instance, all of the United States' capitals and their state flowers. That sure came in handy in life. We developed flash cards and learned every stinking circuit breaker that was energized during flight operations on that stinking plane.

We learned how to perfect our three drills: Bailout, Ditching, and Fire. Bailout was least applicable as I don't know anyone (other than I once *heard* a few Navy Seals doing drills a million years ago) that have intentionally bailed out of a P-3. Odds were not on our side in that situation. Still, as far as the drill goes, we had two minutes to put on our parachute, helmet, SV2, gloves, and flashlight when applicable.

Our signal to the Mission Commander that we were ready to jump out of the plane was that we gathered near the door, looking ready to go, and our hand was on the overhead bar. The only problem with this was that I could not reach the bar with all my gear on. I'd stand next to all the guys a head or so taller than me, their hand on the bar comfortably, elbow crooked, drinking a beer. I stood there hunched over with my parachute straps wrapped firmly around my legs, back hunched over and flailing like a turtle on his back trying to reach the overhead bar. After a while, I realized how ridiculous this looked and just came to accept it just wasn't meant to be, no matter which P-3 I was on. The ceiling never got any lower. I quietly gave up the battle and just kept my arm raised - *simulating* what I was 'required' to do. Blasted P-3 designed for average-height men.

Ditching is when the plane is going down over water and is attempting to land on it. No, we do not have pontoons or any other flotation devices attached to the aircraft. We just hope it works. We secured ourselves to our assigned areas, fasten everything around us, and brace for impact. We then carried out our assigned duties that is determined and narrated on the ditching placard during our plane-side briefing before flight. These are duties such as launching the life rafts, grabbing the water breakers, or first aid kits. My job as a Sensor Operator was to launch the number two life raft in the event of a ditch. This particular life raft is the titanic-size one and weighs approximately 200 lbs. Thankfully, I grew up throwing hay bales. I knew I could launch this raft; it was my job, after all. Besides, if I went out the hatch first and pulled it behind me, there would be plenty of people on the other side pushing to ensure that sucker pops out.

Wrong Place. Wrong Time.

It had been a typically long week of studying with the usual, great finale of tests all day on Friday. By the time we crawled through the door of our barracks room, we were exhausted. A night of just vegging in front of an old movie with some Chinese take-out sounded more appealing than a weekend in Vegas with George W. Bush. After a quick shower, Jenessa and I decided to run out and grab some food and an old movie. She was a stickler for the old classics and *My Fair Lady* was her all-time favorite.

Aylanna gave us her order, but preferred to take advantage of her alone time by placing her nightly dramatic phone call to her husband. We were just excited to have our own phones in our rooms at this point versus the community pay phones down the hall. Though it was not as if she needed the privacy, for she never made any bones about keeping her conversations with him quiet. There were only two tones with which she spoke with him - the whiney, baby-like voice that sounded to the rest of us like a sharp Styrofoam plate edge running along a piece of carpet, or her loud angry-Italian yelling voice. Neither was pleasant and we cringed hearing both.

So in our pajama pants and flip-flops, Jenessa and I hopped into her little white Chevy S-10 truck complete with Texas license plates and a confederate flag bumper sticker, and went to the one place we knew we would be guaranteed the best greasy Chinese food around - loaded with tons of MSG and everything else unhealthy, no doubt. It was at the ever-famous *Chinee-Takee-Outie* on Wells Road.

Coming from the base, it was necessary to make a U-turn to get to the restaurant, as it was on the other side of the divided median. As we swung around, Jenessa accelerated with some force to beat the oncoming traffic and did a quick swerve into the road - not realizing until we were in there that we had undershot the *Chinee-Takee-Outie* entry road and turned into the empty lot just before the restaurant.

"Oops!" Jenessa exclaimed. "Hold on!" [Picture screeching tires like in the movies here.]

We pulled in the empty lot to let oncoming traffic pass. As we turned around watching traffic whizzing past us, looking for an opening, Jenessa popped the truck into reverse.

Suddenly a white cop car with flashing red and blue lights swung into the road, pulling up to the left side of the truck. Then another followed, pulling up on the other side of us. If that wasn't enough, another unmarked car followed and pulled onto the road behind us. We were surrounded by flashing lights!

Our eyes grew wide as we stared out at the cop cars that encompassed us and then looked at each other in disbelief. *What the hell was going on? Was that an illegal U-turn or something?* We had no idea. So we just sat there in stunned silence and each went through a mental check-list together of possible reasons they could've pulled us over. Time seemed to drag on as we sat in nervous anticipation.

From where I was sitting, I could see a policeman in my rearview mirror speaking on his radio. After what seemed like an eternity, the policeman slowly exited his patrol car and made his way towards us. Jenessa rolled down the window as he approached.

He shined his flashlight in the vehicle and in our eyes. "I'm gonna need to see some ID." His face was emotionless. Jenessa fumbled through her purse until she came across her old Texas driver's license and handed it to him. "You girls mind telling us what you're up to tonight?"

As he studied the ID carefully, looking at Jenessa, then looking at the ID as if she was trying to pull a fast one on him, Jenessa began to ramble a long-winded story in her Texas accent that we were simply driving to get some Chinese food, and overshot our turn and turned into the wrong parking lot. I nodded in agreement and filled-in where I could. After we were done speaking, the cop kept the ID and went back to his vehicle and got inside and back on the radio.

He hadn't even told us what we did wrong. He just walked away from the car. We began talking, wondering and speculating about what possibly could be happening. I was nervous and confused. Soon he came back to the truck again. He then asked us if we minded opening the glove box. Slightly perplexed, we slowly obeyed. Then the center console. Then he shined the flashlight all around the interior of the little pick-up until at last he deemed himself somewhat satisfied.

Handing her I.D. back, he went on, "Seems you two girls were in the wrong spot at the wrong time."

I suppose that is bound to happen in life sooner or later, I thought to myself.

"It seems," the policeman went on, "there was a drug deal that was supposed to go down at this place tonight in a vehicle just like this. You wouldn't know anything about that would you?"

Stunned was an understatement of how we were feeling at that moment. If I had a monkey walk up to me and slap my face at that moment I wouldn't have been more shocked. We looked at ourselves in our pajamas and then at each other, and while shaking our head Jenessa replied, "No Sir, no idea!"He stared at us longer - trying to see if our story or expressions would waver I suppose. But the hard part about it was that we were so completely innocent, we felt like he'd already thought we were lying. There's no way he'd believe us.

The police officer scratched his head and quickly scanned the truck one more time with the flashlight. At last he said, "Well, alright then. You two are free to go - but don't let me hear about you getting in trouble later."

I couldn't tell if he was serious or not. We were in our pajamas. How much trouble could we have possibly gotten into? I'm not sure how these situations always seemed to have found us - but somehow they did. In Deer River, it's illegal to make a U-turn. I finally understood why. Apparently, it makes you look extremely suspicious.

The Fire

One of the guys in our group, Gates, happened to have the hook-up of a lifetime. His older brother was active duty in the military, and stationed in one of the 'real' squadrons (as opposed to our 'training' squadron). He was out on deployment, leaving an entire 2 bedroom, furnished apartment at the mercy of his little 19-year-old brother, Gates, to "take care of" for him while he was gone. It was the perfect arrangement that benefitted all. What could possibly go wrong?

One sunny weekend afternoon, Gates decided to throw a 'small, friends-only' party.

Being the good guests that we were, we never came empty-handed.

Now, I didn't have a whole lot of drinking experience at this point. I tried to be cautious as I was underage and they were really making examples out of those that were caught drinking underage. My career was all I had, and one mistake and 'they' (the big boys on top) had the power to take it all away. However, tonight seemed like a safe exception as we were in a home, off base, and with friends.

I didn't even really like the taste of alcohol; however, I couldn't resist a good party with music, friends and a chance to show off my insanely awesome dance moves. Since I didn't like beer then, nor mixed drinks or wine, I naturally decided just a bottle of Absolute Vodka would suffice. I filled up my cup with Absolute and drank it all in one gulp. The hair on the back of my neck stood up and my stomach winced in pain. Fire shot out of my mouth and smoke from my ears. It was no surprise then that much of the night became a hazed blur. I fell asleep by ten o'clock, and have not been able to stomach the thought of vodka to this day. See kids, this is why we don't drink. (And if you're a kid, you really shouldn't be reading this book.)

When I awoke the next morning, I found myself covered with a nice quilt in a room named 'guestroom.' It was not much more than four white walls, a window, and fluffy carpet. I rolled on my side and felt the weight of my bones that had not moved an inch for hours. On the other side of the room lay Emerson in the fetal position, sleeping like a peaceful baby with a cheesy, half grin on his face.

Apparently, I had missed quite an exciting night. While I was violently ill in the bathroom (classy image), my friends dutifully took turns checking on me, and each had an interesting perspective of what I looked like during their shift. For much of the night, the bathroom was my place of resting. Apparently at one point in the night, I had gotten up and decided I was hungry. Jenessa, being the good friend that she was, agreed to make me a grilled cheese sandwich. (Who doesn't crave a grilled cheese in the middle of the night - especially after drinking a pint of vodka?)

This started a chain reaction as the frying pan was left on after the sandwich was made. Before long, a fire of some sort erupted. It was quickly extinguished after it was noticed, but not before leaving black markings up the wall that was behind the stove.

This lead to a massive painting effort the following weekend. We were never invited back. It was probably for the best.

Additional notes of the evening: Sometime in the night Whiner and Jenessa decided that they had been madly in love with each other. Vodka tends to do that. To everyone's surprise (as well as their own), it did not end after that night. Unintentionally, this no-doubt became quite an event as it changed the entire dynamics of our group. He was still a complete jerk in my opinon - but one of my friends.

The lesson? Drinking Vodka is dumb. Additional lesson: If you wake up in the night drunk and hungry - do not use the stove.

The Solution

During that time, as I was struggling to get through the rigorous class-room curriculum, I was also struggling being away from Adam. He was continuing to survive each day at BUDS. Their class size continued to get smaller and smaller with each obstacle. I couldn't believe he was still hanging in there, but then again I couldn't have imagined any reason why he wouldn't have made it. He was the most dedicated person I knew.

I flew out to visit him over 4th of July weekend and had one of the best weekends of my life - watching the fireworks over Coronado Island. Fireworks so gigantic - they nearly touched the ground. Quickly after I returned, we made plans to see each other for the Labor Day weekend. It gave me that extra day to be out there with him. Every night on the phone, we contemplated ways we could be together after our schools were done and we took orders. We were told the Navy wouldn't allow us to be in the same squadron if we were married, but they'd try to keep our orders within 90 miles of each other to the best of their ability. Still there were no guarantees.

I sure didn't want to go to a ship - as that was all I had heard up to this point as a threat of punishment for not passing my classes. However, it was beginning to seem like the only way I could even have the remote possibility of ending up on the same type of base as Adam. I began bugging my instructors to help me look into my options of changing my orders to ship orders. Everyone thought I was crazy. I was just another typical Navy relationship that would go on about as far as I could throw a ball. (I'm terrible at throwing balls.) Our options grew dim and discouraging. So we did the only thing kids our age in the Navy knew how to do at that time when we wanted to be together. We decided to get married.

This 'shotgun' wedding wasn't exactly met with the best response from our family. And was I expecting them to be happy? I wasn't sure. I just knew eventually they'd get used to the idea and that they'd love Adam as much as I did once they met him.

We would see each other in about a month. So we began to plan our wedding. And where would be the easiest place to get married near San Diego? Well Vegas, of course! I called around and began to make reservations. I discovered just how easy it was to plan a wedding in Las Vegas. No blood tests. No waiting periods. No shirt, no shoes, no problem. I called the most glamorous looking hotel I found on the brochures. It was this tiny little place called *Caesar's Palace*. They had it all arranged in minutes. They set up a limo for us to get to the chapel and back - and of course, what wedding would be complete without an Elvis to walk me down the aisle? Yes, I actually reserved an "Elvis." Elvises are really a dime a dozen out there. I just so happened to find the same Elvis that was in the movie *Fools Rush In*. That was his "claim to fame." Everything fell into place perfectly.

And then, for some reason, I began to have a terrible nagging feeling in my gut as I awaited my trip out west.

Young Love

My mom was beyond upset that I was getting married without her present. My dad couldn't fathom the fact that he had never met him and wouldn't be there. Of course everyone thought I was young and rushing into things and should wait - but telling that to a 19-year-old girl that is madly in love is like telling a starfish that they are funny looking. They'll never believe you. They know they are beautiful.

Despite the fact that both of our parents didn't agree with our actions, they were supportive. That was huge. Still, as time went on, I still couldn't shake that something just didn't quite feel right. I couldn't place it. I had never been this happy or laughed so much in a relationship before in my life. I knew we were rushing things because of the military's circumstances. I didn't want to have to sacrifice our careers to be together. It shouldn't have to be that way. I felt that if it was meant to be, we'd follow where our lives took us and it would bring us back together someday.

It was a love of a lifetime, just with all the wrong timing. We both had come so far in our careers in that moment in time and had all of the opportunities in front of us that may never come again. The statistics of divorce rates among Navy SEALS were devastating - over 80% - and that was if he was married to a civilian. I was being told everyday what a mistake I was making as Navy marriages don't ever last. It was mentally exhausting. We had every odd possible against us and it scared me. But then again, is any love ever guaranteed?

Then, he survived Hell Week in SEAL training and was one of 4 of his original class of 95. Still, he promised that he'd give it all up for me if that's what it came down to. For a moment, I allowed myself to think of that possibility. And then it faded as quickly as it came. *How in the world could I ask that of him?* I didn't want to be the wife that kept him from achieving his dream and becoming all that he had worked so hard for. I didn't want him to resent me later in life. He had more motivation and potential than anyone I knew. I knew he would be successful. He already was.

Labor Day weekend came and I went on my trip out to the West Coast. It was wonderful to see him, but something was different. Neither one of us had the courage to talk about it. We didn't know what to say or to do. We kept conversation to surface level things. We avoided the elephant in the room.

We tried to have our usual, carefree fun that had originally attracted us to each other. When we were driving in his truck, I noticed that a few times he had stopped and made sure that his glove box was locked. This was unusual for him and got me thinking. One time, he had to run into his barracks to get some clothes for the night before we headed back to the hotel, I told him I'd just wait in the truck for him and he left it running. I shut off the truck and unlocked the glove box. I felt guilty - but I had to look. My suspicions were confirmed as I saw the white paper bag from the exchange. Carefully, I unfolded it and reached inside to find a beautiful black velvet box. I held it in my hands and ran my finger along the box, feeling its weight and the soft rounded edges. My eyes began to water. I wanted to open it. I knew he would be coming out at any moment and I didn't have much time.

Should I look? Was he going to give it to me or was he returning it? Would he give it to me later? I thought of the time I discovered my Christmas presents before Christmas. It was such a terrible disappointment when Christmas actually came and I knew what each of my presents were. I swore I'd never go looking again. I didn't want to ruin this either. But more importantly, I didn't want to betray his trust. I already had done enough.

I quickly and cautiously placed the box back and folded the bag in neatly the way it was. I started the truck again and stared out the window.

It took everything in the world to hold back my tears.

We enjoyed the rest of the weekend together but still refused to communicate. I just wanted more than anything for him to open up to me - to tell me what he was thinking. I loved and cherished every moment I had with him. I tried to memorize the way he felt. The way he smelled. Everything that I loved about him.

And then when the short weekend came to an end, he brought me to the airport, and we sat in silence for the first time the whole weekend. He carried my bags with one hand and walked me to my gate, holding my hand with his free one. When they began boarding my section, I held him as long as I possibly could and finally gave him one last kiss. I turned to go down the hall leading to board the aircraft. *Why did I let the time pass away?* It was too late to say anything now. I began sobbing uncontrollably as I handed the ticket collector my boarding pass.

The grey old man collecting my pass looked at me and smiled. "It's okay, Honey. You'll see him again." I tried to smile back to be polite, but it only made my tears run down my cheeks faster. Somehow, I knew in my heart, I wouldn't. I spun around to see him just one more time before stepping through the doors to the walkway. I memorized his blue eyes and sandy blond hair. His beautiful smile. I waved a final goodbye, and then Adam, the man that I had gone through so much together this past year - even if it was long-distance, stepped out of my sight forever.

My heart physically ached. I had let him go. We were in love and did not want to lose each other, so we broke up. It was all we knew how to do.

I wallowed in self-pity for weeks, regretting every moment of it. He was my everything. With every bone in my body, I clung with hope that he would call me and tell me that we made a huge mistake, and that we could make it work however we could. But he didn't call. I wasn't sure if he had too much pride, or I had too much pride. I was afraid of rejection, afraid of putting myself out there. *And for what? What did I have to lose at this point?* I had already lost him. But I did not call.

He continued to casually write to me fairly often at first, but they were short and friendly - never addressing any issues at hand. Soon the letters began to trickle off.

My schooling and training that I had been working for well over a year now was beginning to come to an end. Soon I would be graduating and pinning my wings on. I would finally be an AW Aircrewman out in the real Fleet, hunting submarines and traveling the world. It was all I had dreamed of. I should have been elated, but I was numb with a broken heart. It took every ounce of strength I had to muster to get up and go to school every day, and attempt to take my final tests.

How could I have let this happen? How could I have put my heart out there so bad? How could I have let him go? I was supposed to be married right now. A tiny bit of me was relieved I wasn't married. But even if I would not have been with my husband, I would have at least had him a phone call away, just as he had been for the past six months. We had survived the long-distance thing thus far, what was another four years until I got out? I'm sure we could have done it. But for some reason, we just didn't. Apparently, sometimes love just isn't enough.

Picking Orders

In the beginning of our school at Jax, we were given a white piece of paper and instructed to write down where our choice of duty orders would be between the four P-3 squadron locations. Jacksonville, Maine, Hawaii, or Washington. I wasn't even sure if the Navy took these requests seriously, or the instructors wanted to make us feel warm and fuzzy - like we actually had an ounce of control in deciding our fate. The rule was always that the orders would be given to the class to fill the billets with bodies and we would choose them in the order that the person with the best grades went first and so on. This put me... er, somewhere right in the middle.

After much thought and weighing many different circumstances, I had decided that this foreign land of pink flamingos and retirement homes were beginning to grow on me. Really though, what did it matter? I didn't have anyone else to try to coordinate with, so what did it matter what orders I got? I decided that I enjoyed the sun and majestic ocean too much to leave it. I had become hooked on warm weather. Plus, I had already bought way too many sundresses and flip-flops to survive the weather back up North. The thought of Hawaii as a duty station was an awesome one, but I had been feeling somewhat homesick for some time now, and I just could not bear the thought of not seeing my family for the next three years. Travel costs would have been too expensive from Hawaii. So carefully, I scribbled down *Jacksonville* next to my name and folded up my paper quickly as if I were writing down who I picked for homecoming queen. I had a wave of an excited feeling. For a moment I was excited over the possibility. It was nice to have a happy emotion again - even if it was short-lived.

As our graduation began to near, our actual orders arrived, and my excitement quickly dissipated. We all had been discussing our wishes for some time now. Whiner wanted Maine. He thought it would be the closest resemblance to our shared home state of Minnesota. He was a city boy though, and I had no idea what he thought he'd like about Maine. And now that he and Jenessa were officially a 'thing,' of course she would have to go with him. However, she was a southern girl through and through, and I was convinced she would *not* be happy in a northern state like Maine. She had made that clear when she was up there for SERE school. Still, Jenessa had an amazing way of talking herself into being happy. I envied that ability.

Alyanna was picking Hawaii, as that was the one place she and her crazy husband could be together. And I was pleasantly surprised to hear that Emerson was deciding to try to stay in Jacksonville too. At least I'd have my friend down here with me.

The instructor casually walked in with his sets of orders in his hand. There in his hand, he held the keys to our future. I don't think he realized his power in that moment. Or perhaps he did. Either way - no one in the room had remembered to breathe as we all sat there in silence. You could've heard a lemon drop.

One of the instructors, Harris, who was made of steel, ran triathlons, and ate boiled eggs and oatmeal for breakfast every morning as he gave his lectures, called out, "Airman Jones, step out into the hall with me for a sec." He motioned his student, who had a look as if he was just punched in the gut by a zombie.

They both disappeared into the hall. The other instructor continued to page through the stack of papers in his hand. Those magical, magical papers. He grabbed the grade list and meandered to the front of the room.

"We had a pretty good spread of orders throughout the class. Seems as most requests may be fulfilled. And y'all otta thank you're lucky stars cuz this kind of thing rarely happens. The only thing is we are going to be down a Jacksonville order as someone has been instructed that it is necessary for them to stay here - due to a medical condition that can only be treated at our specialized military hospital here in Jacksonville."

It didn't take an Einstein to figure out who this student was - as he was the *only* one not in the room to accept orders. While I may seem a little insensitive over this poor guy's "medical issue," the fact of the matter was that this guy was ranked the lowest in the class. So needless to say - the four orders that they had for Jacksonville were all scooped up right before me and mine being the fifth one - was unwillingly donated to Airman Jones. Not only that - I mean, obviously whatever his 'medical condition' was, it couldn't possibly be *that* bad if they were letting him stay in the Navy, right? Rumor was he had to get an operation to remove one of his testicles. But that's neither here nor there, I suppose. So, in summary, you could say I was a little bitter that I was the *only* one in the class not to get the orders that I had put on my wish list. So, in turn, that is how I ended up getting orders to Maine. Because of a mono-testicular sailor.

I was angry. This was not my plan at all. I hated Maine. All I could think of were smelly open-bay barracks and random people beating me in the mountains. The base had nothing within walking distance. I had no idea how I would spend the next 4 years of my life in Maine. I just knew it would feel like an eternity. However, as they say, life is what happens when we're busy making other plans.

The Mistake

Though I continued with my school, I continued to think about Adam daily. My friends tried to get me out. I'm sure I drove them crazy. Alyanna would get annoyed with me because I'd blow off any guy that flirted with me or asked me out. And though she was encouraging me to 'move on,' I just wasn't interested and I could not understand why she was so pushy about it at the time. She was just trying to help - but really, I didn't feel like it was much help at all.

One night, a bunch of students from my class were going out. At first I declined, but eventually I was talked into it. They promised to take me to Dairy Queen - which is always my weak spot. After some thought, it did beat the alternative of just sitting in my pajamas, watching mindless TV. I had done that for too long now. We were about two weeks from graduation, so there wasn't a lot of studying left to do.

It wasn't my usual group, as Whiner and Jenessa pretty much spent all of their free time together at this point, Alyanna had her usual date with her phone, and Emerson - well, I'm not sure what he was doing that night - but he wasn't around. If only he would have been. Most likely, he was watching Dawson's Creek, as he refused to go out on the nights it was on.

Before I went out Alyanna had a little talk with me I believe in attempt to 'motivate' me. "Go out! Have fun! You're young and single, and have nothing to stop you! Go pick up a guy or two."

"And do what with a guy or two?" I asked, annoyed? Offended? I wasn't sure what she was implying or how to take it.

"Relax. I'm just saying some random crazy sex could do you some good."

"Well, that sounds nice and all - but I'm not really the random sex kinda girl."

She looked shocked and slightly displeased. "Why not?" she asked, as if I were asking her if she wanted fries with her salad.

"Um, I don't know." *Why couldn't I think of a good reason to not have random one-night stands? Obviously because Grandma Henning wouldn't approve.*

"It's *just* sex. It doesn't always have to *mean* something."

It doesn't? I thought about that for a moment. *Hmmm. Maybe I've been thinking about this all wrong for some time now? Lots of people have sex all of the time that doesn't mean anything. That's what people did. I wasn't in high school anymore - and it was a different world out here in the Navy. People didn't judge you if you had sex with random people, did they? Why have I been so hung up on this for so long? Where did that get me? After all, it's just sex. It doesn't have to be a big deal, does it?* I was having this internal conversation in my head. I was talking to my Jiminy Cricket. *Besides, Grandma Henning was in Minnesota and would never know the difference, right?* I think I sat there debating inside my head for too long, because Alyanna got bored and walked away as I stared off into the distance with my pointer finger on my chin.

That night I had a great time getting out. One of my cute classmates, Shawn, had been flirting with me for some time now. I finally gave in and danced with him a few times. The attention was nice, and I had to admit it felt nice to be wanted again.

It was '80s night at the Club on a Thursday night. It was college night - and the one night we could get in being underage. I'm not sure where or how, but we also may have had a beer or two or three. (I wasn't touching any hard liquor this time.) I have to admit - the '80s music was kickin' and I found myself busting out a move or two on the dance floor. It was impossible not to. And then at some point in the night, I ended up kissing Mr. Shawn. It started with just a peck, but you know, the toxic mix of beers, '80s music, and being desperately and pathetically lonely. It seemed to evolve into just a little more than a kiss after that.

So yes, I'm sure you can see where this is going. That night, with

Aylanna's words ringing in the back of my ears, *"Why not?,"* and the combination of my sad and lonely heart, I had my first and only one-night stand.

Well, it wasn't fireworks, I can say that much. In fact, it pretty much sucked. I woke up the next morning trying my best to talk myself out of feeling like I made a huge mistake. I snuck out of there in the wee hours of the morning - before he or anyone else was awake and did the walk of shame to my own barracks.

Okay, it was fun. You were just having fun. You're an adult. You are single. Grandma will never find out. It was okay. I recited this little mantra all morning as I dressed and brushed my teeth.

Emerson and I had planned one of our shopping trips the next morning.

I climbed in his bumper-less truck and made small talk. The previous night was haunting my thoughts.

"You look like ass," he commented. It was true, so I couldn't be offended.

"Thanks. I feel like ass."

"Did you have fun?"

"Yeah, I had a great time. It was '80s night so we danced like this all night." I demonstrated one of my best moves.

"Oh yeah? Did you hook-up with anyone?" Emerson always asked this. He didn't really mean 'hook-up' when he was talking to me. He knew better. Usually. He was just being nosey as usual and wondering if I had met anyone. I don't think he ever would have thought I would have said yes.

"No!" It was my first defensive reaction - but my tone was all wrong. It was unconvincing.

"Whhhaaat? You did! Who!?"

"Well... just... someone."

"Who?? Tell me!"

"No!"

"MAKI, TELL ME!"

"Well, it's someone you kind of know…"

"WHO?"

"Someone in our class…"

"Someone in our class. Oh god. It's not Lee, is it? Man, Maki, he's going to sing to you every night now! (This was something he did every time he was drinking.)

"Eew- no!"

"WHOOOOO then?"

"Well, it's just… Shawn." I said quietly.

"EEEEW- gross, Maki! Shawn? Really?"

"What? He's nice! And good looking."

"He's such a chode." Emerson always had a new word he'd cycle through for a while. "He shaves his chest! Did you… *do* anything with him?" he asked, switching to a big-brother mode all of a sudden.

"No… well, maybe a little."

"What? Are you serious?!" He got quiet. I suddenly felt terrible.

"What, are you mad at me now? You do stupid things all the time! Other people have one-night stands all the time. What's the big deal?" Ugh, I didn't need his judgment now. I already was feeling bad enough as it was.

"Yeah, but *you* don't. I'm just kind of… disappointed." *Oh that's great. My one best friend is disappointed in me. What right did he have?* I stared out the window and tried to hide my eyes that were watering. We sat in silence for a while as we drove along.

"Look," he began. "It's not that. Don't get upset. It's just not… you. That's all."

"Well maybe it *is* me. Maybe what I was doing before wasn't working. Maybe I am the type that just likes to have fun." My voice wavered, and I couldn't help but cry now. I knew he was right, which made me even more defensive. *How did I get to this point?*

"No, you're not. You're just sad because of everything. And I get that. It's okay."

We sat in silence for the rest of the trip. Staring out the window, I got all my tears out that I needed to. I hated crying. But I felt better afterward.

"Com'on," he said as we pulled up to the Orange Park mall. "Now stop being such a pussy. Let's go and get some ice cream."

And then we got ice cream. Because one night stands do not make you feel better. Ice cream does.

Club 5

During those 6 months, in addition to school work, we would do all the things typical 19- and 20-year-olds would do. Go down to the beaches - Daytona and St. Augustine. We would watch the space shuttle launch from our back porches. We would shop and go to the movies. We would also try to go to clubs.

The problem was, that except for Janessa and Aylanna, the rest of us were under 21 and none of the clubs would let you in on any night if you were underage (unless it was a rarely designated event such as the occasional college night). All except for one club. This club was known simply as Club 5.

On Saturday nights at Club 5, you could get in if you were over 18. However; oddly enough, Saturday nights were known as "Saturday Night Seduction" and those were the nights that were the S&M nights. To this day, I don't understand how they let us in for those nights - but not others. And yes, I said S & M. As in chains, bondage, hot wax, girls dancing in cages, whipping, transvestites - you name it. It was a club full of some crazy, kinky foreplay. It was a world I knew next to nothing about. This is something they did not do (at least publically) in Deer River.

The guys played it off as the coolest thing ever, and we girls would be shocked - but intrigued at the same time. The ironic thing was that all we really wanted to do was get into a club to go dancing. And if we had to go to an S&M Club to get our groove on, well that's just how it had to be.

Now, being that my Wings were getting pinned on Monday, November 2nd, and my dad was coming down to pin them on me (this was in keeping up with the Navy tradition of having someone else pin them on for you (usually a wife or girlfriend - though I had neither at the time)), Dad just so happened to be in Jacksonville with us over Halloween weekend. Well what else were we going to do on Halloween night when it happened to fall on a Saturday night? Go to Club 5 of course!

In a matter of a few hours that afternoon, we all came up with some make-shift Halloween costumes. I was a witch - a beautiful witch, of course. Emerson was some '70s porn-star (which seemed to be a perfect idea for Club 5). And we put one of my dad's old velvet 'rain' hats, as he liked to call them, and a white tank top on my dad and called him a mafia guy. He *looked* like a perfect, scruffy mob guy - or at least sketchy enough that he fit in at the club. Eventually, we all gathered up our gear and set out for our night. And try as we may to warn my poor dad, he really had no idea what we were bringing him into.

Emerson, my dad, and myself, and some other little girl that had the hots for Emerson at the time all rode together in his little silver, bumper-less truck to Club 5. She later turned out to be the crazy/stalker type - which I kind of felt sorry for pushing her on Emerson - but I seem to have that match-maker problem when I see two single people. I forget the whole 'Will they have any common interests?' concept and assume since they are both single they will be a perfect match.

As we passed through the beaded entry-way, I watched with a smile as my dad's jaw dropped and his face simply gazed in sheer disbelief. I couldn't help but being slightly satisfied that I could bring something new to the table with my dad. Having worked on the pipeline in Alaska back in the '70s where marijuana and prostitution were both legal, I swore he had to have seen everything. Still, at heart, he was still a good 'ol Midwest farm boy and he was a long ways from home. We both were.

The bartender was dressed as a Playboy bunny in belly-revealing outfit that made it very easy to tell what color her underwear were. She bounced happily towards us, tassels flying all over, and asked for our drink order. Straight out in front of us, the dance floor was hopping with some variety of creatures tall and small. It was a zoo! Up on either side of the dance floors were balconies that were enclosed - in a somewhat cage-like appearance. In these cages were usually scantily dressed girls getting their groove on as on-lookers from below encouraged every move to push the boundaries more than the previous just had. They did not fall short to the challenge.

Our feet stuck to the floor as we walked - there wasn't a dry spot on the black tiles. One could only move so fast, as we were packed in there elbow to elbow. The smell of stale beer and sweaty bodies hung in the humid, un-circulating air.

On stage there was the most beautiful tall, vivacious, curvy, blond transgender singer that I'd ever seen. She had a Madonna-like outfit on, causing her breasts to look more like weapons than anything welcoming. Her hair was the color of gold and hung straight down her back, not a strand out of place as she danced, clutching the microphone in her hand and sang the most perfect rendition of the song "Tide is High" that I'd ever heard. Other than the broad shoulders and Adam's apple, one would have never guessed her to have been a man at one time.

My dad, being the cool country boy that he is, just stood there for several minutes, scanning the scene, absorbing it all in. As he sipped his whiskey on the rocks, he leaned into me and said, "I've been to a few wild discos in my day, but nothing like this."

We all just stood there and nodded. Well said, dad. Well said.

Wings of Gold

Two days later, we stood there in line, all in our freshly pressed dress whites that still smelled of starch. I tried my best to "keep it cool," but could not help the giddy smile of excitement on my face. After one year and four months of being in the Navy, the day I had been waiting for had finally come.

Our class was in a small auditorium – shaped room with inclined fold-out seats. A few family members had joined us. Some were taking photos and the instructors began to routinely read the ceremonial words from a pulpit. They read about our journey. The Navy's commandments and core values. Honor, Courage, and Commitment. It was one of those days we realized we weren't just doing a normal 9-5 job; we were in the world's greatest Navy. All of the blood, sweat, and tears had literally led up to this moment. The physical training, the classroom training, the horrible moments of SERE school and the loss and heartbreaks in life. We were here, we had survived.

As we stood in ranks I glanced to the right and left of me. Everyone looked so great in their dress whites. Except for Gates. We told him not to eat the Cheetos, but he wouldn't listen. Whiner and Jenessa stood side by side and I glanced over in time to see him smile at her. A sign of outward affection that was rare for Whiner. Alyanna looked amazing in her closed-toed shoes.

Various wives or mothers tearfully pinned on their boys' aircrew wings. Soon, it was my turn and my dad came and stood up at the front of the room with me. He was in his best black jeans and button down shirt (Deer River formal wear). He had shaved and trimmed his beard - a signal that this was an event of significant importance in his mind. He had held my prized 'wings of gold' that Emerson had bought for me, and I bought his. It was another simple Navy tradition that you didn't buy your own wings - so it meant the world the day he asked me if we could buy each other our wings. We would be going to different duty stations after this, but I knew he would always be my best friend. My wings were a symbol of that.

My dad fumbled around and eventually got my wings pinned carefully to my dress uniform, above the left shirt pocket, where they would be worn with pride for the next four years of my service. Finally, our day had come. My dad took a step back and shook my hand with tears in his eyes. I finally felt like I had made it. And Dad was proud.

CHAPTER 9

Keflavik, Iceland.

November 1998

Approximate distance from Deer River: 2820 miles

After a quick two-week break visiting friends and family in Deer River, I left home and set out on my first cross-country trip completely by myself to the East Coast. I was headed to my first official duty station in the 'real' Navy at Naval Air Station, Brunswick, Maine, after my year and a half of training. To say I was anxious was an understatement.

My mom had been so generous to pass down to me the old family Chevy Celebrity until I could save up for a new car myself. Shirley (as I liked to call her - as she would 'Surely' do her best to get me where I needed to go) was beautiful pale blue and fully-loaded with power windows, a/c, *and* a cassette player. I was living large driving her around. I gathered all of my best road-tripping cassettes. (Cassette tapes are little devices that we had to use in prehistoric time to play music).

I drove across the top of the country - Minnesota to Wisconsin to the Upper Peninsula of Michigan and into Canada. This was before they had armed guards and rabid pit bulls at the Canadian border giving people strip searches and taking away their houseplants. After Canada, I came back into the US through Vermont into New Hampshire and cut across to the Eastern side of Maine. I had it all planned out and highlighted the roads in yellow across my atlas. I still did not have a cell phone, though rich people and Californians were beginning to get them by this time. My dad did his best to persuade me to pack one of his handguns underneath my seat - in case I broke down and there was a bear I needed to shoot. Thankfully, I was able to convince him that this was not a good idea, considering I had to take it on base with me (which is illegal if I did not register it with them first). I think he finally let the idea go when he realized the gun would be sitting in my car for 3 months while my car was in storage and I was overseas.

The cold weather could damage the gun and *that* would be illogical. It seemed I spent a lot of time in life convincing my dad that I didn't need a gun with me.

I broke the trip up into two days and after twelve hours of driving through extensive, untouched wilderness with very few rest stops, I checked into a nice Canadian hotel just after nightfall. The next morning, I was awakened as the northern Canadian sun peaked through my window. I could tell it was the Canadian sun because it was so friendly and greeted me with a "Good Morning, Aye!"

It was early, so I fueled up on Pepsi and swiftly drove another 12 or so hours through the rest of Canada, continuing into the breath-taking White Mountains of Vermont and New Hampshire. My cross-country journey was an overall uneventful victory and I felt pleased and accomplished as I arrived into Maine just as darkness fell. I had done it. And as I attempted to check into the DET Office of my new command, (the detached office of a deployed squadron run only by a few people) my face turned pale and I suddenly realized that I had left my orders on my mom's kitchen counter back in Minnesota. Without them, I could not officially check into the squadron.

Immediately, I called my mom. I begged and pleaded with her to get them to me the fastest way possible - even if she had to sell her soul to do it. Thankfully, she didn't have to go that far and our old Post Master Gordy said they could get them to me in two shakes of a lamb's tail. I have never paid attention to lamb's tail - but I assumed that meant that he was going to 'overnight' them to me by the next day.

Well, luck must have been on my right side then because I quickly found out that there was a crew landing the next day from Puerto Rico, spending the night in Brunswick and heading to Iceland the next day. If my orders came in time, this would be my transportation, my chariot, if you will, to Keflavik, Iceland, where I would join the rest of my squadron: The legendary VP-8 Fighting Tigers. Did you hear the thunder when you read that? Go ahead. Read it again. VP-8 Fighting Tigers. Boom.

That night I checked into the barren barracks. I prayed for the strength I needed to get through this next phase of my life. I prayed for courage as I prepared myself to live in a new, somewhat desolate country for the next three months with a command full of complete strangers. But mostly, I prayed for my orders to arrive in time so I didn't look like the biggest dumbass of all time in front of my new squadron. Thankfully, these prayers were soon answered.

The Flight

The flight over the Atlantic on that P-3C was frigid and isolating. Just like my old aunt, Hilda. The crew, with their worn flight suits decorated with fancy patches of cool places they had been, was routinely welcoming but I was clearly a fish out of water. I was a rookie outsider and the plane was a foreign land to me still.

Other than my training flights in Jacksonville, this was my first 'real' flight with an operating squadron. And I realized how much I didn't like the P-3C Orion. Most of them were 30-40 years old. They were loud, dirty, and smelled funny. The inside was full of finger prints, grease smudges that it had acquired in its decades of service. They were a four-engine propeller driven aircraft that held a crew of 22 passengers. Eleven of them made up the Combat Aircrew. At the time, for a squadron to be deployable ready, they needed eleven to twelve Combat Aircrews up and functioning. The P-3 has a wingspan of 99 feet and a length of 104 feet from nose to tail. It was built strong and deployed for various missions, but was too great in size to land on an aircraft carrier. Thus, when P-3 squadrons "deployed" they went to a land base overseas and flew the missions from the land. The P-3 had the capability to stay airborne for 10-12 hours depending on the mission, load, and whether or not it loitered (shut down) any engines.

I did my best to stay out of the way of the crew that day, looking out the portside window over the wing, gazing at hundreds of miles of ocean periodically interrupted by clouds. I felt awkward and refused to get up for the entire flight. As I drifted in and out of sleep, I wondered if I would always be unhappy in the Navy as I was today.

By the time I arrived on the unconventional rock they called Iceland, my stomach was empty, my head was swarming, and my bladder was about to burst. I was embarrassed and a bit unsure of how I was to go about using the 'pisser' on the plane - a device that was never intended for female use - so I just avoided it.

We landed, seven hours after we departed good ol' American soil. The time was six hours into the future and a soon-to-be familiar darkness filtered the sky. I watched the ground crew direct our bird into her resting place and put chocks against the tires so they wouldn't roll. Little did I know at the time, but out there on the ramp recovering the plane was the man that I would someday marry. He watched me carry all of my possessions down the ladder and looked over at his friend, Julio, smiled and nodded his head with a look that no doubt meant, *"Yeah, I'd like to bring flowers to her - all day."* Unfortunately, the only thing that I could think about at the time though, was finding out the location of the nearest bathroom. I ran down the ladder on that cold and starry night - a night that was full of new beginnings and lots of snow and ice.

VP-8

So there I was six time zones away from my home and family, and life as I once knew it. At times, it felt as though I was six time zones away from civilization itself. It didn't take long for me to realize how much I despised Iceland in the winter. Perhaps it is nice in the summer, but I wouldn't know. In the winter months, the land was desolate and dark with cursing wind that blew through your stuffed parkas, dismissing them as if they were made of silk, and chilled you to the core. It was so cold that your bones ached. And on occasion, it was necessary to use the rope that had been tied between the barracks in order to get from one to the other for fear of losing your bearings during the white-out blizzard conditions in the mere 20-foot trek.

I soon learned that flying the planes in this environment was altogether a risk of its own. The ramp was completely overwhelmed with a solid, thick impenetrable layer of ice. As the planes taxied along the ice-layered flight line, the crew often had to stand in the flight station of the aircraft behind the pilots to put the weight on the front wheels to give them some sort of traction. On more than one occasion, a plane that was being escorted in by a daring young lineman would spin a complete 360 degrees - temporarily losing all control. There wasn't a thing the pilots could do - just as if it were an automobile on black ice - only a few tons more metal.

Walking on the ramp (flight line) to get to the plane from the hangar was a danger as well. We had to have some type of a reflector pinned on us at all times. That was regulation. There were many times when you could just stand in one place and the powerful wind would literally blow you across the ice.

Also of note were the snowplows. The demonic, Icelandic snowplows could willingly be one's death if pedestrians were not aware of them at all times. The gigantic trucks would get into caravans traveling a good 45-50 mph, blades down on the ice in a horizontal line across the flight line as snow was shot up over the trucks and left in a heap on the side. When the plows got going, they would stop for nothing!

Despite our own personal grievances and complaints, the local Icelandic civilian population absolutely loved it there. They were a fishing community of Viking descendent that dated back centuries. Between the fresh air, wild Icelandic ponies, the puffins, and the hot sulfur springs, they could not imagine living anywhere else.

———————⟙———————

The next day after landing on "the rock," I timidly went to work. I was handed a check list with about ten places to check-in on it. The first was medical. There was a hospital on base, but our squadron had its own corpsman and nurse's office - much like one would have at a school. As I approached the supply-closet sized room in the hangar, I heard yelling coming up from behind me down the hall.

"I've got contact! I've got contact!" I thrust my body back against the wall to make way for a red-headed Irish man that looked slightly like David Caruso in coveralls (the Navy Maintainer's working uniform) running down the hall like a manic six-year-old kid. In his hand he held what appeared to be the inside of a dissected sonobuoy (the microphone-like object that we deployed into the water from the airplane in search of submarine acoustic noises). There must have been a few hundred feet or so of string trailing behind him as he rounded the corner as well as several other people running after him, laughing like a bunch of drunken pirates, as if it were the funniest thing they had ever seen.

"Hi!" The nurse greeted me joyfully in the door. "New check-in?" I nodded, startled, and still distracted by the chaos in the hall. "Here, why don't you come into my office." She ushered me in, closing the door behind us, unfazed by the noise throughout the hall.

Her office was literally a closet that they had somehow figured out how to squeeze a desk into, along with several cabinets, full of supplies. "Welcome to the squadron. I'm Laura," she said with a politely outstretched hand. Her hair was almost black and pulled back into a bun. She wore glasses and no make-up. She looked very plain, but was effortlessly beautiful at the same time.

"Thank you. I'm Airman Maki - er - Julia." I felt strange giving her my first name - as she wore a third class petty officer insignia, however, I was just following suit.

"Julia. So nice to meet you," she replied so politely, so kindly. I wasn't used to many people in the military being this kind to someone below them in rank. Most of the time they were direct. They didn't have time or the need to go out of their way for you.

"Nice to meet you too."

"Well it looks like you have everything I need here in your record." She smiled and closed the folder and handed it back to me. "Here you go. Just be sure to always dress warmly. If you have any sign of an illness give me a call and I'll see how I can help you. And our flight surgeon is in the office on Wednesdays and Fridays - so if you could stop back then, I know he'd like to go over a few things with you." She said with a smile.

"Okay, well thank you so much. I guess I will talk to you later then."

"Oh and Julia," she called out to me as I was reaching for the door to leave. "Do be careful. About half of the sailors in the barracks are being treated for herpes right now," she said with a genuine smile as casual as if she were talking about the common cold.

My jaw dropped and I stammered. "Ah, okay. Um, will do."

Chief

After a few random tours of the hangar and duty office, I was looking down my list when I was suddenly approached by this huge, dark Croatian man in chief khakis. His forehead was pinched in a frown. He had sinister eyes as black as onyx and wore a scowl. His mustache was so thick he could have hid baby birds in there and no one would have known better. As he stood there towering over me, watching my every move, I did my best to hide my intimidation and pull myself together.

"You Airman Maki?" his voice thundered and his eyes glared. I felt pain on my skin where his glare met it. He stood nearly a foot taller than me.

"Yes, Chief?" I said, glancing at the anchors on his collar, feeling very small. "Come with me."

I had only been there for a short time. I couldn't think of anything I could've possibly done wrong already to anger this very angry chief. So, reluctantly, I followed him through a maze of rooms as onlookers gazed sympathetically, for they knew the wrath of angering a chief. Clearly I had already done this somehow.

"Sit." He demanded and I immediately obeyed. We sat in silence. I had no idea what was coming next, though I wished I was anywhere but there at that moment.

"Now, I just got wind that you're gonna be coming to our crew, CAC-9. I'm Chief. I'm the flight engineer on the crew." He said it almost condescendingly. "Know what that is?"

"Yes, Chief." Of course I knew what a flight engineer was. *I think.*

He paused for a moment and looked me up and down - sizing me up, I suppose. I felt naked and exposed. "Maki, huh?" he went on. "Where you from?"

"Oh, a tiny little town in Northern Minnesota."

"Oh ya? Where at in Minnesota?"

"Oh it's small. It's called Deer River. Not many people have heard of it. We just got our first stop light." I always had to add that. I was proud of the accomplishment that seemed to make us a real city now.

"No shit, Deer River, huh? I'm from Hibbing. You know where the Range is?"

"Oh yes, of course I know where Hibbing is and the Iron Range! We used to play the schools on the Range in football all the time." I'm not sure if he cared or not, but I slowly began to relax just a little - as all of a sudden he appeared human-like and not some freakishly huge monster.

"Yeah? I think I dated a Maki or two. Probably some of your aunts."

I didn't really know what to say to that - if it was a good memory or a bad one - so I just left it alone. Maki was actually a very common name up in Northern Minnesota, though I was only related to a handful of them - but I didn't think it was the right time to point that out. I nodded robotically, and he continued on with his introduction speech. Small talk was over - it was back to business.

"Listen up," he said and he leaned down towards me. Without thinking, I instinctively leaned backwards. "There are a few things we need to get straight. First of all, I hate Airmen. Remember that. I *hate* airmen." He spoke slow and exaggerated, allowing the words to resonate in the air. I nodded, unsure what response he was looking for. Should I have apologized that I was an airman? Clearly we would not be having afternoon tea together.

"Secondly, *you* had better keep *my* airplane clean. It is *your* responsibility. If there is ever garbage left on it, if it is not properly vacuumed, windows washed, anything - I'm coming to you and it's not going to be pretty. Got it?"

"Yes, Chief."

"Third," he paused for a second, looking at me. It was as if he was judging, trying to anticipate my reaction. "Don't get pregnant. Understand!?"

I nodded frantically.

"You follow these rules, and we'll get along just fine. If you have a problem, you better come to me first. Do you understand?"

"Yes, Chief." I replied somewhat confused, still unsure of what just happened.

"Welcome to Combat Aircrew Nine (CAC-9)." He stated and mechanically held out a hand. Knowing it was not optional, I shook it hard – well, hard for me, trying to appear confident. I sure hoped I would not let him down.

I was a little fish in a big pond of piranhas. The AWs (Aviation Warfare Systems Operators) pride themselves on eating their young. When we arrived at the squadron, we were in training for about a year. After that year, we would go before our dreaded "board." This was where we would sit in front of a panel of qualified instructors and they would pick our brain apart for a good four to eight hours. In this time, they are squeezing us like a used-up sponge for every piece of information about our job that they could get to bleed out of us. It was a horrible step to a tremendous accomplishment. Until we reached that stage, we were a 'nugget.' A nugget by definition is an imperfect, unpolished rock, waiting to be shaped and molded into a beautiful piece of gold.

The training styles we 'nuggets' faced in the military were less than typical. The student would stand at a chalkboard at the front of the room, getting their brains dissected by the infamous acoustic AW gods of our squadron, at that time known simply as Brian, Chuck, and Johnny. A wild bunch of salty sailors they all were, using teaching methods that had been once passed down to them, such as throwing erasers and markers at the students for incorrect answers. Humiliation was the preferred learning tactic used, and while I hated every second of it, it was quite effective. They sought pleasure in our degradation as if it was an earned right of their seasoned position.

Brian was my "Sea-Daddy." He was my Sensor One Operator. It was his job to train me in everything he knew. Though if I would have spent 50 years learning my job it still would have been impossible to have become half the operator he was. Brian had kind eyes and was a man of few words - but when he spoke them, they were usually carefully selected ones of high importance. Unless he was drunk. Then they were just chicken gibberish. It was important to know the difference. He was always calm and never yelled once or threw erasers. When I did stupid things, (which seemed quite frequently) or answered his questions incorrectly, he was only quietly disappointed. I would have rather he threw erasers.

The Warning

Not too long after I arrived in Iceland, we were scheduled for a long ten-hour burner (flight). After my pre-flight was complete, I realized that I didn't have much to snack on for the long flight that was ahead of me. After checking with the crew how much time we had left, I gaily sauntered to the gee-dunk (food store) in the cold darkness of pre-dawn light.

I have a fear of being stuck somewhere for any amount of time without food - so I always overcompensate how much food I have with me at all times. I'm not sure why - perhaps I starved to death in a past life, or perhaps it has something to do with going hungry on a mountain top for a week. My helmet bag, purse, or anything that I carry always has a pocket or two containing food of some sort. I hoard food like a squirrel hoards nuts.

After gathering my treasured food items I had just bought from the gee-dunk, I began my trek across the icy ramp to where our fine mode of transportation lingered. As I began to approach the plane, I was suddenly blinded by the severe glow that was cast from the taxi-lights above the forward landing gear. Now, for any experienced operator, this should have been an obvious warning sign not to come any closer and to turn back. Still, despite the hours upon hours of classroom training about aircraft safety, the thought had not yet crossed my mind. I had only read the warnings in a book. It had never been demonstrated to me. Most likely, I was thinking about my food. Instead, it was due to this illumination that I did not see the second key warning device of the top and bottom strobe lights flashing, signaling that the RADAR was in use.

As I began to get closer to the aircraft, I realized the complacency of my actions. Complacency/stupidity. Potato/Pa-tatto. I began to casually back up, hoping like mad that I hadn't been spotted. All at once the lights snapped off and the ramp was instantly black. The door flung open hard and fast. At the top of the ladder stood Stanley, the RADAR operator (Sensor Operator 3), with one hand on his hip, and the other waving his finger for me to come toward him. My head dropped and I proceeded forward like a dog with his tail between his legs - knowing that this could not possibly be good.

It was then that he yelled over the APU (auxiliary power unit) the words I feared more than anything. "Chief wants to talk to you." My body was instantly weighted down with dread. I knew it was all over. My head was flooded with a million excuses that were up for grabs. Sadly, I knew none of them would work against Chief. He would not be bothered with such incompetence. All I could do now was to beg for mercy.

I climbed the ladder, looking at Stanley with pleading eyes that screamed "Help me!" He just looked away with the unspoken words that left me to understand that I was on my own. As I reached the top of the ladder, I slowly turned my head to the right, towards the galley where I knew Chief was.

His face wore no emotion, but I could feel in my stomach the penetration of the daggers his black eyes shot through me. He simply pointed his fingers to the seat across the galley table from him. Quietly, I obeyed and sat, trying to appear as innocent as possible. Terror rose through me. How is it possible that one man could make so many airmen so terrified? How is it that I would have rather shot my own foot off than face his wrath? *Maybe I could play dumb - pretend I just didn't know.* I thought to myself. *No, that would probably be worse...*

He looked up at me and then down at the table, squeezing his fists together, as if he was trying to control himself. He looked back up and then came the words that I will never forget. "DO YOU WANT TO FUCKING FRY YOUR OVARIES!?"

Was this a trick question? "Um, no?" I stated, more asking if that was the right answer. He smiled, which confused me even more. We sat in silence. I think he knew I hated silence.

"You're goddamn lucky Stanley shut it off before you got too close." *Oh, that was nice of him,* I thought, slightly relieved. *I can still have children.*

"What is the stand-off on the APS-137 RADAR?"

Okay, this was one of the easiest questions out there. I learned this in VP-30. Don't blow this answer. Was that the big RADAR or the little one? I took a stab at it. "Ahh...250 feet?" I replied. *At least that used to be the answer. I think.* I wasn't sure of anything in this moment. Chief had the ability to do that to me.

He didn't say anything for what seemed like forever. I wasn't sure if that was a good sign or a bad. "Go finish your preflight," he said, releasing me. I turned to go, when he stopped me. "Hey," his voice echoed. I turned back towards him. "That's one." He stated simply, and held up his index finger.

Crap. One strike already! I just got on this crew, and I only had one more freebie to go. Somehow I knew I was going to need it.

Johnny Cox

Johnny was an ambiguous man. His last name was Cox, so everyone had fun saying it. He was a genius when it came to his job, but cold and callous to any of the brand new airmen. It took a long time for one to prove themselves worth Johnny's time. And if we ever made ourselves an enemy of his - we could most likely assume we would be his enemy for life. Johnny was one that was either loved or hated.

Like most, I was intimidated upon first meeting him. I had been warned. He couldn't have been much taller than my own frame, but somehow he still appeared to cast a shadow over me. He had thinning black-gray hair, but very stern, brown eyes. The rumors were that he was known to make grown men cry and had several witnesses to prove it.

One instance of this was with a fellow operator named Ron. Ron, like all of us, was in the middle of getting qualified. He was a smart up-and-coming operator, and had helped me out on several occasions as we would stay and practice memorizing our submarine parameters. Like the rest of us, he had his bad days too.

One flight in particular he messed up a safety training procedure. This angered Johnny in every sense of the word. If there was anything we had to know without a doubt, it was our safety procedures. The whole crew depended on each other to each carry out their jobs in an emergency. That flight he made Ron go around to every member of the crew and apologize for killing them. One of the flight engineers really drove it home by responding that Ron didn't have to say he was sorry to him, but to apologize to his children instead. Johnny clearly did have an impacting way of getting his point across. We nuggets all silently prayed that we were not his next victim.

I learned a secret long ago that continues to help me to this day. This secret was how to soften any cold man (or woman for that matter). Ask about their children (or grandchildren). So one casual morning on duty, we were all sitting around talking, killing the time until our next call. I began asking Johnny a few questions about how his family was doing while he was away. Instantly the usual frown on his face began to cease and he proceeded to tell me all about his five wonderful children. His tone changed and his guard was let down. As he went on to tell me all about their sports and school activities, a light came up across his face and lit it up like a dazzling sparkler on a gloomy night. He must have talked for about half an hour just about his children that he missed so much. It had been over three and a half months since he had seen them. Suddenly Johnny began appearing more like a human and less like a brutal monstrosity.

The Cake

About a month or so later, Johnny came around to me to see how my work was coming. I answered his questions and began to make small talk. He said he was doing well, especially since today was his birthday. Instantly I was delighted. *I love birthdays!* I thought how exciting and yet sad that today was his birthday, and that he had to spend it away from the ones he loved the most. I decided I must do something about it.

I was working as the duty driver, which was the job for the lowest ranked guy on the crew. Naturally, that was me. As a duty driver, aka "squadron bitch," (spoken affectionately, of course) we were at the beck-and-call for crews and personnel that need shuttling back and forth from the barracks to the hangar. Additionally, we were also stuck with all of the mundane jobs, such as cleaning the office, and delivering flight schedules in the brutal Arctic winds while everyone else is out flying around saving the world. Each crew had a rotating week of duty. Every member had their own role whether it was working in Maintenance as duty pilot or flight engineer, or working the front office, standing watch, answering phone calls, and maintaining squadron operations. The disadvantage was that because we were not flying, the week could get extremely long. The *advantage* was that since we were not flying, we had somewhat of a consistent 12-hr on/12-hr off set schedule. We also did not have our normal drinking restriction windows.

When we flew, we had to stop drinking twelve hours before our scheduled preflight time. For an example, it was not unusual for us to complete our postflight and get back to the barracks at 1900 (7pm) and have a preflight at 0800 (8am) the next morning. This meant we had one hour before we were in our 'window.' Most would define this as to have a drink, socialize a bit, and to relax and unwind before heading back to our rooms to begin 'crew rest.' However; most sailors interpreted this hour as an opportunity to pound as many shots of alcohol as possible within that hour so they could enjoy the next few hours with the intoxicated effects - though I cannot confirm nor deny this theory of actually occurring.

The white US Navy-issue vans that we were given to us to drive were usually on their last leg. They had been known, on several occasions, to break down in the middle of nowhere for no good reason. They did not sport four-wheel drive which was often a necessity in Icelandic winters. Many times, the shifter labels were old and worn, which would force us to have to guess where the gears actually were. If we did not know how to drive a stick, it could make for an interesting time.

So in the few moments I had to spare, I began to put them to good use throughout the day. When I had to run an errand near the commissary (the military grocery store), I ran in and bought some cake mix and decorating tools. In the minutes I was at the barracks, I popped a cake into the oven. And in the minutes I was in my room alone, I did a jig. This is where the problems began.

Somewhere in my balancing and timing act, I was unable to get back to the barracks in time for the 35 minutes of allotted baking time. It was more like 50 minutes. This made for a very crisp and dark cake. I knew that I had failed as soon as I opened the doors to the barracks and was greeted by the lofting stench of black smoke. Devastated but determined, I started the entire process all over. I went back to the store and bought new cake mix. I didn't do a jig this time. After a few trials and errors, by the end of the day I ended up with a baked, frosted, and decorated cake. I even used skittles to spell out his name. It wasn't pretty - but at least he wouldn't have to go without a cake on his birthday. Mission accomplished and I was all excited when I thought about how surprised he would be.

That night, I gathered some of the junior guys like myself, and we all went up to the First-Class Mess to seek out Johnny. The First-Class Mess was a great little hangout intended for First-Class Petty Officers. When they were feeling generous, they would let the other ranks enter their humble abode - since there really were not many other places to hang out. Inside, you would find pool tables, dartboards, a television, radio, and of course, the ever-popular well-stocked, and dimly-lit bar. This was often our refuge and outlet during those cold and lonely winter nights on the other side of the world from our families. You may be thinking by now, *my word, sailors must drink a lot from all of her references to alcohol*. To which I would simply reply, yes.

I entered the room, cake in hand, as everyone paused to watch the scene unfold. I delivered it to Johnny and excitedly exclaimed "Happy birthday!"

He stood there, with a surprised, confused look on his face and a beer in his right hand. Soon, someone in the back began a loud rendition of the "Happy Birthday" song. Everyone else quickly jumped in and the entire First-Class Mess sang in unison. He looked so happy, thanked me, and I for the second time, I saw Johnny Cox smile. I was pleased with myself, hoping I had helped him feel a little human-like in this place where birthdays seem to be forgotten about.

Quite a few years later, I was reminiscing one night with some old Navy friends over a few cups of tea. Someone just happened to slip up and informed me that it never really was Johnny's birthday that night. He was just messing around with me earlier that day, not realizing how gullible I actually was. When he saw that I had gone through the trouble of baking a cake (or rather two), he did not have the heart to tell me the truth. In fact, everyone in the Mess knew, but failed to tell me. They went along, no doubt entertained. That night I did NOT learn "Don't believe everything you're told." But perhaps looking back, Johnny was the one that learned his lesson that night.

Akureyri & Aerosmith

During our six-month deployment overseas, we were oh so *generously* given the choice of four days of liberty that do not count against your leave days, or you can take seven days of your own leave. Most people did not have the money to go home or would have rather saved their leave days, so they opted to take the four days of liberty. It just so happened that our crew's R & R (Rest and Relaxation) days were to be over Christmas. Normally, one would think this would be scoring big; however, when you're all by yourself in a foreign land, extra time off (while it's nice to get a few hours of rest) really just makes the time drag on even longer. This also happened to be my first Christmas away from home. I had no idea what I was going to do with myself.

Lucky for me, I didn't have to think too much about it. The enlisted guys on the crew had been planning to take a small trip just to get off of the base for a bit and see a little of the island. Island meaning ICEland. After talking to the little travel agency on base, they had it all arranged to get a rental and drive to the top of the island to a remotely quaint little fishing town and rent a cabin for a very affordable price. So the five of us enlisted guys from the crew that didn't have any better plans piled into a 1960s-style, Scooby-Doo-like van that the MWR (Morale, Welfare, & Recreation) Center had concocted for us. Bright and early, we set out on our journey, seeking an adventure, armed only with a change of clothes and an Aerosmith cassette tape that was worn nearly to shreds by the end of our inexplicable voyage. [*Love in an elevator...*]

We drove for a good eight hours. We trekked up snow-capped mountains, along the sparkling cliffs, and all around the threatening Arctic waters. The roads twisted and turned, snakelike along a narrow, but paved road. Often the snow would whitewash across it, leaving you to guess where the actual path was. Where the mountains were too steep to climb, dark tunnels would protrude through and some even ran underneath the ocean bays. It was a fabulous, scenic excursion - much like a picture of an uninhabited Arctic from the pages of a National Geographic magazine. [*Oh, oh it's Amazing...*]

We arrived at the cabin that evening and survived on a cooler full of beer and snacks that we had so domestically packed. The cabin was a cozy rambler situated snuggly among the mountains that cascaded into the shores of a bay in the Northern Arctic Ocean. It had two bedrooms in which I, the only girl, respectfully got my own. The boys could have cared much less where or even if they slept. The cottage had a built-in hot tub situated outside on a roomy patio. The place was picture perfect - a scene from a Christmas card. [*Dream on...*]

The hours of that night were filled by drinking and the hot tub, which occasionally can be a dangerous situation - especially when the hot tub was on the outside patio, surrounded by sub-freezing temperatures. This led to several mishaps throughout the night. During all of the ins and outs of the hot tub as we replenished our beer supply, a nice, solid crest of ice was formed upon the patio. This led to several fabulous spills - of our beer - and our bodies. Okay, mostly mine. During one scene, I seemed to have forever lost my toe-ring, as it became lodged in-between the cracks of the wood. It was then that the toe-ring was ripped from my toe, but not without first permanently removing a good chunk of flesh in the process. My entire thigh soon became all one nasty black bruise from hip to ankle. [*Walk this way...*]

Because people often seem to come up with the greatest of ideas while they are intoxicated, and often feel invincible (a scary combination), Stanley casually came up with the idea of making snow-angels. Of course, we thought that was genius. Surely we would make the best snow angels the Icelandic puffins had ever seen. (I'm sure they were secretly watching us.) However, if you've ever decided to make a snow-angel in a bathing suit, fresh from a hot-tub - well, you aren't very smart either. But like so many bad ideas in hindsight, it sounded like a good idea at the time.

Following Stanley, I leapt like a gazelle on fire out of the hot tub and ran barefoot down our snow-encrusted path. We climbed up onto one of the snow banks and, with a literal leap of faith, fell back trustingly into the powder. It was gloriously refreshing until I suddenly realized that I could not get up. My wet hair had frozen almost instantaneously to the snow that was packed beneath it. As I lie there in the fluffy snow, steam rising off of my wet body, I reassured them it was okay to just go on without me. It seemed like the right thing to do. Save yourself. I'd just hang out for a while until the snow beneath me began to melt enough to free me. But good 'ol Chief knew all too well the "no man is left behind rule." He dutifully took it upon himself to rip my frozen hair from the ice, leaving a patch of it behind. The following morning I arose battered, bruised and with a small section of missing hair. I had been wounded in the battle, but I was going to survive. [*Rag doll living in a city...*]

Our second day was filled up with a tour of the city of Akureyri. It was a gorgeous, snowcapped fishing town set deep in the northern waters. Everything seemed so clean that it sparkled in the sunlight. The townspeople were very patient with us English-speaking folk as we attempted to shop and ask for directions on that Christmas Eve day.

When we returned to our cabin, some did a bit of housekeeping, while others decided to do a bit of "exploring." We were actually on a mission. We determined that it would be such a waste to let such glorious mountainsides go untouched, never knowing the full potential of their dramatic angles.

At the bottom of the sharp hill near the waters sat a tiny little boat house storage shed. Oddly enough, we could not find any sleds in the building. Never missing an opportunity to get creative, it was then that I was educated of a much more exciting purpose in life for a tabletop. Together, my second flight engineer, Dave, and I soared like the wind down that mountain, stopping only short of the chilled blue waters. It was truly an unbeatable experience.

Not to be outdone, Stanley was always trying to come up with bigger and better ideas in life. Down by the water's edge in the small storage shed, there lived a long, wooden kayak. Now I have seen plenty of great pictures in my short lifetime, but I would have to say that Stanley and Dave coming down that mountainside in that old kayak is one that stands out vividly. At first it seemed like a genius idea. They all do. Then the kayak began picking up so much speed that no one would have guessed a long, nearly aerodynamic-shaped object like that would begin to spin out of control on its way down. Ours, like many sledding stories before us, also ended with all of us in a substantial crash. [*I go crazy, crazy...*]

It was then, in those last moments of the dusky light of the afternoon, that I realized a deep emptiness in my back pocket where my credit cards and military ID are normally kept in during outings in which I did not want to lug my purse around. Somehow they had fallen out during the crazed ordeal. A panicked search ensued in which we began combing the snow on the side of a mountain. Do you know what it is like to comb the snow of a mountainside looking for a credit card in near dark? It was like looking for, well, a small piece of plastic in a snow-covered mountain side at dusk.

Here I was, at the top of a mountain in the middle of nowhere, in a country on the other side of the world, with no identification or access to my money. But what I did have was Dave. I was just about to go into my ugly, panicky, freak-out mode when Dave, to all of our astonishment, put on his CSI hat and discovered each one of the cards hidden in the white crystals that lay on the frozen ground just before the darkness of 2:00 p.m. fell upon us. I felt like I had been given an "idiot move" pardon by the grace of God. It was not my finest moment; however, I did learn that night that if one decides to go sliding down a mountain in the middle of nowhere, it is important to first remove all of their most valuable assets from their back pocket. [*And I don't want to miss a thing...*]

In addition to our fabulous beer, Chief and Brian also smuggled off base one of the juiciest steak tenderloin. For some reason it was against the rules to bring meat off base. Dare I say illegal? I plead the fifth. Besides, who the heck makes it illegal to take a steak off base? Can you imagine getting arrested for that?

"What are you in for?"

"I bought a steak, then drove it off base." Hold the phones.

Did I mention it was the rarest steak I'd ever eaten and was grilled to perfection? It ruined all other steaks for me. They will never be good enough. Never. Who would have thought the best steak I'd ever eat would be in some cabin at the top of Iceland. Do they even have cows there? I'd never seen any - but I'll tell you what I did see - wild Icelandic Ponies. Hmmm...

That Christmas Eve was the epitome of untraditional. It consisted simply of a bunch of Navy guys sitting around playing cards, drinking beer, and eating pony steak. And while we were all enjoying ourselves and each other's company, we all had a constant preoccupation in our minds of our families back home. I could only imagine the guys were wondering if their kids and wives (those that had them) were doing okay and getting excited for the arrival of Santa Claus. They would have probably been putting cookies and milk on the table by now. Perhaps asking for another book - too excited to sleep. *Were the kids thinking of their fathers?* The men at my table sat with smiles on their faces, but at the same time, their minds drifted. I thought of their wives - no doubt being strong for the kids, keeping with the usual traditions, but secretly dying inside as the holidays are constant reminders of family. I thought of how a void in one's family is undoubtedly magnified with the holidays. These men had left behind a huge void that was held apart by the Atlantic Ocean.

That night I once again saw my crewmembers in a different light. I realized they had all been so worried about how *I* would react being away from home for the first time - trying to make it as nice and distracting as possible for me. At that time, I was single, and I missed my mom, dad and sisters. I didn't understand the unbearable pain of being separated from your spouse or child. They knew all too well. These guys were the bravest people I knew. This was their sacrifice.

So after pondering this over a few beers, I wandered back to my room and watched *Armageddon* (the movie - not in real life.) Then I cried. And not just because it was more Steven Tyler music. I decided I needed to call my dad. So I did. I drunkenly called my dad collect from Iceland on Christmas Eve. And he accepted the call and listened to me ramble on and on until I stopped crying without once mentioning the price of the call. Now that's the true love of a parent. [*Sweet Emotion...*]

That night I was abruptly awakened by a single stream of light cascading through the blinds. This light was so bright that I was sure someone was standing over me, shining a spotlight in my face. Instinctively, I checked the clock. It was near 4 o'clock in the wee hours of morning. Still blinded, I sat up and realized this glowing light was nothing other than the moon beaming into my window, lighting up a narrow trail across my eyes. I felt it beckoning me to the window.

Doing my best to keep silent, I ungracefully tip-toed to the window, tripping over at least three items of clothing. When I finally arrived at the window,

I could not help but take in the sheer magnitude of it. There it sat, glimmering with robust pride. Instantly, I felt its peace. It had been a while since I'd admired the moon.

All at once it occurred to me that as I was away on the other side of the world from my family, the moon was my connection home. It was the same moon that hung over Minnesota. It was the same moon that sparkled over the ocean during our night flights. It watched over me when I would walk home alone to the barracks in the dark, and the moonlight guided me along the right path.

In some of my loneliest hours, the moon began to serve as my sense of strength and comfort. On those nights, I would look up to the sky and know that I was looking at the same moon my mom, dad, and sisters could be looking at, at that very moment.

Crossing the Line

On New Year's Eve 1998, I had been the duty driver for the duration of the day and still had a couple hours to go on my 12-hour shift. One of the jobs as the daytime duty driver was to deliver the flight schedules for the following day to various places around the base. Had I known what a fiasco this simple task would turn into, I may have saved the job for the next on-coming shift.

I had just about completed the task and had only a few schedules left to deliver. Since it was later at night than usual, most people had gotten off work for the 'holiday,' and there were no planes around, I decided to take a slight short cut across the flight line instead of driving all the way around it to the other hangar. Little did I know, I was about to make a terrible mistake.

I was cruising along going about my business at a speed probably a tad more than what was acceptable on the flight line, and jamming to the only American station that came in. It didn't matter if it was *Bayou Frog Leg Jam* if it was American. It was in English and I missed English-speaking radio stations.

Suddenly, out of nowhere, protruding flashes of red and blue caught my eye in the mirror, rudely breaking my driving trance. Annoyed at the delay, but not overly concerned, I obediently slowed the van to a halt. *What the hell? Maybe*

I was going faster than I had originally thought? I began to fumble through my wallet for identification, making sure my seatbelt was still in place. Perhaps this was a routine check? I couldn't think of anything I was doing wrong- I wasn't even speeding. Well, not by too much.

Without warning, I suddenly heard muffled shouting at my window. I jumped, and alarm instantly changed to petrified, as I observed an Air Force security guy with an M-16 pointed in a disturbing position towards my truck. "Exit the vehicle immediately! Keep your hands where I can see them! I need some ID!" The dark figure in camouflage shouted, and I found myself staring down the barrel of a rifle. My limbs were paralyzed in fear. I slid off my seat and froze. I couldn't have moved if I wanted to. It was the Air Force.

"Ma'am, I need your ID. NOW." His young voice boomed. I slowly obeyed, still dumbfounded. What else could I do? He led me away from the van, but remaining in the stream of the bright headlights. It was then I noticed out of the corner of my eye that we were slowing becoming surrounded by more security men and vehicles. Again, he yelled at me, "On your knees, hands behind your head." I was in disbelief and still had no idea what was going on. I was in uniform - a 19-year-old girl in an American US Navy uniform and driving a government vehicle. And yet, I was still being treated like I had a turban on my head and a swastika on my shoulder.

My aggressor walked a few feet away from me and began talking and pointing all over the place to his partner. He also made intermittent calls on his radio. I began to notice the ice on the ground melting from the heat of my flesh under my uniform onto the skin of my knees. All I could think about was what was going to happen to me and what kind of trouble was I going to be in. *How did this happen?* I still had two flight schedules left to deliver!

Eventually the partner, a seemingly much more compassionate individual, came over to me. Noticing the look of fear on my face, he spoke to me reassuringly. "It's alright ma'am. We'll get this taken care of."

Noticing an opportunity, I jumped in quickly. "Can you *please* tell me what's going on?" I pleaded. I tried to keep my voice as neutral as possible. I was terrified, yet furious that they could treat me like this. Me, fellow military. I was also mortified. I kept looking around to see if anyone came out of our hangar, which wasn't too far away and still within good viewing range. I felt the embarrassment one feels sitting on the side of the road as they're receiving a ticket for speeding while seeing all rubberneckers passing by - only 1000 times stronger due to the M-16 in my face.

I thought of how my dad always warned us to never point a gun at anyone at any time. Even if it is unloaded - which I'm sure this one was not. Clearly this guy was not too conscientious of his gun aiming. Dad would have been livid with his poor gun etiquette and would not have been afraid to tell this shmuck how things really are.

The two glanced at each other as if they were sending out secret messages above my head. *Why won't they tell me what was going on? Such nerve.*

"Do you know what a 'red line' is, Ma'am?"

I stared at him as if it were a trick question. Of course I knew what a red line was. It was a boundary line painted red. The Air Force had them surrounding all of their military planes that were parked around the base. *Was he referring to something else I should know about?* I was confused. It didn't help that my legs were going numb from the cold and my nose beginning to run, but I was too afraid to move my hands to wipe it. And why did he keep calling me ma'am? He clearly knew I was enlisted - and probably younger than him. I was wearing my dungarees AND he had my ID. "Um, yes?" I answered, sounding more like a question. *Did I know what the 'Red Line' was?*

Just then, the callous guy with the gun came back. "What are *you* doing on the flight line?" he asked sounding more like an accusation than a question.

"Well, I was delivering flight schedules for my squadron. I *have to* drive on the flight line to deliver them. I am the duty driver for VP-8. My hangar is right over there," I pointed it out to him.

"Oh, VP squadron, huh? Hmmm. Well, it seems as though you have crossed over a point of no entry."

"Where?" Again, I was confused. It wasn't the first time I had driven onto the ramp with the duty van delivering schedules. In fact, I had just delivered them the night before. *Why now was all of this chaos happening?*

He shot out his finger into the direction that I had come. "Right over there is where you came from. The point of entry is approximately ten feet to the left of that."

I squinted out into the blackness of the night. I strained to look at where my tracks had come from. Maybe it was the darkness, or maybe it was the endless snowdrifts, but I saw no red line and had no idea where this guy was talking about. Still, I nodded in agreement. I just wanted this to end so I could go home.

"Here, stand up, but keep your hands up." I guess his moment of empathy was trying to show me that he wasn't a horrible guy, just one doing his job. I didn't buy it. *Ten feet. Really?*

"Is there anyone who can vouch for you and your location?" He asked.

"My squadron is right there." I pointed to the hangar that was a good baseball's throw length away. I'm horrible about estimating distances. Okay maybe a professional baseball player's throw. Not one of my throws. "My pilot, the SDO (Squadron Duty Officer, the officer I was on duty with) is there. He can vouch for me."

Man, I was in trouble. I can see it now. I'd been in this squadron barely over a month now and look at the predicament I was in. This wasn't looking good - especially if the SDO was to get involved. *Thank heavens it was Kennedy. He seemed like a nice guy. I mean, his call-sign was Sweet Pea, for god sake. He wouldn't yell at me. Or would he? I barely knew him - except that he was on this absurd new diet called Atkins where he would only eat the burger and the bacon from a bacon cheese burger. Crazy! Didn't he know that he should be eating high-carbohydrate, low-fat diet to lose weight?* All kinds of thoughts flooded my head. I was shaking now. Partly due to the cold that was taking over my body, and partly due to the anxiety that was steadily increasing in me.

Mr. Rifle Man stepped away from me and began to talk on his radio again. I couldn't make out a thing he said. Meanwhile, the guys surrounding us began to relax their positions somewhat. The guy next to me (the nice one) began making small talk. At that point, he could have told me that he enjoyed licking spotted frogs in his spare time - I would not have remembered a syllable. All that I could think about was what was going to become of me.

Then, in the small light from the hangar, I could make out the SDO trudging down the snowy flight line. I was flooded with relief upon the sight of a familiar face. As he approached I shot him the best *I'm-so-sorry-please-don't-be-mad* face I could muster. He simply shook his head.

I don't know what he said to Rifle Man, but I knew it would be better now. I wasn't going to be hauled away in handcuffs ringing in the New Year in some Icelandic prison. I've never heard of Icelandic prisons. But these Nordic people were descendants of Vikings. How friendly could their prisons possibly be??

Soon after, they released me to him. We drove back to the duty office in silence. At last, I broke it by saying the only thing I could. "I'm so sorry, Sir." My voice wavered. *Don't do it. Don't get emotional.*

"Airman Maki, stop," he said followed with a long pause. "It's okay." More awkward pause accompanied by silence, then in a business-like tone, "I trust you will be more careful around the red lines from now on."

"Yes, Sir, I'm so sorry."

Somehow, I already knew I would never hear the end of this. And I never did. That night in fact, the entire barracks had heard the story before I had even gotten back there when my shift was over. Everyone thought it was the funniest thing in the world. Still feeling humiliated, I did not agree. Being that the knees on my dungarees were still wet from where I had been kneeling, it took a while. However, after a few New Year's Eve drinks, my anxiety began to melt. True to my word, from then on, I avoided red lines like the plague.

Crash

When our crew was on duty, we had it all worked out so the driver would drive to the barracks and swap out the van with the oncoming driver. Then the new driver would assume and take the other guys back to the hangar to relieve the others.

One night that I was driving, it happened to be snowing a bit. This was not unusual for Iceland. It had been a particularly long day of answering to the usual demands that duty entails and I was ready to hit the rack. I began to recite the day's crazy events to my off-going ASDO (Assistant Duty Officer), Stanley. As I backed up to turn around in the tight parking lot, I was really getting into the heat of a story. All of a sudden, there was a thunderous crash, and we were instantly jolted to a sudden stop. I just froze, unsure of what to do next as I heard Stanley mutter an "Oh, shit."

My stomach dropped and a dreadful feeling crept into my body. It had only been a couple of weeks since my last "driving incident" with the red line. I was beginning to make an irresponsible label for myself already. At the same time, we turned to see my victim was a small white car. A white car in the white snow. It could've happened to the best of drivers. Unfortunately, it also happened to be the only car in the parking lot that contained a driver.

I was quietly petrified as I glanced over at Stanley. I didn't know what people did when they hit people while driving government vans. *Did I have insurance?* Normally laid back, Stanley began to very openly freak out. "Get out! Get out and talk to them!" He said shoving me out the door.

"What do I say?" I had never been in an accident before that involved another person.

"Just go and tell them you're sorry and give them your information."

Information. What information? I slowly opened the door to the stupid van that became more of a pain in my side each day that passed. Meekly, I crept to the car, rehearsing my lines with every step. As soon as the stranger saw me, he opened his door. I shouted at him, "Oh my goodness! Are you okay? I am so sorry," before he could say anything or react in any way. I was expecting him to come out of the car yelling or swinging at me.

"I'm fine. I guess we should call Security," he said. The thought made my stomach turn. I was hoping for an instant that we could just pretend it never happened.

Someone called Security. All that I could think about was what was going to happen to me now. *Would I be arrested for damage to the government vehicle? Maybe they'd send me home? Maybe I'd get my pay docked to pay for the cost of the damages.* Stanley came over, still shouting directions. "Okay, security is on their way, so I'm going to get another ride over to the hangar! You wait here and fill out a report with the cops!" I'm not sure if the fact that Stanley was yelling at me or leaving me was making me more upset. I suddenly couldn't control it any longer and my eyes began to well up with tears.

"Don't you dare cry!" Stanley began to yell at me louder. This only brought on more tears. "Stop it. You can't cry. I can't handle that right now! You'll be fine - you need to take care of this! I've got to go!" And then he ran away quickly as his ride pulled up.

And there I stood. *Did he really just leave me?* Security showed up shortly after and we went through the apparent usual routine. I was surprised at how easy it all turned out to be as far as the law goes. I had hoped by the time they sent the bill back to the squadron, we would be on our way home. I lost points on my license on the base in Iceland. This did not bother me. If they wanted to take me off duty-driver watch, that would be just fine.

That evening, we all hung out in the ever-popular First Class Mess and retold the day's events. Stanley, although one of the best storytellers around, was also an extremely *dramatic* storyteller - so you kind of had to listen with a filter. By the time he was done, it had sounded like I had left the other car as a pile of aluminum. This was in part a contribution to my reputation as a poor driver. Well, that and my poor driving record.

Later that night, he came up to me and apologized for leaving me so suddenly. He explained that when I began to cry, I reminded him of his 14-year old daughter, and he just couldn't take it. He hadn't seen her in five months now. I forgave him.

That night also solidified my first nickname appropriately entitled "Crash." Even though I was an experienced Minnesota driver, I did my fair share of slipping around the flight line. The following week, I slipped across the roadway and into the big metal dumpster. This only left a tiny scratch on the van. Two days later, I smacked into the hangar backing up. Thankfully no one was around and it wasn't hard enough to cause any visible damage - in the dark. It was somewhere around this time I gave up attempting to defend my driving capabilities. I was a pretty terrible driver. I ended up losing several points off my license during those three months. Yet they still continued to schedule me as duty-driver.

$$\vdash\!\!\!\!\!\dash\!\!\!\!\!\dash\!\!\!\!\!\dash\!\!\!\!\!\dash\!\!\!\!\!\dash\!\!\!\!\!\dash\!\!\!\!\!\dash\!\!\!\!\!\dash\!\!\!\!\!\dash\!\!\!\!\!\dash\!\!\!\!\!\dash\!\!\!\!\!\dashv$$

Bodo, Norway.
December 1998

Approximate distance from Deer River: 3680 miles

Many of our anti-submarine warfare missions were conducted in the Northern Arctic Ocean as it was a high submarine traffic area. In order to get there, we often had a transit flight of three or more hours - not to mention the eight+ hours on station. Considering the usual length of time a P-3C can stay airborne in normal conditions is about twelve hours, when we are "yanking and banking" (flying around the pattern at a low altitude, dropping sonobuoys), that time is substantially reduced, even if we loiter (shut down) an engine to save on fuel. This, however, is often not even an option in dangers of Arctic weather. Therefore, after we completed our missions, we would head to Andoya, Norway, to refuel for the trip home.

Andoya, Norway, is the location of a small Norwegian base in the middle of nowhere. It is located on the northern most point of Norway, what seems to be miles from any civilization. It is really the top of the world; well, other than the North Pole.

The night was a particularly stormy one and the plane jerked one way and was bogged down another. I felt my dinner in the back of my throat. We were flying low and deploying sonobuoys. The sonobuoys we shoot into the ocean transmit sound waves back to the airplane to detect under water occurrences. (Reference: *The Hunt for Red October* - or *My Mom Hunts Submarines*. You know, whichever you prefer.) The smell of the burning cads that fire the sonobuoys out of the plane wafted in the air, causing my stomach to ache even more as I sat sideways blinking my eyes hard, as if that would help me focus better on the green screens that were in front of me.

"Flight, TACCO. [Tactical Coordinator calling the flight station] I need you to come hard left to try to drop this buoy on top of the last one that failed."

"This is Flight. We're working on coming left back on the circle; however, the winds are playing a hard offense right now. Holy shit - we're getting sea spray on our windshield right now flying at 300 feet. The waves are about 20-30 feet high right now."

"Well that explains why none of our buoys are working!" Exclaimed Brian, in a frustrated voice. He slid back and dropped his pencil that he was using to take logs. "We aren't going to see a darn thing out here tonight." The unforgiving icy waters crashed below us - black in the night without a moon.

"Conditions are even worse north of us. We'll never make it to refuel in Andoya at this point so we're detouring to Bodo for fuel," Flight announced [pilots].

"Calling off-station at 1910 Zulu." Even the world's largest Navy doesn't stand a chance when Mother Nature is running the show. The power of the massive ocean never ceases to amaze me.

As we touched down in Norway, I could faintly make out mountains behind us in the dark distance. The Arctic winds protruded through our thin flight suits and jackets as the flight-engineers attempted the agonizing refueling process swapping out every few minutes for moments of relief. Others ran inside swiftly for a chance to smoke a cigarette or gather some warm coffee for the ride home. While everyone was carrying out their routine duties, suddenly a pungent smell of burning wires accompanied by smoke began to consume the tube of the plane.

Immediately the emergency fire bill was activated and everyone swiftly carried out their duties that had been so well rehearsed over and over again. It was such a mini-thrill when it was the real deal! Quickly the power supply that was generating the smoke was located and the circuit breaker was pulled. It turned out that the windshield wiper had been left on and ended up shorting out. Not a gripe that would cause the plane to become unable to fly; however, in that moment, about half of the crew - the ones that were working up in the front half of the plane - consumed a dangerous amount of smoke that caused an immediate headache. So we decided it was in our best interest to spend the night in Bodo, and allow time for the crew to get examined to ensure they were still fit for flight. Dizzy pilots are not a good thing.

Iceland was essentially my first time in a foreign country. (I cannot really count Canada as foreign, although Quebec is pretty outlandish.) However, Norway was the first time I was really out into civilization in a foreign country. It was quite a learning experience.

We checked into a local hotel and decided on a time to meet in the lobby so we could eat, and peruse the town. It was a very nice hotel; however, the room itself was very unique from anything I'd ever seen. The bed was a single, very low resting, with a full-sized pillow top to lie on. There was a bidet in the bathroom - and this was the first time I'd ever seen anything like that. Luckily, I'd heard of them, so I quickly realized it was not a drinking fountain as my first thoughts were for a flash second. Still, I only had a rough idea of how they worked and it was not exactly one of the things they covered upon check-in. Thankfully, there was also a regular -functioning toilet alongside of it. My favorite part of the room, however, had to have been the heated bathroom floors. Oh yes. They were so amazing; I could've slept on them. It was like candy for your feet as you walked across them.

I had packed a change of clothes with me in my helmet bag. We were told it would be a good idea flying where we were flying. Unfortunately, I forgot to pack a change of shoes. So I changed into a sweater, jeans, and put my flight boots back on. I did my best to straighten up quickly and head downstairs to meet the rest of the crew. However, I was stopped short when I could not budge the door. I twisted and pulled and jiggled all to no avail. After about five minutes of this, I began to panic. *Oh my god - I'm locked in my room!*

Naturally, everything was written in Norwegian. I picked up the phone - I had no clue which button to push - so I started pushing random ones until I heard a voice at the other end. It was speaking in Norwegian.

"Yes, I am in room 323, and I am stuck in my room," I replied to the voice slowly and loud - as if it would help them understand English.

The lady on the phone responded so fast and so broken, that I could not make out a word she said - even though I believed they were a form of English.

"What? I'm sorry- I don't understand…"

"jibber jibber jibber- *PUSH*- jibber jibber jibber."

"Oh, okay." I said, still confused. Surely I had tried that already. I sat the receiver down and made my way back to the door that had caused me so much anguish. I forcefully turned the knob and threw my shoulder into the door to push it from its jammed location. The door flew open and I followed, slipping and landing on the floor. I quickly stood up and checked to make sure no one had seen. *Was I seriously pulling that entire time? Who had ever heard of doors opening into the hallway of a hotel?* It was absolutely absurd. But apparently this had happened before to Americans if this lady did not miss a beat explaining to me to push.

I went down to the lobby - and realized I was a bit early, so I still had time to take some cash out of the ATM that was just outside of the hotel gift shop. *Twenty dollars should be about enough.* Of course, as I inserted my card - English was not an option yet on that particular ATM. So I fumbled through - doing my best to decipher. Entered pin number. Check. Sjekking eller Sparepengerer? I just picked the first selection and hoped it came out okay. Someone had mentioned the translation between the dollar and Kroner was just moving the decimal two times. *Or was that the Lira?* I couldn't remember. So I selected the option that I thought was translated to $40. Somehow, I ended up with the equivalent of some $200, give or take a little in Kroner. *So I guess I will be buying all the beer tonight.* Thankfully, the money looked fake and it did not feel like I was spending real money. Besides, it's not like the money would be worth anything anywhere else. Of course most banks will do converting - but even going to the bank is challenging when you do not have a car. So, I took the lazy route and decided it was a good excuse to spend it.

After dinner, which by the way, I had no idea what I ate, but it was good. Jeg spiste fisk og fisk til middag? I have found it is best to just order the house special when you cannot read the menu. They usually are the best dish. Ask the server to bring you their favorite.

After dinner, and a few rounds later - Chief, Brian & I moseyed around the buildings surrounding the hotel. There was a disco of some sorts that we wandered into. Me being a short, tan (hadn't been that long since I was in Florida), brunette in flight boots, it was a bit apparent I did not fit in among all the tall blonds with pale skin.

While Chief and Brian sat down and ordered a tall beer, I could not help myself and had to run off to the dance floor. It was like an inner driving force I could not resist.

So there I was on the dance floor surround by blonds at least a head taller than me, all wearing wool sweaters of some sort. I decided to break out some of my awesome signature moves, like the sprinkler and running-man (which is not easy to perform in flight boots by the way). This was not the type of club I was used to from back in my Florida Club 5 days.

Suddenly, I heard someone behind me asked me my name in English. I replied. It was a tall blond guy. He handed me a drink. I thanked him and began sipping on it. Then the blond stranger with crazy accent I could never imitate (every time I try it comes out like the Swedish Chef from the Muppets) commented, "You're not Norwegian."

"Nope."

"Where are you from?"

"I'm an American," I replied.

"American? Well, are you here for business or pleasure," the tall blond stranger asked me with a smile.

"Oh, I'm in the Navy." *Who the hell comes to Bodo, Norway, in January for pleasure?* "We came here to refuel because of the blizzard and our plane broke down - so we're here for the night."

"Oh really? What do you do in the Navy?"

OPSEC you say? Yes, here was where I was turning into an open book at this time. "I track submarines and blow them up during war time," I replied to him casually, like it was one of the top ten most common jobs in our country.

As the words left my mouth, I felt a strong hand grab my shoulder and drag me off of the dance floor. I turned around just in time to see Chief let go of me. He was sitting at a tall table with Brian, who was casually sipping on some mixed drink.

"What the hell are you doing?" He demanded.

I wrinkled my nose. "Just talking." *God, I could never make this man happy.*

"Where did you get that drink?" He asked, snatching it from my hands.

I shrugged. "I don't know. The guy I was talking to bought it for me."

"Are you a damn idiot? You just take drinks that people hand you? Don't they teach you anything where you're from?"

Now to be fair, I left home when I was 18 - well under the legal drinking age. Aside from not being old enough to go to clubs back home - there were no clubs back home. So *no*, I guess I'd never thought much about it. But there was no use in telling Chief that. He already had his mind made up and was continuing to share it with me, whether I wanted to hear or not. Besides, he knew where I was from. The same place he was from. A place where we played a little game called *Duck, Duck, Gray-duck*. But I decided not to remind him of that right now.

"And what the hell are you doing telling them you're an American in the Navy," he went on and on.

"I didn't see why... "

"Do you know where we are?" He cut me off. "We are in Norway. Do you realize how close that is to Russia?" He continued without giving me a chance to answer. "Have you been paying attention to the news at all - a little massacre that just happened a few days ago in Racak? You have no idea who is who in these parts and you don't go spouting off your mouth to everyone making yourself an easy target. Do you understand?"

"Yes Chief." I replied.

"And don't go calling me Chief out here, either!" He hissed low and under his breath.

"Okay." I hung my head and turned to go on the dance floor. I don't know what the heck he wanted me to call him. I certainly wasn't about to call him by his first name. It would be like calling my dad by his first name. Disrespectful and awkward. I smiled to myself at the thought. *Chief was so funny sometimes. This drink was really good!*

Some many, many beers and dances with tall blond strangers later... Brian and Chief came up to me and said they were going to head home now. Not missing a beat - I replied in my happy-drunk voice, "Okay! Bye! I love you guys!" Because I sincerely love everyone when I drink and feel it is so important to let them know.

They wandered off through the crowd, shaking their head. I continued to dance. Sometime later (as I had no concept of time at this point), I turned to see Brian.

"Hey Brian!" I smiled a big smile, because I thought how much I really had missed him.

"Hey Lady, you're coming home now." He stated simply and looped my arm through his. We made our way through the crowd and I was sure to tell all of my new friends goodbye before I left.

As we got out on the street, I saw my good ol' Chief sitting on the bench.

"Hey! I thought you guys had gone home!" I was so excited to see them. It was then that I got the "You-Never-Leave-Your-Crew-Out-In-Town-By-Themselves" Lecture. Apparently they were just testing me and had come outside, smoked a cigarette, and came back in to get me. I didn't exactly understand, as I was a perfectly responsible adult that could survive just fine on her own. But I allowed them to walk me back to my room; to be sure I made it back to my room safely in this foreign country that must have been friends with the communists. I mean, they sold Cuban cigars right in the hotel gift shop. That was the beginning of many nights where I would appease them and let them escort me back to my room to be sure I made it safely. They were always worried about something.

The Dance

It was the night of our squadron's post-Christmas, Christmas party. Celebrations on deployment were few and far between, so everyone was there. Besides, what else were they going to do? Work, workout, practice their Swahili, or sleep.

My crew met up ahead of time and arrived together. I had painted them all our crew patch on a Christmas ornament, because I could not go without giving gifts on Christmas. They seemed really touched by this and it was nice. Naturally, Chief gave me a hand-held vacuum cleaner for the plane as a Christmas gift. In his mind, he thought he was hilarious.

We arrived at the squadron party and it was the first time I had seen any of my squadron members dressed up in 'real clothes.' It was strange. I wore a little black dress and heels for the first time in months. As my crew and I walked into the party, I felt the usual eyes look up and see who the cat drug in. It was always so funny to see everyone we worked with every day all cleaned up. I barely recognized some of them. I did my best to look sophisticated as I carefully began down the steps. As I hit the second step down, naturally I mis-stepped and fell down to my knees. Unharmed, other than my pride, I quickly recovered and kept walking as if this was something I did all the time. Because in actuality, it was.

Our squadron devoured the fabulous dinner because it was anything but galley food or Wendy's. (The only fast-food restaurant on the base. I still cannot bring myself to eat another square burger.) We dined, drew door prizes, and celebrated like normal people do. Then, because we didn't want the night to end, went to the famous "Top of the Rock" (the base's dance/night club) to go dancing.

My crew drifted off and I mingled with some of my new maintainer friends. (Aircrew and maintainers often found themselves at odds with each other. It's an ego thing.) Among them was a Tron (an Avionics Technician) that was so handsome, I couldn't help but choke on my gum every time he looked my way. He wore a black leather jacket and had dark captivating eyes. His hair was combed back and he smoked his cigarette like James Dean. Cigarettes completely grossed me out, but somehow he made it sexy and I could not figure out why. His laugh was infectious. To strangers he came across as cocky, but they just didn't know that he was the type that would pull over on the side of the road to help turtles that were trying to cross.

Word was he had a motorcycle back home. The thought made me weak in the knees. I had always had a thing for a guy on a motorcycle. I was warned numerous times by my over-protective friends and co-workers to stay away from him. This only intrigued me more and I could not help but find myself drawn to him like a magnet to a frying pan. He was so easy to talk to. I hung on every word he said - but did my best not to reveal how smitten I felt. He was Italian so I knew he liked noodles. When I found out he liked to fish - it was all I could do not to run away with him right there. I loved to fish too. Of course I did not realize at the time this meant he loved to fish for 12-hours-at-a-time fishing marathons. I do not have that kind of an attention span.

I am not sure how it happened, but for some crazy and unexplainable reason, I found myself uncontrollably falling for Aaron - hook, line, and sinker. On this night he had on a white button-down shirt with brown buttons and a pair of dark blue jeans, which was dressy for deployment standards. His dark hair was combed back and his eyes took away my breath. We both had been drinking a bit which helped loosen the atmosphere. I talked to him every chance I could think of something clever to say.

"Did you know Venus is the only planet that rotates clockwise?"

"What?"

"Did you know in Kentucky it's illegal to carry ice cream in your back pocket?"

"Um, no. Nope I didn't know that," he said with a smile. He was so cool.

I stood there talking and sipping my drink. There were others around, but I cannot remember too many of them. Some songs I danced when others asked me, other times I sat out - wondering if he would eventually ask me. Suddenly, the upbeat mood was broken by a provocative key as a slow song sieved into the base club, instantly affecting the disposition of those enclosed in the balmy space. It was a sign that the night was nearing its end, as almost to signal a last chance song.

Junior, his obnoxious side-kick friend had been hitting on me all night. Junior was the gross type of drunk who would pee in inappropriate places such as indoor plants and coin-returns on vending machines. Oblivious to my heart's true interest, he asked me for a last dance. I glanced up at Aaron with pleading eyes, screaming for help. (Not literally, of course, that would have been awkward.) He took the cue and reached for my hand, explaining to Junior that he was a moment too late. I was rescued.

Aaron and I fit perfectly together. He smelled sweet, yet masculine, as I rested my head on his shoulder. As my heart began slipping away, ignoring all rational messages my brain unsuccessfully tried to send, I thought to myself, *I'll bet you're the kind of guy that refuses to use a hamper.* Turns out I was right. However, I also knew in that moment, that it was all over for me. I was falling head over heels for this handsome man I scarcely knew. As Garth Brooks' words sang on, I knew if nothing ever came of this incredible night, we had this moment. We had "The Dance."

The Phone Call

The next day I could only think of one thing. *Will I see him again? Did he want to see me again?* And, *man I could go for some ice cream.* Okay, those are three things. But time did not stop and after a long day at work, I was studying in my barracks room with a couple of the guys from work. All of a sudden, the phone rang and it was him! I was so excited, but instantly realized that my company was composed of onlookers/listeners.

"Hey, so I was wondering if you would like to go to a movie this Friday? They are showing *The Waterboy* on base." Aaron asked, sounding dreamy. Still, this was horrible timing. I could not let the guys know about this or I would never hear the end of it. I had to get him off the phone until they were gone.

"Oh, thank you. But I'm sorry - this just really isn't a good time," I replied quickly.

Surprised at my answer, he went on "um, okay. So you *don't* want to go to the movies with me then?" He asked a second time. Apparently he wasn't used to rejection. It was killing me inside. The guys were watching me now.

"I'm sorry - I just can't talk right now," I said quickly and hung up the phone so there would not be further discussion. *Oh man, I sure hope I will get the chance to explain*, I thought.

"What was that all about?" One of them asked.

"Oh nothing. Someone downstairs needed help." Then the phone rang again. I turned around and picked it back up. "Hello?"

"So why won't you go to the movies with me?" *Oh my gosh.* He was relentless. He was not going to take no for an answer. That was hot.

"Okay I will. Wecantalkaboutitlater. Bye!!" I said in one breath and hung up the phone and whirled back around again.

"So you *are* going to help them then?" Ron asked me.

"Yeah, I guess I am," I said, attempting to contain my ridiculous smile.

First Date

"Let's kick some names and take some ass!" I tried to laugh quietly to myself - I did not want to look like I was too amused by the stupid humor in front of me - but in truth, I was dying inside. It was hilarious. Just then my date, the handsome Italian boy I had been eying for some time now let a heartfelt belly laugh out. It was my cue that he had the same stupid sense of humor I did. I mean he did ask me to watch the movie "The Waterboy" with him. I instantly relaxed. Besides, how could I ever possibly have a second date with someone that didn't enjoy Adam Sandler? (Not counting Mr. Deeds and the one where he played his own twin. Those were horrible - but they had not come out yet.) I was relieved we were on the same page. And I was relieved that he did not seem to mind that I ordered a large, extra butter, extra salty popcorn with no intentions of sharing.

As I adjusted myself in the hard chair, I did my best to make my hand look lonely, and available for holding. The hand with the least amount of butter on it. Everything was going perfect and I was happily surprised that for a first date I was having such a great time. It was so easy.

Suddenly, I felt an object pelt me in the back of the head and stick in my hair. I reached back in time to pull out a buttery piece of popcorn. Trying to be discrete, I turned around in the darkness and glared at the couple behind me.

"Don't look at me!" The guy whispered right away. "It came from back there." He pointed behind himself into the dark abyss. As the light on the big screen in front of me flashed to a brighter scene, I could make out the faces several rows behind me in the half-empty theater. There sat four of the guys on my crew. Almost in unison, they smiled and waved back at me. I shot them an evil glance, shook my head, and turned back to the front before Aaron could figure out what was going on. The last thing I wanted to do was to scare him off by informing him he was actually on a date with me and my four big brothers. Apparently, it was a package deal.

Warning #2

I was so exhausted one night after our 10-hour burner, but I wanted to check my email quickly before going back to the barracks. It was 3am and I had been up since 4am the previous day, but I was really growing homesick and was hoping to have heard from my family. My grandma had passed away a few weeks prior after fighting Alzheimer's for over ten years. There was no way I could go home to her funeral and I did not know how badly it bothered me until after it was all said and done. As I was sitting in Operations room, there were only a few others around during this late hour. Suddenly, I had the eerie feeling that I was being watched and slowly began to turn around.

I almost screamed when I saw the dark shadow towering over me. "Oh my god, Chief, you scared me half to death," I said, not relaxing.

Ignoring my comment he replied with his usual angry tone, "Can you tell me what the hell this is?" He held up a transparent trash bag that clearly was full of items. I never knew where to go with these questions. *Did he want the obvious truth? Or was it a trick question?*

"Um, garbage?" I said quietly, unsure of what else to say.

"Thank you, Airman Maki," he replied condescendingly. "Yes, this is *garbage*. And do you know where I found this garbage?"

Oh shit. Did I forget to take out the garbage? I was so deliriously tired, I must have missed it. But instead of simply telling me, *Airman, you forgot the garbage*, Chief always had to turn it into a horse and pony show.

"I'm sorry, Chief. I must have forgot - I'm so tired. I promise it won't happen again."

He stood there and stared at me. Awkward silence. I felt like making a crazy face at him so he would stop staring at me.

"Okay?" I asked. I wanted to scream - *I messed up! What do you want from me!?*

Instead, he opened his hand and the bag dropped at my feet. "That's Two."

He stared at me for a few more seconds. "You don't get any more fuck-ups." And then he turned and left.

I just sat there and stared at the trash. I was not sure if I was going to cry or pass-out from sleep deprivation.

Lisbon, Portugal.
January 1999
Approximate distance from Deer River: 4100 miles

This one time, on the grounds of extra training, I got to go to Portugal with a different crew. My new crew, CAC-4 (which I would be an honorary member of on a temporary basis) and I landed swiftly into Lisbon, Portugal. Riding from the base to the hotel was quite a wake-up call. It was my first real glimpse of an impoverished part of a city. It looked devastating - and this place was not even bad compared to a real poverty-stricken area. The hills of beautiful mountain-sides were not lined with wooden houses, but rather cardboard and tin shacks. Electricity was a privilege in this neighborhood, and a washer and dryer were unheard of. As we drove by, the faces wore little to no expression.

The inner-part of the city exploded with history. The streets were lined with cobblestone, and ancient architecture adorned buildings everywhere. The smell was very stale and I had to hold my breath going past the fish markets and sewer run-offs. I soon realized just how young America really was.

We checked into our 5-star hotel - which really by American standards wasn't much more comparable to that of a Holiday Inn. Although it was nice and comfortable, nothing extremely lavish. We changed out of our flight suits, cleaned ourselves up, and became situated in our temporary living quarters.

Chuck, always the events planner, coordinated five taxis - enough to fit us all in - and set out to see what a good time Lisbon had in store for us that night. I climbed in, always stuck in the middle of the back seat between two guys be-cause I had the short legs. No sooner had I sat down when the driver planted the accelerator to the floor. I clutched for dear life as we raced around buildings and people, keeping up with the one in front of us. I am pretty sure there was no such thing as a speed limit there, as the goal was to get your speedometer as high as it could go until you had to slam on your breaks for the next red light. In fact, I think it was optional whether you stopped for the red light or not. It was all quite fascinating - that is until we realized that the taxi in front of us decided to stop at the last minute for one of the red lights.

The driver of our cab slammed on his breaks, but it was a moment too late. The tires screamed a horrible noise as we plowed into the cab in front of us, bringing us to an instant halt. Thinking the worst was over; I relaxed my death grip on the seat in front of me. Not a moment later, the third cab demolished our back end. Someone somewhere uttered the perfect words, "Holy shit." I couldn't have said it better.

As the first two cabs drove off, unaware of our situation, we all somewhat checked each other out for damage as we staggered to the sidewalk. It was then that it got a bit chaotic. All three of the cab drivers began shouting words in a language that we could not speak, but we all felt we understood just from the tone and arm waving. Before we knew what was happening they got into their crippled vehicles and sped off.

Stunned, we all looked at each other unsure of what our next move should be. *Did they really just leave us? And not one of us knows what part of town this is - or where anything is located.* As we stood in the middle of this foreign city with no transportation, it was then good 'ol Chuck stepped up to the plate and just began walking. And because no one had any better ideas, we all just followed him.

I am not sure how long we walked. We attempted to communicate with all kinds of people. The people were not very receptive and we were often met with cold stares. Still, everyone else walked along as though they did not care, so I did my best to ignore it as well. We seemed to walk forever, following many different versions of foreign directions, and just when my shoes were beginning to blister my feet and I was walking sideways on them, miraculously, we ended up on the waterfront - which was our initial goal when we initially set out in the taxis.

It was a stunning location despite the smell of fish wafting through the air. The waters that lined the pier were black as the night. The moonlight danced and sparkled on the smooth waves. They rose gently and fell without a sound, causing all of the fishing vessels that lined the pier to softly sway back and forth. Many of them were old and built skillfully of wood. They appeared to be the kind that had been passed down for generations, the only surviving witnesses throughout the victories and defeats of the city's history.

As we walked along taking in the scene, a handful of familiar faces came into focus seated in the outdoor bistro tables lining the front of one of the restaurants. Of course, they were wondering what our hold up was all this time.

And as the crew of American sailors reunited under that Portugal moon, the festivities soon began. Shots of tequila were bought. Ughh. Tequila or Jäger. Every time. Of course I wasn't old enough to be picky yet because all that I cared about was the fact that I could legally drink here. Another round of shots and a round of raw oysters were bought for all. How could I say no to the delicious sea creature with the texture of a cup full of cool snot? Not that I have ever tried a cup full of cool snot.

More tequila was brought. Then more oysters. A round of Guinness. My lips began feeling numb. I patted them to make sure. Then I slowly sipped on what tasted like a cup of molasses. Baskets of assorted fried unknown greasy items. A shot of tequila. Some monkey meat on a stick. I started smiling and could not stop. Everything suddenly became funny and I had to force myself to concentrate on important things such as talking and walking. All of the food began tasting the same. I checked my lips again just to make sure they were there. Then the overwhelming urge to "bust a move" entered my head. *What a fabulous idea.* I went out on the dance floor. A round of Jäger. Ugh. More dancing. I was starting to discover my inner-dancing queen. I was a fantastic dancer. At least in my head.

Another oyster? Don't mind if I do! Followed with another shot of tequila. Had to wash it down, of course. This led to dancing on a speaker because I suddenly felt I was just too short to dance on the dance floor. No one seemed to mind. Things started getting a little hazy. Somewhere after, I was happily thrown over the shoulder of our TACCO, and set to rest outside the door. It was the only way I was getting down from my speaker. Eventually, we all waved our goodbyes to our new friends (I love new friends) and gaily sauntered down the pier under the stars.

And then…

The most annoying sound in the world penetrated my eardrum and caused my head to throb. I opened my eyes, panicking, unable to figure out where I was. *Home? No. Wait, I was in Iceland. But I'm not anymore… we went on a trip to… Portugal.* I looked around to discover I was in a hotel room. Alone. [sigh of relief]. The annoying sound was coming from a clock next to me that read the numbers 6:00. I looked down to see that I was still dressed in the clothes I wore the night before. *Wow, I don't even remember coming back here. That's pretty bad, Julia,* I thought to myself. *You can't do that anymore.*

And then I had the realization that no matter how reckless I was in a given night, that my crew of big brothers would always make sure that I would get home safely - and alone. Sure I had many civilians come up and talk to me. But somewhere in the night, they were quietly pulled aside and warned or threatened. They would all eventually leave soon after. Of course, I never realized this was happening at the time. I could not see the fires they occasionally put out either when someone did not take to kindly to their instructions. But I knew I would always be safe. And perhaps that was not necessarily the best realization, as it essentially gave me a free ticket to be a little careless and not have to worry anymore. After all, I was now 20 and immortal.

That morning, we had to go in for a brief and preparation for our flight the following day. Everyone seemed to be doing relatively fine. We headed back to our hotel around lunchtime. Somewhere in the mix of it all, people began fleeing off to go use the bathroom quite abruptly. It began to have a chain reaction. Not for all, but most. We retired to our hotel rooms, with plans to meet up for dinner later. No sooner did we get there, did everyone start calling around saying there was no way they could go and eat, as they could not leave the bathroom for more than five-minute intervals.

After much debate the final verdict was that the common link was: Consumption of raw oysters the previous night. It soon became clear. We had all gotten food poisoning. At once it occurred to me that it probably wasn't the best decision to eat raw food that comes from the water where the waters are condemned.

If you've never had food poisoning, the only way I could describe it is to imagine your intestines are tying themselves in a knot and squeezing every last bit of the contents out - both up and down, anywhere it can get rid of the toxins. You're not exactly sure if you should sit on the toilet or hang your head in it. Don't go in that order though. If you're lucky, you had a sink right next to the toilet. This lasted all day. Then through most of the night. So much for our last big night on the town. I despised being sick and missing out on the fun that the non-oyster poisoned people were having. I was so hungry - but food would not stay down. Then, out of nowhere, my Knight in Shining Armor (aka Aaron) brought me some fried rice from a Chinese restaurant in Lisbon. It meant more than all the flowers and jewelry a man could buy for his girl. I did not know if it would stay down, but I was so starving that I knew I had to try.

By the next morning, I did not completely feel like death anymore. However, our pilots were still not up to par. As a result, we were unable to make our flight home to Iceland. The pilots that were tag-teaming the toilets were just not capable of flying an airplane. This lead up to a small problem with our billeting. The hotel did not have room for us all to stay another night. As our saving grace so that we did not have to take turns huddling over a burning barrel on the street for the night, they called around for us and found room at another hotel for that night - on the *other* side of town. They even arranged for a bus to take us over there.

That bus ride was unlike any other. Though my stomach was still slightly queasy, I had begun to feel somewhat better at this point - though others still did not. Just like everyone has their own way of sneezing - I learned that everyone also has their own way of vomiting. Some are discrete; others are extremely loud - and not a bit shy. In the fifteen minutes it took to get to the other side of town, those that were not ill were lucky enough to have to listen to a round of people throwing up into their bags. Continuously. Nonstop. It was deafening. And the smell. Oh how the smell was uncontainable and something else altogether. By the time we arrived at the hotel, even the ones who did not eat the oysters were getting ill. Our bus was left with a stale, acidic, fishy smell. We were a ghastly looking crew, if I have ever seen one. Somehow, by the grace of God, we were able to make it back to Iceland the next day.

Going Home

Iceland's landscape in itself is brutally breathtaking and the Icelandic natives could not be more biased in its favor. I would catch my breath every time we flew above the jutting terrain made up of jagged snowcapped mountains and steaming volcanoes that plunge directly into the ocean with vengeance. The unique Northern Lights that were made of walls of green, gold, white, and crimson that looked like dancing walls of light suspended in midair. They were best seen on the chilled nights that were so silent and still that our old plane even appeared to fly more quietly - leaving only a gentle rumble in its wake. The lights would appear out of nowhere and shown like a wall of glass in the sunlight, delicately, as if they would shatter if the plane threatened to protrude their barrier.

While I was in Iceland, I was beginning to find a love for the dirty old P-3. I will never forget the day I was able to fly the plane myself (with the co-pilot in the other seat of course). He taught me the fabulous concept of cloud-surfing. It was just like riding the banks of snow on a snowmobile back home in Minnesota - only much smoother. As I weaved the gentle plane in and out of the white pillows 10,000 feet above the Earth, it was a moment of pure elation. Of course, the guys in the back would probably beg to differ. That day, I flew my first plane, and also made three guys puke in twenty minutes.

Keflavik, Iceland, was my first far-away journey full of challenge, reward, and endless memories. I earned my Bluenose Certificate for flying over the Arctic Circle. I found new friends and new love, and was introduced to many new parts of the world. I made plenty of mistakes, but from them I learned a great deal and was also part of some incredible missions. I literally saw the world from a new point of view that really impacted my outlook on life. After living in this new world for three months - a world where wild ponies that roam freely as icicles cling to their chin whiskers and wind that could pick up a small child, I definitely had a new appreciation for my country.

And though I had a hard time believing the day would ever come, after going to bed and consecutively waking up enough times, the last day of our deployment finally arrived. There was a contagious buzz in the air - an extra energy encircling everyone in its path.

The long flight home to America seemed twice as long as it did to get out there. There were several times in which I had to remind myself to slow down and breathe, as my stomach would begin to ache a sweet, anxious ache. I felt like I was going to throw up one minute and the next I was bouncing off the walls, talking a mile a minute. Restlessness set in, and even though I tried my best to behave myself since the Skipper was aboard, I could not help it. I just could not sit there and be a 'yes-sir-no-sir' kind of sailor on that day. So I slapped the Skipper. No, that part didn't really happen.

That day, we were all just a bunch of guys and girls anxiously waiting to go home. Everyone was joyful. It did not matter if I were to have just cut off their finger, because they were going home. Even the airplane shook with excitement as we fired up the engines. The first one, then second ignited. Soon the third and fourth followed. As flight announced to set condition five, everyone quickly secured themselves and their belongings.

As we taxied to the runway, I watched from the observer station, facing backwards, looking at where we had been. These were the last few moments I may ever see of this country. Iceland. My first foreign country. My first deployment with my first squadron. So much had already happened in such a short time.

The mighty P-3 came to a halt at one the end of the runway and paused for just a moment. Seconds later the engines began to spin faster and faster. The propellers became a blur of gray. The plane began to shake, holding in place, almost as if it was shaking with excitement. It was being teased. *Do you want to go? You ready to fly? Are you sure you're ready?* YES, YES!! It replied back. *Well... then... GO!!* The brakes released and she bolted forward, first slowly as she was weighted down with a load from hell. Then, increasing speed with every second that passed. Faster, and faster. So much runway had passed already. More than usual. But she was so much heavier than normal as she had to have enough fuel and the responsibility of carrying this full crew of sailors across the Atlantic Ocean to their beloved families that no doubt were anxiously waiting. I leaned forward and could make out the lights at the end of the runway quickly approaching. And then... *rotate*. When the precise speed met the calculated weight, aerodynamic engineering was at its best and we had... lift. The mighty P-3 dutifully climbed and climbed. The ground grew smaller and smaller as we rose above the clouds and could no longer make out the island below us. We were going home! Nothing was changing that because now we were in the air. Over the ocean. Nothing could stop us now. (Well, I have learned to never say never - and not to count on anything until wheels were actually on deck in the country of our destination, but we were getting closer with every passing moment.)

We were the last flight to arrive in the states on that sunny February afternoon in 1999. That was the reason the Skipper was aboard - he is always the last to return home. After seeing endless blue ocean and faded strands of white clouds, the serrated islands and jutting rocky shoreline of Maine outstretched their arms to us. The mighty aircraft performed a flawless, gentle landing and began taxiing to the hangar filled with anxious on-looking family members filled only with ecstasy. Home.

After the ladder was brought down, Customs came and passed unusually swift. That rarely occurred. It was an unforgettable sight as the reunions began. Children had changed in six months as they ran to greet their parent, gleefully beaming, unable to contain their excited squeals. Fathers were meeting their new infants that they had yearned for so long now to hold for the first time. It all was a truly a spectacular display of the human spirit - to be welcomed home to the best country in the world.

The best thing was that there were people on the deck to put the plane to bed that night - so there was no pisser-dumping for me (which was great since it was beyond full after such a full and lengthy voyage). No post-flight cleaning this day. We didn't even download our own bags. The guys on deck did it all for us.

When it was my turn, I slowly exited the plane in a line with my crew. The cheering from the crowd was intoxicating. It was as if we were walking the red carpet as we stepped down the old ladder that had served us daily for the past six months. I stepped cautiously. It would have been a bad time to fall down the ladder.

My foot hit the cemented taxi-way. It was American cement. The best cement ever. I was home at last. Carrying my helmet bag, I carefully walked past all the wives and girlfriends with tears in their eyes, at last reunited with their long lost loved ones. Thankfully, I was able to bum a ride from the duty driver to go pick up my car from where it had been stored in security. Luckily, it started right up despite not having run for three months. I drove past all the "Welcome home boys!," and "I Missed You Dad" signs. I stopped at McDonald's and grabbed some dinner to go, since I knew my fridge in the barracks would be empty.

CHAPTER 10

Brunswick, ME.

February 1999

Approximate distance from Deer River: 1400 miles

A few days after the entire squadron returned home, Aaron came by my barracks. "I want you to meet my best friend," he said as the tall stranger sauntered in behind him. "This is Tayte."

I reached out and shook his hand and he reciprocated.

"How's it going?" he asked. He was tall and thin. He had blond hair and a round baby-face and a nice smile. However, his most striking feature was his blue eyes. They were the bluest eyes I'd ever seen. I almost wanted to sing that to him in a song. Almost.

"Good! So nice to finally meet you. Aaron talks nonstop about your fishing adventures together."

"Oh yeah? Well hopefully we'll get some good days in this spring in the Androscoggin." The Androscoggin was the river that ran through the Brunswick area. It had great fishing; however, we were never able to eat anything out of there due to old factories that used to dump their waste into it up until the 1970s. The river and its contents were still impaired by the lasting effects of the pollution three decades later.

As we all walked down to the parking lot talking about all the fishing holes they had planned to visit, we climbed into Tayte's Ford F-150 pick-up truck and he started it up. All of a sudden *The Divinyls* blared on the radio, "*I don't want anybody else. When I think about you I touch myself...*"

Tayte's face grew the color of a cooked Maine lobster and he quickly switched off the radio. Aaron busted out in a rage of contagious laughter to which I immediately joined.

"Ah, yeah. That cassette tape is permanently stuck in there, so it's all I can listen to - over and over," he added with dramatic exaggeration.

"But luckily Tayte is gay, so it doesn't really matter." Aaron interjected with a straight face.

"You're...gay?" I asked, my surprise sobering me up. *I mean, I didn't judge...*

At that, both Aaron and Tayte could not contain their laughter anymore. "No, no. I'm definitely *not* gay," Tayte replied, giggling like a school girl as he flicked his wrist in the air.

As I hung out with the two friends, all I could think of was how great it was to be home in America again, to eat American food, drive American trucks, and listen to great American music. Like the *Divinyls*.

Old Enough to Fight

I could not stop thinking about the thick, succulent steak and lobster I would devour that night. I had it all planned out in my head. I would order the steak cooked my favorite way, medium rare, knowing I would not have to worry about contamination. It was going to be heavenly. Maybe I would throw in some surf with my turf - just not oysters. Not yet.

I could not stop staring at my handsome date, my new love. Tonight we were going to be 'real people.' I smiled and squeezed his arm close to me as we walked inside the restaurant. We sat across from each other at a table that overlooked the water, holding hands. The waves glistened in the moonlight and crashed upon the shoreline. No expense was spared as we celebrated our homecoming at our favorite restaurant.

I glanced around and was met with stagnant expressions from my fellow diners. I wanted to shake them and say, "How are you not smiling? Don't you realize we are all here and that all of us have it so good?!" Instead, I just fashioned them the biggest grin I could. Surely, they thought I was daft. Or drunk.

The waitress read the specials of the night in English. Her New England accent was music to my ears. A funny music. She asked to start with our drink order.

"I would *love* a glass of your house Merlot and a side of water, please," I requested, thinking how wonderful the wine would taste with my steak.

"Can I see some ID?"

Without thinking, I handed her my military ID - the same green rectangle card that dictated whether or not I was allowed to pass through the safety and familiarity of armed American gates in the middle of a foreign country. It was the rectangle that held my entire identity and fate for the past six months.

"I'm sorry Hun, but you're not of age. I'll bring you that water though." She placed the card on the table, and headed back to the kitchen.

It took me a second to register what just happened.

"Welcome back to the states, Babe," said my date, smiling at me across the table.

Embarrassed, I sat back in my seat. Maybe I was going crazy. In my head I felt seventy - I had worry lines around my eyes and dark circles to prove it - despite their mere twenty years. It had felt so long now that I was away. I had simply forgotten that I was not old enough to drink a glass of wine with dinner in my own country - though I was old enough to fight for it.

The Difference

Towards the end of 1994, the USS *Eisenhower* became the first aircraft carrier to allow women as permanent crew members aboard a combat ship. Shortly after, they opened up the combat aircrew (CAC) rating to women. As you can imagine, this was met with some resistance by the older, saltier sailors who were not ready to conform to a "kinder and gentler Navy" in which they had to wear pants at all times, keep the jokes cleaner, and the work spaces free of pornography magazines (in theory).

Most male sailors in the 1990s were fine with it, as they had been raised by mothers from the women's lib era. The military was always just a few decades behind the rest of the country.

Combat aircrew meant flying over enemy lines with the chance of going down and getting captured - hence the reason we attended SERE school training. But it was easier for society to accept as we were not performing face-to-face frontline combat that everyone has been so afraid to open up to women until the

War on Terror. Flying was different.

Now I whole-heartedly with every bone in my body believe that men and women are created equal. Some may disagree and that is their opinon. You should stop reading my book, though, because we cannot be friends anymore. Yes, men are built differently and generally physically stronger. But that is not to say that there are not women out there that are just as strong or stronger.

In my opinon, there should NOT be a sliding scale when it comes to physical readiness for a combat position. Either you can launch a 200-pound life raft, or you cannot (man or woman). And if you cannot pick that cookie up, I do not want to put my life on the line and fly with you. As long as a woman can perform the same job as the man, there is no difference.

Oooh, except for one. Little. Thing. I don't have a penis. There, I said it. Hence, I was not made to stand up to pee. Yep. We're going to go there.

The P-3 head (bathroom) contains a "honey bucket," which is basically a dry bucket seat in which one can sit upon to perform all #2 operations. This type of action is quite discouraged, as the head contains no ventilation system and will cause grave nostril distress to fellow aircrewmen in the tube during flight. Should this occur, the offender would be responsible for disposal of the hazardous material as well as compensation to fellow aircrewmen upon completion of flight in the form of a case of beer.

Should an aircrewman find the need to relieve himself of liquid matter, (a common occurrence, considering our flights can be extremely long) one would simply unzip flight suit bottom, flip the forward-facing lid up on the free-standing urinal, and let it all go.

If this aircrewman for some reason did not come equipped with their own penis apparatus attached to their person, this process suddenly becomes a wee bit more complicated. I said wee.

A penis-less aircrewman must first unzip the entire flightsuit from the top to bottom and half undress to get to the essential parts of this operation. Then, because there is almost always as trail of urine down the front of the urinal leading to a small puddle on the floor, (bad aim or short penis - I've never been sure) it is necessary to tie their flightsuit sleeves around the knee area so as to not drag it in this puddle.

The penis-less aircrewman then must unfasten and lift off the entire top of the urinal, often releasing a horrendous smell of coffee-hydrated fellow aircremen's liquid waste. At this point, unless the penis-less aircrewman is over six foot tall, they would need a bit of lift to hover over the bucket of urine that comes up to about waist level (well, my 5'4" waist level). This can be achieved by stepping one foot onto the honey bucket seat and the other onto the toilet paper holder on the opposite wall. Also to note, the aircraft is not stationary during any of this time. It is necessary to be prepared for maneuvers, turbulence, or just asshole pilots who think it is hilarious to yank the plane if they have found out someone is in the head. After all, it's not their mess to clean up. And that, my friend, is how you use the urinal in flight without a penis.

Of course there are other techniques that have been used throughout the years. A cup. Go in a cup and dump it into the urinal. My problem with that method was that I didn't want to be responsible for a dirty cup afterward. I had tried a disposable coffee cup once. Additionally, after holding it that long (I would try to space it so I would only go once a flight) - an 8-ounce coffee cup does not cut it. Unfortunately, I came to this realization about 6-ounces into the process.

There were even rumors about these packs that we could order from the PR shop (Parachute Rigger shop that housed and kept all of our flight gear in tip top working condition) that turned the urine to gel. Again, what do I do with a bag full of urine gel for 5 more hours on the flight? As crazy as the "hang-like-a-monkey" method was - I found it to be simplest. No forward thinking/preparation involved as there were so many other things to worry about before a flight - especially when you are the unqualified aircrewman.

I will spare you the additional details of what a new level it brings it to when it's that time of the month. Yes, I can hear the salty old sailors cringe when someone goes there, but the fact of the matter is, it is our reality. Although by the end of my first deployment, I was like a bathroom ninja. Rarely was I noticed going in and out of there. I don't think the guys even realized I ever used the head on the airplane. I learned not to bring attention to myself when I have to go. I would just sneak in and out. I also learned that owning a penis definitely had its perks. Haha.

Roommates

"Approved." The request chit was stamped and signed. Because the barracks were short on rooms, I had been approved to move out and live on my own as a little old airman. And I had 30 days to find a new home or it would be denied. Now on an airman's salary, it would have been darn near impossible to afford a place on my own. I had been planning on moving in with Janessa - that is until she found a place to rent from a sailor in a deployed squadron. The problem was he only wanted one person living there while he was not.

Plan B. Aaron nonchalantly invited me to live with him and Tayte to help them really save money by sharing the rent. I had only been officially dating him for a little over a month now. I'm sure in the books somewhere this was listed under 'Really Dumb Idea.' However, my blissful heart sang with joy over the idea and thought it was the most wonderful thing that could ever happen for two people. I could live in my very first apartment outside of base with my handsome new love. Aaaand his best friend. What could possibly go wrong?

Flash forward three months later and we have this ominous recipe: A shiny new boyfriend that worked nights. The new boyfriend hated housework in any form. A new girlfriend that wanted him all to herself. The new girlfriend could be a slightly-controlling neat-freak at times. Slightly. Two best friends that loved to fish together from sun up until sun down every weekend. One single bathroom for all to share. The young, strapping best friend enjoyed baking cookies with various women on the weekends. An apartment that had very thin walls. A long-haired cat that the two best friends decided to adopt together that chronically sneezed boogers all over the house.

The result: a lot of passive-aggressive silent treatments between best friend and girlfriend. Some raging arguments between boyfriend and girlfriend as a result of boyfriend being stuck in the middle. Occasional overly-dramatic storming out actions.

It was hard. It was ugly at times. Tayte and I developed a love/hate relationship as we both competed for Aaron's time and our different life styles. We both offered things Aaron loved. Fishing and boobs. Eventually Tayte and I began to resent each other. Aaron and I had both fallen quickly in love with each other, so quickly that we didn't see each other's flaws and how different we were from each other until later. I began to feel like the house maid, cleaning up after two men who were out fishing all day. The laundry basket was always full of clothes, the bathroom was always full of hair, and the walls always full of boogers from the cat. One day after a particularly loud fight about cleaning, which equaled feeling neglected, I had enough. I packed my bags and stormed out into the parking lot. I was not going to be a maid or second-string anymore.

As I was fumbling for my keys in the dark, I noticed a tall shadow walking towards me. Assuming (or rather hoping) it was Aaron coming to apologize, I didn't look up and continued to load up my bag.

"Watcha doing?" I looked up, surprised to see Tayte standing over me.

"I just have to get out of here," I sniffed, trying to hold back my tears. "I can't take it anymore."

"Can't take what?" He asked, his tone kind, which caught me off guard. I wasn't sure if he was going to yell at me too, siding with his friend. I was also pretty sure he could hear everything Aaron and I had been fighting about.

"*Everything.* I can't do this anymore. It's too hard. We're just so different."

He was quiet for a few seconds. "Yeah, you are. But that's what makes it a good relationship."

Now I was confused. I didn't think he wanted us to be together. I was taking away his best friend. I was the enemy.

"Well it's not good. We're just fighting *all* of the time."

"Yeah, you're learning how to live together. And you're fighting over the stupid stuff, like laundry and changing the cat litter. But the big stuff's good. You guys still love each other, don't you?"

"Yes, but...."

"But that's what matters. Aaron is messy," he smiled. "We know this. But I've never seen him so happy before with someone. You guys are having a rough patch - but you're perfect for each other."

"I know. I just - I just don't know what to do anymore. I feel so lost," my chin began shaking and I turned away so he couldn't see my tears welling up again.

"Com-mun-i-cate," he pronounced each syllable. "Running away won't help anything. Go back in there and talk to him. Some days you just have to suck it up and remember what's really important." As I looked up at him, I couldn't believe the words he was telling me. All this time I had thought he wanted me to leave. Here he had come back out to stop me.

I took a deep breath and had calmed down quite a bit by now. "Okay," I slowly nodded. "I'll talk to him."

"Okay good," he grabbed my bag and as we started walking back he put his arm over my shoulder. "You alright?" I nodded again.

"Good. And I promise to start helping more around the house, too," he smiled.

And he did.

The Recruiter

"They're sending you where?"

"Portland. Just down the road." He shrugged his shoulders.

"A recruiter? You're seriously going to be a recruiter?" I repeated the word - hoping if I said it enough I could believe it.

"It was the only way I could stay in Maine." I shook my head at the thought. At him. "So you're going to get that guy they call Rugged for a Sensor One I hear. Sounds like he's pretty good."

"Yeah, I guess. It won't be the same though." I sounded like a pouty kid, whining over receiving Cheerios for breakfast instead of Fruity Pebbles.

"It never is." Brian said as he ran his whole hand down his face and over his thick mustache. "It's just part of the job. You get used to it."

"Well I hate this part of the Navy. And I hate that the Navy makes the dumbest moves. You're like one of the best acoustic operators in the Fleet. And they're going to make you a recruiter. I just can't believe it," I said. I knew how I sounded. I knew I should try to think about his feelings rather than just feeling sorry for myself, but I just couldn't help it. This was going to kill him inside and I knew it. Everyone who knew Brian knew this. But the Navy had never exactly been known for its good decisions when it comes to its people. It's all about the needs of the Navy. I hated that. I hated everything.

"You keep your nose in the book, okay?" I nodded, keeping my head down. "I'll miss ya kid." He said and gave me a strong hug. My first "sea-daddy." I looked up to him with the pride that a child would to her father. There was no one smarter than Brian. I owed everything to him. He turned and got into his car and I turned and walked into the NEX to grab some lunch.

Blond Moment

"Take the tapes out to the plane and start pre-flighting. And don't skimp on running the long tests. I want a full preflight. I'll come out in an hour to check on your progress. If you do well, I'll sign it all off on your PQS (Personnel Qualification Standard)," Rugged instructed in his all-business tone.

"Okay. Got it." *Gosh, this new guy didn't mess around.* I went out to the plane carrying ALL the gear I could at one time, like a weighted down mule. I fired up my station and began the pre-flight. It was the first time I began ENTIRELY on my own, but I wasn't too worried. I felt like I knew what I was doing - for the most part.

"Good morning, Chief," I said as he walked by me in the tube.

"Goddamn piece of shit aircraft from a piece of shit squadron…" his grumbling voice trailed off. I sighed. I had read the gripe book as we just received the plane from our neighboring squadron. There were definitely a large number of discrepancies on this one.

As my preflight went on, I watched the screen. When it was time to test my hook and trackball (basically a 'mouse' and 'clicker' for the plane) my screen was frozen. I could not get the trackball to move at all. *Oh great.* I thought I remembered a discrepancy in the book about the display… *what was it again? Crap. Rugged was going to kill me for not writing them all down.* I recycled the overhead circuit breakers. I messed around with the trackball. After about ten minutes, I was out of ideas. *Crap.*

I went up to the flight station and made a radio call to maintenance, explaining that I had an avionics issue and requested they send someone out to troubleshoot. They said someone would be on their way and I went back to my station to wait for them.

I felt the plane move gently and heard someone on the ladder. As the door opened and the maintainer stepped into view, removing his cranial, I saw my worst fear. It was Aaron. My stomach leapt. I didn't want to appear as if I didn't know what I was doing in my job in front of him. We did our best to keep our relationship quiet in the squadron. It wasn't a big deal, as he only outranked me by one level and we weren't in the same chain of command. Still, I worried about gossip and tried to hold off on everyone knowing as long as possible- though I was a terrible actor.

"What seems to be the trouble?" He said casually, and I did my best to look as professional as I could. I couldn't help it though. The sight of him still made me smile and blush.

Pull yourself together. "Well, I'm not sure what's going on with the trackball. I can't get it to display. It seems to be locked-up. When I do this, it does this," I said as I demonstrated. I continued to ramble more and more details as he just watched.

Finally when I was done, he leaned in, moved the trackball for a few seconds. Then he opened the door to the controls underneath the display and flipped the Channel 1-2 switch. The display then began working effortlessly. I sat there for a few seconds pretending that it just didn't happen. I nodded. It was probably one of the first functions they taught us back in Jacksonville. It was the most obvious solution staring right in my face. And I had overlooked it. But instead of having my 'blond moment' between me and my sensor one who should've been out there training me, I had to have it front of Aaron. The one I wanted more than anyone to impress. I was mortified. Turns out, it was only the beginning of my 'blond moments' that he would come to witness. Thankfully, he never held them against me. In fact, he was usually quite entertained by them.

Squishy

Once upon a time, there was a man who really wanted to go far in life. Perhaps it was for the money. Perhaps the fame. Or perhaps he was beat up in high school a lot for being socially inept and swore one day he would get back at the world if it was the last thing he did. Somehow "Squishy," who never did learn the basic etiquette of socializing with others, made the rank of Commander in the Navy and was awarded a squadron of his very own. That squadron was us.

It wasn't just that he was an awkward man. Many people are awkward. I can be quite awkward at times. But only sometimes. And it wasn't the fact that he leaned in to read your name tag every time he spoke to you, making it an uncomfortable chest stare-down. Or that he incorrectly classified whale noises on the monitor in flight as a "classic Sierra" (a Russian submarine). Heck, it wasn't even the fact that he would continue to scratch his balls excessively every single time he spoke to you. (Although this was quite disturbing and left me wanting to scream, "Just because I am looking in your eyes doesn't mean I can't see what your hand is doing!!") By far the biggest problem with Squishy was that in his eyes, you only mattered if you had some value to him, or he could get somewhere by knowing you - and everyone felt that.

On one particular day, as I was duty driver, (*again*) we happened to have an admiral visiting our command. This was a very big deal. Anytime an admiral comes, the entire squadron takes a week to clean every space and crevice throughout the hangar spaces. We pressed the linens and baked a cake. And just before the admiral arrived, Squishy came in to make sure we all knew our roles.

"…And Airman," he looked over at me, "Be sure you grab his bags right away and carry them out to the airplane for him."

"Yes, Sir," I replied and Squishy disappeared.

Not too much time had passed before the admiral and his assistants arrived. As he stepped out of the vehicle, I took notice of what a mammoth-sized man he was. He had to have been over six and a half feet tall with extremely broad shoulders and a muscular build. The SDO and I nearly tripped over each other to get out to the vehicle to greet him. As the SDO introduced himself, I began to reach for the bags, my head barely coming up to his chest. "Here Sir, let me just bring these out to the plane for you," I said as I reached for them.

"Thank you, Airman, but I can get them," the admiral refused.

"Oh, Sir, I insist," continuing to reach out for them.

"No, please. I would prefer to carry them myself," The admiral repeated, looking me square in the eyes. Of course it was the Navy, but I have no doubt it felt odd to the admiral, who was probably raised as a gentleman, to have a 20-year-old girl half his size carry his bags for him. In any other setting it would have been socially…weird.

"Oh, okay. Yes, Sir." Sensing that I should let the subject go, I turned to go inside, holding the door for the admiral and his company as they made their way through the hangar and out to the aircraft that had been pulled up into prime parking on the ramp.

A few moments later, Squishy bolted around the corner - having caught a glance at the admiral walking across the hangar bay.

"WHY IS HE CARRYING HIS OWN BAGS!?" He shouted at me. "DIDN'T I TELL YOU TO CARRY THEM OUT TO THE PLANE FOR HIM!?"

"Yes, Sir, but…"

"THEN WHY AREN'T YOU?!"

"Sir, he insisted. I tried to grab them from him, but he insisted on carrying them himself," I said, nervously.

"Well…" I don't think he knew what to say next. "Whatever." And with that he threw his arms up, turned and walked away. Disgusted.

Anthrax

During that home cycle, as all home cycles went, we were constantly in a state of preparation for the year, working towards the efforts of our next six-month deployment. Maintainers were getting the planes ready, and aircrews were getting their crew qualifications completed. Before our upcoming deployment to

Sicily in 2000, we had to prepare ourselves for the talk of biological warfare. The big craze at that moment was anthrax. So, the Navy decided it would be in all of our best interests to get our anthrax immunization series, to complement all of the other toxic live disease vaccinations that were currently crawling through our bodies at this point.

As this was going on, there was so much media hype on anthrax, it was mentally exhausting. Being that our squadron was going overseas to support efforts with Bosnia/Kosovo Campaign, we were prime candidates to be experimented on.

Over and over, the squadron leaders (CO, XO, & Flight Surgeon) assured us that there were no harmful side effects at all. Still, it was a hard concept to swallow when we heard news reports of people dying and suffering major life-long side effects. This was a major live virus that was relatively new to the public. And I couldn't help but think, sure they may have done a few studies here and there, but what were the long term effects? And how much of the studies were really done with women - given the fact our bodies function in much different ways.

Would it be something like the drug DES (Diethylstilbestrol) that was given to mothers to prevent miscarriages before it was stopped being prescribed in 1971? It worked to prevent the miscarriages; however, the female offspring of these mothers then grew up to find some twenty years later that they were infertile. How would I know what possible effects a drug like anthrax would have on my children? We would not know for a couple of decades. The military did not exactly have the best track record for protecting its people from being an experiment. (Agent Orange?)

Stressful did not even begin to describe it. The most stressful was the fact that we had *no choice* in the matter. There were people that protested; however, upon refusal of taking this drug, we were promised a dishonorable discharge. Of course, that meant no McDonalds jobs or ever having a job again the rest of our life. As Chief would say, they had our balls in a vice grip.

I did as much research as I could on the matter, printing off any negative reports I could find. And it was not hard to find many. In fact, it was quite alarming all of the information I was uncovering. It was also a tricky line I was walking, as I knew we were not allowed to object, and any protesting could have serious consequences. Still, I felt that I had to do everything I possibly could.

After I had this bundle of information, I went through, highlighting pertinent and alarming headlines and facts "Nervous system side effects have included dizziness, seizure, tremors, aseptic, meningitis, encephalitis, transverse myelitis, cerebrovascular accident, facial palsy, hearing and visual disorders, Guillain-Barre Syndrome, sepsis, systemic lupus erythematous, polyarthritis nodosa, spontaneous abortion, and multiple sclerosis have been reported... Hematologic side effects have rarely included aplastic anemia, neutropenia, idiopathic thrombocytopenia purpura, lymphoma, leukemia. Psychiatric side effects have rarely included mental status changes, psychiatric disorders, and mood-cognition disorders. Cardiovascular side effects have rarely included myocarditis cardiomyopathy, atrial fibrillation, syncope, endocarditis, angioedema, and collagen vascular disease. Renal side effects have rarely included glomerulonephritis and renal failure." The list went on, but always happily ended with "casualty has not been established." Oh good. At least I won't die directly linked to the shot - it will be from one of these other diseases. And the funny thing is that although they were nicely prepositioned by "have rarely included," they still are included - and there are a ton of side effects listed. I didn't even name them all. I would have bored you to tears and frustration in the pronunciation of the diseases alone. The point is - well, I think you get the point. (https://www.drugs.com/sfx/anthrax-vaccine-diede-effects.html)

I bound these papers neatly into a report-like essay. And I carefully typed an anonymous note (well, probably not so anonymous after this - it was ME!) addressed it to my Skipper, pleading with him to stand up for us - and to stop this from happening based on all of my research. I felt good. I felt like I had at least spoken my piece. I would not go down without a fight - even if it was a tiny little slingshot against a dozen grenades. I also thought of writing to my Congressman; however, time was running out. We were scheduled to have our first series of shots within days.

The next day we were all called to quarters. We filed into ranks and listened as Squishy addressed us, explaining how displeased he was with our behavior. My stomach sunk. I began to realize all of my efforts were in vain at that moment. He assured us that we would be fine. The drug had been around for decades now. He did not appreciate this type of negative rumor spreading around.

As I stood in line next to Aaron, with my paper in hand, waiting my turn to get my injection and my paper signed off by the Corpsman, I felt the sinking feeling of defeat. I had lost the battle. I had no voice. It didn't matter what I had to say - no matter what point I had or the fact that I was only going to be in the Navy for a few more years. Here, I had signed up to serve the country, defending the Constitution which clearly gave all Americans the freedom of speech. Ironically, none of us serving had the right to free speech.

"Next." Doc called out. I stepped forward and took a deep breath. I was too consumed with the grief of defeat - I wasn't even afraid of the massive needle this time. As it punctured a hole into my skin, stinging it immensely, I felt a piece of myself die. It was the tiny bit of belief I still had that one person could make a difference. The pasty substance was squeezed into my arm, leaving a golf-ball-sized lump under my skin. It was excruciating. It was a helpless, crushing feeling. I always had thought I could make a difference. But I didn't.

JTFX

JTFX (Joint Task Fleet Exercise) is an annual training we would conduct with our entire Battlegroup off of the coast of Jacksonville, Florida, during our home cycle. The Battlegroup consisted of an aircraft carrier at the center. It was accompanied by its protective ships (destroyers and cruisers), subsurface contacts (submarines and sharks), and other aircraft (helicopters). Since the P-3 is land-based and too large to land on a carrier - we had the privilege to perform reconnaissance flights and uphold the outer most protective layer to the Battlegroup. We were manned with crews "flapping" or flying back-to-back missions around the clock- relieving each other on-station. It was always exciting to be working with the real-deal versus simulated contact in a computer-like trainer scenario.

Our flight from Maine down to Jacksonville (where the operation area was) grew more and more delayed as our crew continued to preflight new planes and find discrepancies as we went along that would 'down' the aircraft. This seemed to be a recurring theme for our crew - or so it seemed. Maintenance soon began to dread us and I'm sure if given the option, they would have preferred to put a 'closed for business' sign over their door when they saw us coming. I'd like to think we were being thorough and efficient, finding the gripes on the deck vice in the air - which is not the place you want to find out that your engine has a massive oil leak the size of a whale's raincoat. Most of these planes had been flying longer than I had been alive. Clearly, they had issues, but we kept repairing them because they were all that we had.

By the time we landed in Jacksonville, it was dark and we were on our third plane of the day. That makes for a long day, considering most of our full pre-flights take three hours and just the delays in general take a few. Tack on a few hours long flight down to Jacksonville and a post flight (cleaning up, putting the airplane to bed) - and you've got yourself a long day.

When I checked into my barracks room on base in Jacksonville that night (my roommate had already arrived there and reserved our room), I was greeted with a note left on my door from Aaron, who had landed with the Maintainers hours earlier. It was safe to say I was expecting him to be quite belligerent by the time I saw him. The note he left for me which was stuck in place by some make-shift labeling stickers we had been using to put names on our mailboxes, relayed which room he was in so I could find him. (Before we had cell phones, it was necessary to fight off the dinosaurs to get to one of those phones with a cord thingy.)

I unpacked my luggage, and went to find him. Earlier, he had mentioned that he was going to be sharing a room with his friend Jay, so I also was looking for a man I had never met before that went by the name of Jay. I decided to just go to his room and see if they had already retired there, despite the gathering going on below in the courtyard just outside our barracks.

The barracks were set up motel-style, with a balcony and doors that went directly outside in a square. The open courtyard made up the center of the square with volleyball nets and barbeque pits. When you walked through the door, you were in a little corridor-like area in which there were four separate rooms (complete with their own bathroom) attached to a lobby. They went respectively by the names of A, B, C, and D, as the military frowned on creativity. Aaron was in room 224B - two hundreds being second floor.

So when I got to the lobby and searched for room 224 (Aaron said he'd leave it open a crack for me), I was immediately struck by the sight of a man passed out outside of the door on the floor. Now for many people, this could be an alarming scene. However, in the Navy (or college dormitories) these sights are not uncommon. Of course I ensured he was breathing. I'm not a caveman or anything. And despite the commonality, I just didn't have it in me to leave a poor sailor that I had never met before passed out in the hallway by himself all night. I yell-whispered, "Jay! Jay! Wake up!" in his ear. I shook is shoulders. No response. So then I actually yelled in his ear, "Jay!" Still nothing.

Carefully, and like an assessor to a crime scene, I stepped over him and pushed the door to 224B open. There was Aaron, passed-out like a drowned rat on his back, mouth wide open. My first thought was to put something funny in it, but I quickly reminded myself that this wasn't the appropriate time.

"Aaron! Wake up!" I shook him.

Nothing.

"Aaaaaairrr-roooon." I dragged it out the way I do when I'm impatient with him. "Waaaaaaake uuuuuup!" In that moment, I could have driven an M1 Abrams tank full of lizards playing the tuba through the room and he wouldn't have budged.

Well this sucks. I thought of my plans for the night being erased. Maybe I could still catch up with my crew. But I couldn't leave with Jay lying in the middle of the lobby.

I reached down and tried to hoist his arm around my neck. It was dead weight from a man that was probably over 6 foot tall and 200+ pounds. Everyone is taller than me it seems, so I'm terrible at estimating. His arm alone was heavier than a lead-filled bucket. I grabbed his wrists and stretched his arms over his head and began to pull. I leaned forward, digging my high heels into the carpet, putting my whole body weight into it as he slowly began to move. His head bounced along the floor. He didn't care, so I didn't care too much. I was doing him a favor, dammit. Inch by inch, I drug his body like an ox pulling a California Redwood into the bedroom until his feet could finally clear the door enough that I could shut it with him safely in there.

I gave Aaron's dirty face a peck on the cheek and told him goodnight. *He's lucky I like him so much*, I thought, shook my head and closed the door behind me.

The next morning I awoke to the phone in my room ringing.

"Hello?" I said groggy - trying to place where I was. *I'm not in my bed. I'm in some barracks room...*

"Good morning, Babe!" The familiar voice replied all cheerfully. *Oh, right, I'm in Jacksonville today. Crap - did I oversleep!?* I frantically searched for a clock.

"What time is it!?"

"It's 0600."

"0600?"

"Yeah, I thought you'd be up by now. What time do you have to preflight?"

"Oh, we landed late - so they pushed our preflight back to 0900. So we could sleep in." I was quick to add.

"Oh, I'm sorry. Is that why you never came by last night?"

"Ah, I *did* come by last night. You wouldn't wake up." I said, trying not to sound too annoyed.

"Oh, I'm sorry, Hon. We had waaaay too much to drink."

"Yeah, I kinda figured. Well, did y'all have fun," I asked, trying to be nice - but still not wanting to wake up all the way yet. If I get off the phone quick - maybe I can still fall back asleep before my long flight today.

"We did. Thanks. Jay's bummed out he got stuck on the night shift so he had to stay behind and fix parts all night - but the good thing is you guys should be good to go for your flight today."

"Jay stayed behind?" I sat up. "Isn't Jay your roommate?"

"Yeah, he is - we're just working opposite shifts, so you may not get to meet him this trip like I had hoped."

"Oh..." I was confused.

"But tonight you can meet my friend Brian. He's a cool guy. Somehow he ended up in my room though last night - musta passed out on the floor talking or something. He's such a tool!" He laughed like it was the funniest thing he had ever said.

"Actually, I think I *have* met him."

Jacksonville

Pre-flighting in Jacksonville in the middle of the summer is just straight-up miserable. Our Northern-based planes complained about the heat like a pair of old southern belles sitting on the front porch. They whined every morning. The electronics protested with every initialization. They just straight up were breaking-down with every loophole they could find.

"I HATE Jacksonville!" Chief complained as he came in from fueling the plane and shook the sweat from his brow like a dog. "It's hotter that two rats fucking in a wool sock out there," he grumbled and staggered to the front of the plane to check the gauges. Chief always had a way with words.

The ground air-conditioning worked on rare occasion. We had one standalone unit that was jostled from one plane to the next, bringing with it any relief it could muster through a tube blowing cold air into the old bird for her and her crew. Even the airplane sweated and would require a good dehumidifying every chance she could get. A time-consuming, miserable but necessary evolution for everyone involved. And even still, the ground air that was spitting forth from the auxiliary power just could not compete with the scorching Florida August sun that shined high with vengeance upon its new arrivals. It was not enough to be beat down from above - the cascading rays would bounce from the tarmac upon which plane and human alike stood before every evolution. It was all a 30 year-old plane could take.

They were breaking left and right. Never before had maintainers worked harder on a 'peacetime' evolution to keep those birds in the sky. Aaron in particular, showing his genius, (not penis) disassembled our plane vacuum and rigged the hoses directly (with the assistance of a little duct tape) from the air vents directly into the electronic racks - giving them just enough extra direct cooling so they would not activate their thermal cutoff switch from the heat being too much to withstand.

We flew day and night around the clock, searching for and localizing our own American submarines. Some days we would drop a 2-ton torpedo on them and blow them into millions of particles. Some days they would shoot us out of the sky, getting the best of us with their anti-aircraft missiles. It was a marvelous sight. All simulated of course. Some days our job was one badass video game. That is why true AWs love what they do more than anything. They are hooked on the thrill of the cat and mouse game. Only the strong prevail! Kill all; spare no one from our wrath!

And then, some days life in the Navy can be a big day of broken planes, buffing decks, scrubbing the head, and dumping piss. At least we knew we were never going to be stuck doing one thing for very long.

Bar #1

"So what brings you boys into town?" The big-bosomed blond asked coyly as she slid a round of Guinness's across the bar. Chief picked one up and began passing the others behind him. He handed one off to Dan, who was sitting to the left of him. Sometimes if he had enough Guinness, he would allow a smile or two towards the big chested waitresses. But if they showed an ounce of stupidity - forget it. They were not even worth his time.

"Construction," Dan said and took a long gulp of his brew.

Chief looked over at him, smiled a half smile and turned back to the blond. "Yep. Big Dan here's the boss man. We're just in town to build some things."

"Watcha all building?" Another busty woman walked up. She was shorter than the blond with long brown hair and a tight white t-shirt on and fingernails two inches long that were painted a fire-engine red color. Neither one of them seemed to notice that Big Dan was actually the smallest guy on the crew.

Dan never wanted to miss an opportunity to captivate an audience. "Well, you see, we're gonna be tearing up those beaches out there and we're installing a gigantic carousel that can fit two hundred kids on it at once." His arms stretched wide as they would go as he demonstrated the size.

"You're going to tear up the beach?" The blond chimed in, bringing her hand to her chest as if she had just been informed of a death in her family.

"Oh yeah. We have to. For the carousel. But see," Dan went on, "they're not going to be just horses on the carousel. Nope. There are going to be sheep and kangaroos and lions and hyenas for the kiddies to ride on."

"Hyenas? What in Jesus' name would you put hyenas on a carousel for?" The brunette piped in.

"Ma'am, I don't know about you, but it was my childhood dream to ride on a hyena. Honey, we are making childhood dreams come true tomorrow," Dan said without blinking an eye. The rest of the crew was standing behind him now, no doubt overhearing the interesting conversation, nodding their heads in unison and quick to turn their heads away when they could not contain their snickers.

"I can't believe you guys are tearing up our beach. Why haven't we heard about this?" Blond girl asked, now alarmed.

"Oh, it's kind of a big surprise for the city from the mayor," Dan said. "We're under contract to keep it on the down-low." He winked.

"Well I can't let you do that. Not these beaches. Why, I've been going to the Jacksonville Beaches my whole life. Now you just see here. You ain't gonna stick a big ol' carousel right in the middle of them. I don't care what kinda animals you are putting on it. I won't let you!"

"Now just calm down there, Ma'am." Chief tried to reason with the girl - taking sheer pleasure in torturing her. It wasn't so much that he enjoyed being mean - which often that was the case. Mostly, Chief just figured if they were dumb enough to believe their drunken stories, well, then they probably deserved it.

"You know that's Big Dan, as in Dan's Construction Company, sitting right next to you. If you don't like what the city has decided to do, well he's the one that can stop it all."

Dan glanced over at Chief with a beaming smile of thanks for handing him over a damsel in distress.

Bar #2

The heavy wooden doors flung open much easier than expected. Through the dimly lit room, the bartender looked up from his register. Two men were sitting at the bar. Both stopped and looked up, right in the middle of their conversation to check out the riff-raff that had just strolled in.

Off in the corner was a couple that was completely enchanted in each other's company - so much that they didn't even glance up.

We strolled in like our own private gang and filled in the empty seats around the bar. Of course a new bar meant a new round to order.

And then - before we could even get our drink order out, we spotted it. Over in the corner beneath a pale spotlight lay a perfectly good set of drums on a raised platform - along with a microphone. Just sitting there. All by themselves. And of course, if something like that is just sitting there in plain sight with no one around (well not too many people) - well, this was just an open invitation.

Bar #3...Wait...

A few rounds had now passed. We had all begun our talks about moving onto the next bar. When out of nowhere, a drum began to beat. It wasn't just pounding either. This single drum beat had a bit of rhythm behind it. It was the toe-tapping kind of drumming that made sitting still irresistible. Slowly we turned to the stage where the sound was being generated. Sitting under the spotlight in a near-empty bar was Rugged behind the drums of a near empty stage. When he noticed he had our attention, he looked up, smiled and waved, winked his eye and began to lay it all down hard into the drum in pure Van Halen style.

In unison, our jaws hit the floor as he continued for his ten-minute solo. *Who was this man?* Surely not *my* sensor one. My sensor one was a crabby stick in the mud that made me clean the tapes on the plane for half an hour until they were up to his standards. Where did this style and musical talent come from? All at once, Rugged appeared in a new light before me. He. Rocked. The. Drums.

And of course, he wasn't on his own for long. In less than two shakes of a drummer stick, Stimpy (the navigator) got up on the keyboard and revealed his own secret talent as he did a perfect impersonation of Stevie Wonder. Shortly after Big Lovin' (TACCO) got on the stage and revealed his not-so-much-talent-but-ever-so-entertaining self. The rest of us watched in awe as the drunken talent of CAC-9 spewed forth. And even though The Monkey's Uncle in Jacksonville actually allows dancing on the tables, on this night I resisted the urge, as I wanted to show the new guys on my crew how responsible I was. This night.

The Ride Home

Since I was a minor again when I returned to the states, I by default was the designated driver. It made it an easy decision and I had no problems escorting my now very drunk crew back to the safety of their own barracks in Jacksonville. Good ol' Jacksonville.

I was driving some government van - as Big Lovin' had used his magical powers to find us a form of transportation. I quickly learned that Dan always felt it was important to get naked when he drank. Thus began the music selection for the ride home. As I'm driving a white government vehicle, a chorus breaks out set to the tune of "The Wheels on the Bus." However, the lyrics were now replaced by a much more popular round of, "The AT on the bus gets naked, naked, naked. Naked, naked, naked. Naked, naked, naked. The AT on the bus gets naked, naked, naked. All through the town."

And it did not stop there. Oh no, this entire round of musical joy went around until each and every crewmember had been accounted for. And what resulted from the cadences of pre-school songs made Navy version? Clothes flew. Drinks were spilled. Joy was in abundance.

Sure, this is normal, I thought shaking my head. Dutifully, I kept my eyes glued to the road (for my own sake AND theirs) as I could only imagine the HAZREP (Hazard Report sent upon a mishap) the next morning. Government vehicle crashes. Various naked sailors strewn all over the pavement and one clothed female driver. It was just an ugly thought all around. As we crossed the infamous Buckman Bridge that night, someone thought it would be hilarious to throw Dan's clothes out the window. Over the side of the bridge they floated, drifting ever so lightly into the dark waters below. Of course it was dark, so I'm mostly just assuming this. They very well could have landed on the car's windshield behind us.

With each passing second, my fingers continued to grip the steering wheel. I cautiously drove under the speed limit. I obeyed the two-second rule at a stop sign. I didn't back-up, because, well, you know. However, it wasn't until I approached the gate to get on base that I really began to get nervous. How was I to explain driving naked sailors around? Thankfully, I was able to get them to stop singing - for just a moment.

I put on my best 'innocent' look as I approached the guard and dimmed my lights. Slowly, he began his walk over to the vehicle. I held my arm as far out of the van as I could - so he could read my military identification without getting any closer than necessary.

"How are you doing tonight?" I looked at him and smiled as sincerely as possible.

He looked up at me with a scowl on his face - as if I had just asked him the dumbest question possible. *How do you think he's doing? He was on night duty - and it's one in the morning.* I'm sure all he cared about is going home and going to bed. And here I come driving through with a van full of drunken sailors that are just wasting his time. Yes, I realized he had the power to lock us all up right now on several charges.

But for some unknown crazy reason that I'll never quite understand, he waved us on. I'm assuming he just wasn't in the mood to do paperwork.

One never knows exactly what they will encounter when driving through the gates. There are days in which you could flash your library card at the guard and he'd wave you through as his mind was complacently in another place. And on other days - the guard may act like a Studio 54 bouncer - overly eager to throw anyone who missteps out of line into a pair of handcuffs and toss off to a cop driving by.

I guess that night was our lucky night.

A couple weeks later, LT Burke and Big Lovin' passed out professionally embroidered T-shirts that read "Dan's Construction Company" that they had made up. Because, why not?

The Outsider

"Hello, VP-8 AW Shop?" I held the receiver to the shop phone in my hand. It was what I liked to describe as absent of color - also known as beige, or tan, or the color of boring. It smelled of old cheese and I was careful not to touch the receiver on my chin. I could only imagine what was possibly growing on it in a shop full of men. I was attempting to study in our room reserved for the AWs in the squadron.

I heard a click on the other end of the line as I was disconnected from whoever was calling. *That's odd*, I thought to myself. I sat on the orange davenport - it was so old it was from back in the days when my grandmother called a sofa a davenport. Its cushions were hard, and the seat was long - causing my feet to stick up and unable to reach the ground when I sat all the way back.

On my lap rested my trusty green Navy-issued notebook. I had been staring at the numbers and acronyms on the page for so long that my eyes could no longer see them. I was studying which countries had 16 cylinders on their diesel electric submarines and which countries had 12. Of course the acronym to remember this (like them all) was a small poem that always had a woman's name and some random sexual act she performed. How else could you expect sailors to remember hundreds of parameters? It was a tried and true method that, believe it or not, worked like a champ. Though I was a little disgusted with Carol and the things she did on a Saturday.

It was a quiet day in the Shop as the SS-2s that weren't flying were working on their PQS, or studying for their SS-1 board. "See," I overheard Joe explain to Myron. "It has a big slope on the bow - like a ski slope that would cut your nuts off if you slipped. That's how you can identify the Russian ship Kuznetsov."

Suddenly my thoughts were yet again interrupted by the phone ringing next to me. There were a few other guys around the table in the room studying, but it was an unspoken understanding that if you were the one next to the phone - you were the designated phone bitch - er secretary.

"AW Shop."

This time I wasn't disconnected, but there was silence on the other end - followed by an impatient sigh. *"I need to talk to Bill."* Her words were short and curt.

I pulled the receiver back from my ear and looked at it. I raised my eyebrow and wrinkled my nose. *Wow, this woman is having a bad day.*

"Oh-kay…" I replied to her carefully. "Bill, it's for you," I said, giving him my best *good luck with that* expression. I got off the couch and went to the table to continue my studying and try to give him some privacy in a room full of sailors. I glanced at the clock. One hour until we break for lunch. Ugh. My stomach already ached with hunger.

"Yes, Baby, I know," Bill mumbled into the phone - his voice was as low as he could get it. Everyone in the room had their nose in their books, but was more than likely listening with one ear, just out of sheer boredom.

"No, Sweetie, she is an AW." He was barely audible now, however we could all hear him all too well. "Can we talk about this later? Because you're being ridiculous. No, Hon. No. Trust me; you have nothing to worry about."

At this point other eyes began to glance over at me, carefully without moving their heads out of their books. *Are you fricking kidding me?* I thought. *There is no way he is talking about me.* But everyone else's casual glances indicated otherwise. *What the hell? Had Bill casually forgot to mention that he worked with another woman? And was that seriously an issue for this lady? Did she honestly think I was going to do something to her precious Bill at work?*

If I had not been so angered at the situation, I would have laughed. On a daily basis, I not only saw these guys as burping, farting, reading porn, and talking in grave detail about their Saturday night escapades and who they planned to bang next. But I also saw them as my peers - my big brothers. We helped each other. We spent hours in a given day together. We became each other's therapist and support system. We would tell each other when we were being stupid or unreasonable. We would pick each other up in the middle of the night if someone needed a ride and cover for each other to keep from getting in trouble by the higher ranking guys. I was one of them - or at least I had always thought I was.

First East Coast Crew

Because CAC-9 was the best crew ever - no really - we got the best score on our TORPEX (shooting a [simulated] torpedo at a submarine), we were selected to be the first crew on the East Coast to shoot a SLAM (Stand-off Land Attack Missile) exercise in Point Mugu, California.

We were pumped! Excited for the opportunity and excited for the mid-home cycle trip to California. In fact, the morning we began our preflight out in sunny Point Mugu, we were so overzealous that some genius on the crew thought it would be so Hollywood of us to sign the fabulous missile that hung off of our portside wing for a perfect photo opportunity. Like a monkey with a grease pencil, I joined in with everyone else. I'll have to say - it did make for a pretty awesome picture.

Ten minutes later, Chief came out (who besides being a flight engineer, he is also an AO- ordnance man) and seriously lost his mind on us.

"What in Jesus H. Christ's name were you idiots thinking?"

"It's all good, Chief," Burke said, trying to keep the peace. "We're going to drop it and no one will know the difference."

"Oh really, Sir? And what the fuck happens if we can't drop it because of weather or a hung store? Then what?"

And before Burke could say anything, Chief used his magical powers to curse our crew just to prove his point. The clouds rolled in over the clear skies and made them an ominous gray. You know the song, "It never rains in Southern California"? Well Chief made it rain that day. He had that kind of power.

Our crew took off that morning and flew for hours until we were bingo (just enough fuel to get home) and not once had a cloud opened long enough to get a clear shot to deploy the graffiti missile. The end of the flight was ceremoniously concluded by Chief stomping down the tube of the plane with the dirtiest of curses littering from his mouth like little crumbs of demise. I thought I had heard it all by this point. Turns out, there were all sorts of adjectives and nouns I had never even thought to put together before.

The next day was our last scheduled flight and last chance to remove the now cursed missile from our wing. But this day was different. We had all apologized to Chief for our reckless John Wayne ideas about signing a missile. It was wrong and morbid. We were scum. And finally, at some point in there I think he decided his point had been proven and he decided it was time to restore the clear blue skies again. It didn't take long either. Not fifteen minutes from arriving to our on-station point, we were able to get a clear shot and on the third "weapon away" we dropped that blasted SLAM into the soils of Southern California's firing range and CAC-9 became the first East Coast Squadron to drop a SLAM on a land target. The crew first breathed a sigh of relief and then a round of cheering ensued throughout the tube of the plane.

Broken Foot

"*How* did you do it?" Rugged stared at me in disbelief.

"I don't know. I just threw on a pair of shoes that were by the door to grab the cat food from my car this morning. I just stepped wrong and rolled my ankle. You know, when you step wrong and it hurts but goes away? I figured if I walked on it long enough it would go away," I shrugged.

"What kind of shoes?"

"They had a heel of sorts… platform I suppose," my voice trailed off.

"Seriously?" Rugged said in his annoyed tone.

"Yeah, they were the closest thing to the door."

"You were running in platform shoes to get cat food? You've been limping on the damn thing all day. Take your boot off and show me." He was so bossy.

We were sitting at the station flying just off the coast of Maine. We had already completed our event and now were just 'burning hours' and getting some pilot training in. I unlaced my boot and pulled out my throbbing foot. The pain ensued and it instantly began to swell up twice the size as it was in my boot. As I pulled down my manly tube sock that I wore with my flight boots, I revealed my foot with flesh that was the color of night - topped off with pretty green toenail polish. It looked like a zombie's foot.

"Oh my god. You need to show that to Chief right now!" Rugged insisted.

"No way - why on God's green earth would I do that!?" I protested. But it was too late. He had already repeated it on the ICS.

"Go up to the flight station and show him. Now," Rugged ordered.

So with one bare foot that I could barely put weight on, I glared at Rugged as I trekked up to the flight station. It hurt so much more now, without my boot to stabilize it.

Chief examined it for about five seconds. "Goddammit Maki. Lieutenant, turn this plane around. She's got a goddamn broken foot."

"No, I'm fine..." I began when Chief leaned into my face and spoke as clearly and concisely as possible. "No, you are not fine. When we land this plane, you will go straight to medical. Understand?" He was so close I could smell the chew on his breath. I tried not to make a repulsive face. Why was this man always so difficult?

I nodded and turned to walk back to my station. I don't know why I ever bothered to argue with him. It was like arguing with a gorilla. No one ever comes out a winner.

"And Maki?" he called out to me.

"Yes Chief?"

"If you ever fly with a fucking broken foot again, I will break the other one to match. Do you understand?"

He was always so logical.

I went to medical. Turns out I actually did break my foot. One of the stupid little bones that are not even that useful. They cast it up to my knee and for the next 6 weeks I was medically "downed" which meant I "flew a desk."

I returned to the hangar that afternoon and as I crutched down the hallway, I heard the voice that always sent my hairs up on the back of my neck.

"Told you it was broken, didn't I?" he looked satisfied with himself.

"Yep. I suppose you were right."

He came closer and examined my cast. "Now that's a broken foot, alright." He smiled, and kept walking past me. "Oh and by the way, your toenail polish isn't within Navy regulation color. You'd better get that fixed by tomorrow, Shipmate. They're putting you on plane wash duty, since you can't fly."

"Yes Chief." *I'm sure washing a plane with crutches and a cast that I'm not supposed to get wet won't be a problem at all.*

Family

"Petty Officer Maki?"

"Yes, Sir?" I had recently made Third Class Petty Officer and was loving the way it sounded.

"I'm going to need you to stand watch on Thanksgiving, okay?" The commander informed me. Initially, I was bummed out as it wasn't my crew's turn and I had already made plans.

"Okay," I replied. "Did something happen?"

"No, nothing happened. I am just re-working the schedule and putting all the single people on it. You know, since you don't have a family."

I was confused. *Um, I had a family. What a sad thing to say.* And then I realized he meant I didn't have children.

"Oh, you mean I don't have kids?" I asked, slightly confused.

"Well, yes, and you don't have family here either," the commander went on.

"Okay, well I can stand the watch, Sir, but I wouldn't say I don't have a family. I mean, maybe not in the way you think of family." I had Aaron now. And Tayte. And Janessa and Whiner. I had been with them for years now. They were my entire support system and who I spent my time with when I wasn't working. If they weren't family, then what were they?

"Okay, well thank you, Petty Officer. I'm sure you do."

The Last Day

"We are at war, folks." Squishy went on during Quarters the day before we were to deploy to Sicily. It was the end of January, 2000. We weren't really at war, but our CO, Commander Squishy, [not so] secretly wanted us to be at war. It was good for his career. We could win more command flags.

All of our spaces in the hangar were packed up and we were ready to fly out. We just had to get through this looong speech so we could go enjoy our last day in America for 6 months. The truth is I had so much to get done, that there wouldn't be much enjoyment. Not during the day - but we did have a nice traditional Brunswick lob-stah dinner planned. I couldn't wait. I began dreaming about food as usual.

"We will be getting shot at as we fly these missions ahead. We need to be prepared - always," Squishy continued on. For a second I stopped thinking about melted butter and I let my mind wander to the 'what ifs.' *What if we really did get shot at? What if we ended up going down over Bosnia? What if we were captured in a prison camp and were sodomized until we gave them information?* The only information I knew was about submarines and I couldn't imagine they'd really care about submarines. For a brief second, a slice of fear crept into me before I quickly dismissed it away. *This is what you signed up for, Julia. You will not give them your secrets on how sound travels through water.*

Knowing that I had an early morning pre-flight made it impossible to sleep that night. I kept checking the clock every hour, thinking of all the things I needed to remember. 2:42. *Ugh.* I was nervous and excited. But also sad. Mostly sad for my crew that I knew was spending their last few moments in the arms of their loved ones that they would not see for the next six months. I was lucky enough to have mine going along with me. We had been together for over a year now on home cycle. He was my family.

CHAPTER 11

NAS Sigonella, Sicily.

January 2000

Approximate distance from Deer River: 5120 miles

Our missions out of Sicily were rarely anti-submarine missions. Instead, we were directed to gather intelligence - one of the many multi-uses of the P-3 war-fighting machine.

⊣ Background ⊢

"Beginning in 1992, Bosnian Serb forces targeted Srebrenica in a campaign to seize control of a block of territory in eastern Bosnia and Herzegovina. Their eventual goal was to annex this territory to the adjacent republic of Serbia (which, along with Montenegro, constituted the rump of the Yugoslav federation). To do so, they believed, required the expulsion of the territory's Bosniak inhabitants, who opposed annexation. In March 1995 Radovan Karadžić, president of the self-declared autonomous Republika Srpska (Bosnian Serb Republic), directed his military forces to "create an unbearable situation of total insecurity with no hope of further survival or life for the inhabitants of Srebrenica." By May, a cordon of Bosnian Serb soldiers had imposed an embargo on food and other supplies that provoked most of the town's Bosniak fighters to flee the area. In late June, after some skirmishes with the few remaining Bosniak fighters, the Bosnian Serb military command formally ordered the operation, code-named Krivaja 95 that culminated in the massacre.

Srebrenica massacre, slaying of more than 7,000 Bosniak (Bosnian Muslim) boys and men, perpetrated by Bosnian Serb forces in Srebrenica, a town in eastern Bosnia and Herzegovina, in July 1995. In addition to the killings, more than 20,000 civilians were expelled from the area - a process known as ethnic cleansing. The massacre, which was the worst episode of mass murder within Europe since World War II, helped galvanize the West to press for a cease-fire that ended three years of warfare on Bosnia's territory. However, it left deep emotional scars on survivors and created enduring obstacles to political reconciliation among Bosnia's ethnic groups.

The International Criminal Tribunal for the Former Yugoslavia, established before the massacre to scrutinize ongoing military conduct, concluded that the killings at Srebrenica, compounded by the mass expulsion of Bosniak civilians, amounted to genocide. It pinned principal responsibility on senior officers in the Bosnian Serb army. But the United Nations (UN) and its Western supporters also accepted a portion of the blame for having failed to protect the Bosniak men, women, and children in Srebrenica, which in 1993 the UN Security Council had formally designated a "safe area." In a critical internal review in 1999, UN Secretary, General Kofi Annan wrote, "Through error, misjudgment and an inability to recognize the scope of the evil confronting us, we failed to do our part to help save the people of Srebrenica from the [Bosnian] Serb campaign of mass murder." Although Serbia was not legally implicated in the massacre, in 2010 the Serbian National Assembly narrowly passed a resolution that apologized for having failed to prevent the killings."

"Srebrenica massacre." Encyclopedia Britannica. Encyclopedia Britannica Online. Encyclopedia Britannica Inc., 2013. Web. 02 Jan. 2013 http://www.britannica.com/EBchecked/topic/1697253/Srebrenica-massacre

Sigonella, Sicily's Naval Air Station was just a hop, skip and a jump to various locations in which we would be working over various parts of Bosnia and Kosovo. The flights we flew on were considered dangerous enough to warrant 'hazard duty pay' and we would actually carry a parachute bag full of bullet-proof vests on each flight. Still the lowest ranking member on our crew, not only did I get to dump the pisser after every flight, I also had the privilege of loading the plane with the parachute bags full of the vests, another full of radios and maps along with my usual audio tape boxes, helmet bag, flight bag that contained a Naval Aviation Training and Operating Procedures Standardization (NATOPS) manual, Circuit Breaker book, PQS book, and an In-Flight handbook (IFH) to cover instructions for the software. I was a weighted-down mule. It didn't take long before I quickly learned to steal - I mean temporarily borrow - loading carts from the maintenance shops for the transportation of these items to the plane. Still, I had to get them up the ladder most times on my own.

On one of these occasions as I had the parachute bag full of bullet-proof vests over my shoulder, I made it up about ten steps on the ladder when I suddenly lost my balance and fell backwards. Thankfully, the large bag hit the flight line first and actually caught my fall. And there I lay, sprawled out on a parachute bag full of bullet-proof vests at the bottom of the ladder. Uninjured, I did the first thing anyone does when they fall down a ladder. Quickly scramble to get up and look around to see if anyone saw. And if they did - act like you meant to do it - like halfway up the ladder I suddenly grew very tired and decided to fall back and rest for a few minutes on the bag. Luckily, no one was in view - so I determined no one saw and I had never heard anything to believe otherwise.

If you look at a map of Europe, Sicily is the island off of the coast of Italy. Italy is shaped like a boot, and therefore looks to be an asshole boot that is kicking the poor defenseless country of Sicily. When we were there, the temperatures easily made it past 100 degrees on a daily basis. As if that wasn't bad enough, we usually had to walk to work from our barracks to the hangar. It wasn't far, but between the gear you carried, the extreme heat, and the screaming mee-mies, some days it became quite unbearable. The screaming mee-mies could best be found stuck upon the unavoidable layer of sweat on a person's skin as they walked. They were a pesky little nit that bit hard (often leaving a spot of blood), and stuck to any surface- hair, shirt, and or tongue as they would fly in and stick to the back of your throat as one was walking along. They didn't actually scream, so much like the Pleasing Fungus Beetle, I'm not sure where they got their name from.

From the base we had a great view of Mt. Etna, an active volcano. It was a marvelous structure that you couldn't help but be slightly nervous when watching the red lava trickle down the sides and never-ending ash spew from the top. Rest assured, an active volcano is the safest volcano, we were told. It is the volcano that sits below you asleep until she decides to awake that causes more devastation than all other natural disasters combined.

However, the constant ash piles that spilled from Mt. Etna left much to be desired. Before every pre-flight, it was necessary to clean this ash from the aircraft windshields. This was not an easy task for a short person. The maintenance ladder only went so high. After that it was almost necessary to straddle the nose of the aircraft. Or balance on our tip toes with one foot propped on the plane, while hanging onto the wiper with our other hand. However, we did not do this when anyone from maintenance was around. Just like a lot of things in the military, they wanted it done, but they didn't really want to see how we got it done.

Driving in Sicily

Driving off base on the roads of Sicily was a choice we had to make ourselves, as we were often taking our life into our own hands. Were we feeling particularly lucky that day? If not, it was best to stay home.

In Sicily, there may have been a speed limit. I never saw it - nor ever saw law officials enforcing a speed limit. They probably have much more important things on their minds. Like controlling the Sicilian mafia, monitoring the outsourcing of tomato sauce, and keeping the Umbrella Girls at bay.

What are these "Umbrella Girls" I speak of? Well Umbrella Girls are the nicknames given to the "fancy-dressed" ladies that would linger just outside of the bases' gates. We called them Umbrella Girls as an umbrella was all that they had sheltering themselves from the scorching afternoon sun. They were very shiny with perspiration, as anyone who spent all day working under the sun would be. They were nice enough girls - always willing to help you out with *any* desire you may need fulfilled.

Be warned, though. These ladies that twirled their fancy umbrellas under the pounding heat of the Sicilian sun were not just anyone's friend. You had to pay them for their "friendship." However, they were more than willing to be a "friend" to any homesick sailor in a time of need. If one should mosey along, I guess the story was that an Umbrella Girl would duck off into some shrubbery or car or whatever was available, make the sailor less homesick, (baking him some cookies?) and resume business shortly afterward alongside the road again - not missing a beat - just perhaps missing a shower. (Cookie baking can get so messy!)

The country roads that surround the base were very narrow, old, and windy - so visibility wasn't always the best. Now say one is driving along, minding their own business and a car is coming towards them. They check in the rear-view mirror and happen to see another car coming up from behind at a fairly decent speed. They laugh out loud and think, "There is no way this guy can go anywhere. Why, there is another car coming in the opposite lane."

Well, that person is quite mistaken. It is actually their job (the slow car) to move to the shoulder (no worry about slowing down or anything logical, though). Actually, it really doesn't matter if they want to move over or not, because the car coming from behind is going to get on their ass and move them to the side, as the oncoming cars meet and both pass by - now turning the skimpy, shoulder-less highway into a 3-lane racetrack. It was best to always just get the hell out of the way because we didn't know what we were doing, and we sure as hell didn't know what the Sicilians were doing.

Geep

While we are on the subject of driving - there is one more thing to be mindful of - the geep. A geep is exactly what it sounds like - they are a combination of a goat and a sheep. They are dirty, white, straggly little creatures (much like a Kardashian) that like to hang out in the middle of a narrowly winding Sicilian road. Sure there are shepherds that are watching them, but they are usually nowhere to be seen. Perhaps they are having afternoon tea and cookies with the Umbrella Girls.

The point is, whatever you do, you cannot run over, hit or even nick these things. Not even by accident - and if you do, it is best to get out of the car and just run away. Take your registration with you. Actually, I'm sure that's not the best advice either. No, burn the car - pay the difference at the rental station and just run back to base and pretend to be asleep. It'll be cheaper to do that than to pay for the geep. Swerve and hit an on-coming car before you hit one of them.

If one hits a male geep - they must pay their value to the shepherd. We were warned that they weren't cheap either. Now if one hits a female, they must not only pay for her, but every geep she could have theoretically produced in her lifetime. How is that figured? No idea. But it sounds like something the Sicilian mafia probably came up with, right? Anyways, just run, because the outcome isn't going to be pretty either way.

Misjudgment

If I ever thought the duty vans in Iceland were ancient, the ones in Sicily were from another time all together. Air conditioning was a luxury that we were not afforded in the 100+ degree weather. Why, that was simply what windows were for. There was no power-steering for this van, so one had to use their body weight as they pulled down and nearly hung off one side of the steering wheel. It often felt as if I were a cowboy throwing down a steer by their horns in a rodeo in order to make the beast turn at slow speeds.

Half of the time the floors had holes in them (aka floor air conditioning). It was necessary to hold onto our belongings during our travels, or it would end up bouncing out and down the middle of the road behind us.

To top it all off, not only was it a stick-shift, but the stick was on the steering column and the gears were completely unlabeled. It wanted us to guess which gear we were in by trial and error. Sometimes one just had to grind a few gears and figure out the hard way which one we were really in. When I say grind, I mean man-handle the shifter with my entire body weight as it fought back - screaming and calling me dirty-whore names when I forced it into the wrong place. It was like trying to thread a needle while trotting on a horse. There was often much stalling and squealing involved. But the Navy trusted that we could drive these beasts, so why should we question our driving abilities in a foreign land?

One day, after being pestered endlessly for a non-related-to-work ride by my pilot, Algae, I finally gave in. Truth being told, I was usually eager for any excuse to get out of the duty office, and was really more than happy to take him. Still, I could not let on to that though. Everyone was always very anxious to get a ride from place to place rather than have to walk in the sweltering heat. Sailors were always striking dirty deals to catch rides back and forth. "I'll shine your boots for ya. I'll give you my alcohol rations. I'll try not to crash the plane the next time I'm flying your ass around." Pilots were always striking deals that were hard to say no to. So, Algae and I loaded up into the hefty lump of metal duty van and proceeded to go on our way.

As we were pulling out of the parking lot, I thought I had seen another officer whom I thought I knew further down the road. Of course, when I thought I saw someone I knew, it was only natural to do stupid things to get their attention, such as swerving and pretending to run over them. I'm sure everyone does.

"Oh wow, it's Robertson. Watch this," I said, getting all excited. I laid on the gas pedal, swerved, and proceeded to drive mindlessly towards the pedestrian that began to come into focus, laughing, because it was going to be so funny to scare him.

All of a sudden, sheer horror came across my face as the man began to come into focus. "Oh shit!" was all I could say as I realized not quickly enough that this was not someone I knew, but rather a very high-ranking officer from the neighboring H-53 (helicopter) squadron. He just stared at me dumb-stricken as he clenched the wall behind him with terror in his eyes.

Mortified, I quickly whipped the steering wheel around at the last second (because I was planning to anyways), and continued past the officer. I gave a quick wave, as if this was normal, and looked the other way, in my best effort to remain anonymous. I continued to drive along very quietly now while Algae, being the supporting man that he is, decided to point and laugh as if it was the funniest thing he'd ever seen.

Another Misjudgment

It had been a long day in the Operations Office in between flights. I was able to quickly sneak in some time on the computer and fire away a couple quick emails to my sisters and best friend back in the states.

"Why the hell do we have to burn more hours this quarter rather than roll them over so we have that much more to work with next quarter?"

"Because we won't get as much money then and who knows - we may need it next quarter," the Operations Senior Chief replied.

"Oh yeah, 'cause that makes perfect sense," the junior officer said with a sarcastic tone.

As I sat there, typing and semi-listening to the conversation that was taking place on the other side of the room, I subconsciously reached over without taking my eyes off of the screen for my pop (Minnesota talk for soda). As I grasped the bottle and removed the lid, I slowly brought it to my mouth. Just as I tipped my head back to take a swig of the liquid, I caught a nauseating whiff of tobacco. I peered into the hole to find a sea of brown with white bubbles floating around on it. The insides were lined with small brown strands of tobacco and seeds. The saliva slowly edged its way down the inside of the bottle straight towards my opened mouth, leaving behind goopy strands of spit down the side. But it was too late. The warm saliva from an unknown source just touched the edge of my lips.

"AHHHHHH!" I let out a gut-wrenching gag, nearly throwing down the bottle of chew. I wiped my mouth with the sleeve of my flight suit. My throat began to burn. My stomach was uneasy. I was not going to make it. I raced down the hall to the bathroom, hearing faint laughter behind me. Instantly, I was hit by the smell of Simple Green. This, mixed with the smell of the tobacco, caused a spontaneous eruption of my breakfast into the toilet. This went on for several minutes.

Finally, when I felt I was finished and had nothing left in me to vomit, I washed my face under the faucet and made my way back into the Flight Ops Scheduling room.

I opened the door to hear LT Albertson shout, "So I say rectum - I damn near killed him." This seemed to be his signature line that he would shout off random-ly as if he had a weird version of Turrettes.

He spun around and his gaze met mine. Several other onlookers - well they looked on. "Petty Officer Maki - I hear you were so thirsty you had to drink from my dip bottle," he said with a smirk.

My stomach flipped again at the thought and I swallowed hard. "Sir, I would greatly appreciate it if you didn't leave your nasty-ass spit bottle lying around on the desks in here." I knew I was out of line speaking to an officer like that, but in that moment - I didn't really care. What could he do to me? The worst had already been done.

"Well *yes ma'am*. I'll surely see what I can do about that." I could hear the sincerity in his mockery. Satisfied enough, I nodded and grabbed my bags to leave.

"Senior, I'm going back to the barracks. Suddenly, I'm not feeling so hot."

"I'm sure you're not, Maki." Senior Chief replied with a grin. "Alright, see you tomorrow."

I turned to go back out the door. All I could hear behind me was "So I said Liquor? I hardly know her!" And LT Albertson laughing like he was the funniest man on Earth. I couldn't help but laugh either. He was pretty damn funny. And disgusting.

The Measure of Happiness

It was an exceptionally beautiful day and we finally had a flight that was during daylight hours. I finally felt like I had accomplished a goodnight's sleep - a rare commodity on deployment. We were in the middle of our preflight and Rugged was performing the preflight tests on the acoustic software. I had just finished washing the aircraft windshield and went into the galley of the plane to put away the cleaning solution and throw out the paper towels. Chief was sitting at the table with a frown on his face as usual, charting his fuel weight and balance calculations. I sat down across from him and he didn't look up.

"I just cleaned the windshields," I said with a bit too much enthusiasm, as if I was expecting a gold star.

"Wonderful." Chief replied without an ounce of enthusiasm. Silence followed. "Chief, what would make you happy today?" I looked at him thoughtfully. It bothered me severely that I only made him angry.

He continued his calculations. I'm sure I made him even angrier for interrupting his thoughts. I was beginning to wonder if he even heard me. Finally he put his pencil down and looked up at me. It felt like his dark eyes could look into my soul. "You know what would make me happy? If you fucking AWs could learn how to fuel a plane or do something useful instead of just gallivanting around on it like a bunch of squirrels in heat."

"*Can* I fuel the airplane?!?" I asked, as if I had just been given an all-expense paid trip to the Caribbean.

"*You* want to fuel the airplane? You know there is more to it than just hooking up a hose to the plane right? You've got to get the weight balanced and calculated just right between all of the tanks."

"Yes, I can totally do it!" I replied. I was excited to do something different for a change. I loved the idea of being in charge of something as important as the aircraft's fuel.

"Well alright then. Maybe I can teach you how to do fuel samples too," he said, and for the first time in my life, Chief looked at me for a second with something other than a frown on his face.

I could hardly contain my excitement. Not many AWs knew how to fuel *and* do fuel samples. *Maybe if I learned everything there is to know about being a flight engineer and an AW, Chief would really be impressed.*

As we headed down the ladder of the plane Chief asked me, "Do you know what the three most important rules to live by in the Navy are?"

"Nope."

"Beer is food - there's a pork chop in every beer. Sleep is overrated - there will be plenty of time to sleep when you're dead. And NATOPS are for new guys."

"Okay. I won't forget."

AW2

The sound of the phone rudely broke the spell of my dream. Confused, I opened my eyes, squinted, and looked around. *Where was I?* I looked over and saw Jenessa was asleep in the bed on the other side of the room. She stirred and rolled over - no doubt irritated by the annoying sound. *Barracks room. Sicily. Still here.*

I reached over for the receiver. "Hello?" I mumbled, wondering what hour it was.

"Hi can I speak with AW *two* Maki?"

Half asleep, I replied, "This is- ah- AW *three* Maki."

"No, it's AW2."

This person was obviously very confused and too stubborn to listen to me. I was getting even more annoyed by the minute.

"Who is this?"

"Julia - shut up." The voice was a familiar one. "It's Chuck. You made second class. The results just came in."

"What? Shut up! You're lying."

"I'm as serious as a heart attack."

"I don't believe you. I only took the test once! No one makes it on the first shot."

"Well, you did. So there." I was stunned.

Jenessa had turned over and was listening now. "Did I make it?" She asked, hopeful.

"Who else made it?" I asked Chuck. "Did Jenessa?" I asked excitedly before he could even answer my first question. *It would be so wonderful if we...*

"No, she didn't. But Whiner did! And Myron and Graves. I've got to go call them now. Congrats! Don't party too hard now."

I hung up the phone slowly. I looked across the room at my friend and shook my head. Suddenly I was no longer excited.

"Did Whiner?" Jenessa asked, reluctantly.

"Yes."

Knuckles

The place was called Jox. It was the only sports bar on base in Sicily. (At least at that time.) Or rather the one place to go after work where all of us carless sailors could stumble home after a few rounds. It was also nice because the drinks came at a military-discounted price and the toilets still had seats on them - a luxury that we were not always afforded out in town. It was in Jox that I watched some crazy girl deep throat a beer bottle neck (and then later someone had to explain to me what she was trying to do). It was also in Jox that I also learned that our beer that was sent to us overseas had formaldehyde in it. (Ironic, since I shop organic now.) I guess my guts have been well-preserved.

Many nights it was dead in there, but tonight - ahhh. Tonight was different. Everyone in the squadron who wasn't working the night shift was there celebrating the advancement results. [General] Quarters had been held that day and the Skipper 'pinned' on all of our crows. (i.e. we sewed them on our uniform in advance and then conducted the ceremoniously rank award recognition.) From that point on, everyone proceeded to "tack" on our crow. (Punch us in the arm, as was Navy tradition.) By the end of the night, my arm was quite sore, but it was quickly forgotten pain. My shop, my crew, my seniors were all congratulating us and of course rounds of drinks were bought nonstop. Tayte had also made Second Class Petty Officer [AT2]. Aaron had made First Class Petty Officer [AT1]. He was always such a one-upper. (To be fair, he had been in longer than both of us.)

Music and beer flowed freely as the night went on. *All those hours of studying in which I felt I hadn't retained a single thing and doubted myself countless times - maybe this Navy thing might work out after all*, I thought to myself. Just then Chuck walked up to me.

"Ah, you might want to go check on your girl - she just went into the bathroom."

"Okay, why? What's up?"

"I think she's had too much to drink and she and Whiner were fighting about something as usual," he muttered and began to wander off into the sea of people. Probably to go find a girl to bake bread for. Chuck had a bread maker in his room. No joke. Girls always flock to carbs.

"Okay, thanks for letting me know. I'll go see what's up," I hollered back to him over the music and began to weave my way through the crowd towards the bathrooms.

"Hey." I was suddenly stopped outside the bathroom door by a guy I didn't recognize. He had to have been from one of the other squadrons, as I pretty much could recognize every face from our squadron at this point.

"Ah, hey."

"Did you just pin on Second today?"

"Yep."

"Nice job."

"Thanks!" I replied. I was beginning to grow impatient, but he was directly in my path to the bathroom entrance.

He took a big swig of his beer. I hesitated to see if that was the end of his conversation - I didn't want to be rude - but I was getting anxious to check on Janessa. I started to go past him and he put his arm up to block me.

"You know, the only girls I know that join the Navy are either dykes or hoes." He leaned down, closer to me and his breath smelled of rank alcohol, burning my face. *Surely I had misheard him. There's no way he could've said what I thought he just said.*

"Excuse me?"

"I said, are you a dyke or a ho? Cuz I could really use a ho right about now." I clenched my jaw and every muscle in my body. *Was he seriously saying this to me right now? Tonight on **my** night of celebration? After everything?*

The next few seconds were a blur. He reached to put his hand on my shoulder and before I knew it, I jerked my left shoulder back and swung my right arm around at the same time, making direct contact with his jaw and my fist. He stumbled backwards, no doubt about as shocked as I was that I had actually done it. He tripped over the chairs behind him and fell into a group of people.

Just then I heard from behind me a familiar voice. "Maki! What the hell did you do that for!?" It was Rugged. I didn't know if he was going to discipline me or praise me.

"He just - he's a complete asshole!" My eyes began watering and I was shaking. *Ugh, why did I always cry when I was angry!?*

"Are you okay?" He asked as a couple others walked up now too.

"No, I'm not okay!"

"You just clocked the shit out of him!"

Just then the guy came to his feet and staggered in our direction. Clearly, he was beyond drunk. "What the fuck's your problem, bitch?" Now I was worried. I wasn't sure what this guy - who was clearly much bigger than me - was capable of. Unfortunately, I hadn't considered this when I instinctively punched him in the face. I didn't care.

"Hey, why don't you get him the hell out of here," Rugged yelled at a couple of guys next to him. At first they looked annoyed, but then as they surveyed the scene, they did as instructed.

As the night went on, the story grew bigger and bigger around the bar. Inside I felt horrible. Not for what I had done - but by what he had said. I couldn't shake it. I thought we were beyond this point in the Navy. It was a realization that there will always be ignorant people everywhere - no matter what decade or century it was.

I grabbed Janessa and brought her home. We both lay in our beds and talked about all of the great things we were going to do and foods we were going to eat when we got back to the states after this deployment was over. Then we talked about how much better it would be when we got out of the Navy. Eventually we both just fell asleep.

The next day on the flight I was finally able to upgrade my name tag on my flight suit to AW2 Maki. Although I was thence forth deemed "Knuckles" by the crew. The story of how I earned my call sign was one that I was both proud of and humiliated by. As a result, it was rarely told.

Big Ol'

"Love in an elevator... loving it up while I'm going down..."

"Ugh, stop, would ya?" A disgruntled voice broke the cheerful singing over the ICS of our PPC (Plane Patrol Captain), LT Burke - the man that once was voted the funniest man in Boston. The man who paid for his college by doing stand-up comedy.

"Oh, what's that Stimpy? You don't *love* my beautiful singing?" Burke asked. "Tell me Baby, does it make you horny?" Burke was always impersonating Austin Powers. Or Dr. Evil. Or Squishy. Or anything he could impersonate.

246

And crazy enough, he was always dead-on.

"I don't care if you sing… just no Aerosmith songs please."

"Whaaa? You don't like Aerosmith!?" It was as if Stimpy renounced his love to a dying parent. "Are you a communist or something? Who *doesn't* like Aerosmith?!?"

Stimpy replied, "I just had this ex that used to play that album over and over and over. I just cringe now anytime I hear Steven Tyler."

"Oh, man, that sucks." Burke replied with sympathy in his voice. There was about ten seconds of silence on the ICS that passed. And then the melody resumed, "So I took a big chance at the high school dance with a lady who was ready to play," he sang again. "It wasn't me she was foolin' 'cause she knew what she was doing when she told me how to WALK THIS WAY! TALK THIS WAAAAY…"

Unanimous laughter broke over the ICS as we all sat at our stations listening to the conversation over our headphones. Suddenly, another work of Aerosmith broke out from Big Lovin.' Then Dan in the back with another one. It was catching on like wildfire as Stimpy made protesting sounds of a drowning rat in retaliation. Suddenly, in mid-song, the Aerosmith serenade was paused and Dan spoke randomly.

"You know, I was thinking last night. If I ever have a kid, I think I'm going to call him Big Ol.' Instantly more laughter broke out as everyone silently put Dan's last name into the mix. Big Ol' Cox.

From that moment on, Dan would forever be referred to as Big Ol.' And for the rest of that deployment, it was the unspoken mission of CAC-9 to break into Aerosmith songs whenever we could think of a new one in Stimpy's presence. I also learned on that deployment that there were a LOT of Aerosmith songs. Chances are, around your brothers-in-arms, you will always get the opposite of what you ask for.

Big Ol's Bad Day

It had already been a painful day. We had pre-flighted three planes and 'downed' all of them. Engine oil leak here, cracked wing there... We were always to be quick and efficient, though to be efficient - it was impossible to be quick. Finally, on the fifth hour of our 3-hour preflight, we deemed the fourth plane good enough to trust with our lives. We relocated our gear once more and took off.

The Mission: Deliver three Commanders to ground forces "In Theater" so they could show how efficient our operations were. It was not a typical flight day - it was a show-and-tell day. The Skipper trusted his best crew, good ol' CAC-9, would accomplish the mission with ease.

A couple of hours later, after dropping off the officers, we took off for the sky. Somewhere in our transition, a gruesome realization struck our unfortunate In-Flight Technician, Big 'Ol. Instantly his face grew as pale as a ghost. I thought him to be ill and quickly searched for an empty bag as I sat across the fuselage from him.

"You okay?"

He hesitated, mumbled something and then spit out, "I forgot the antenna!" Surely I hadn't heard him right. "What?!"

"The antenna! I FORGOT the fucking antenna! I left it on one of the other twenty effing planes we pre-flighted."

"Oooh." I racked my brain for a plan - but fell short. There was no way of transmitting video to the ground without the antenna. I strained to find words of comfort to my poor friend. I had nothing. He shook his head and accepted the inevitable - he was going to have to tell them.

Over the hum of the engines, I watched up the tube of the plane as Big Ol' hung his head and informed our TACCO of the situation. It was like watching your best friend march off to the firing squads.

For Big Lovin', our beloved TACCO that stood well over six feet, it was rare a day that this man's face did not hold a smile, or a song upon his lips. He was the size of a grizzly, but had the heart of a saint. I had never seen him angry before.

I watched in that moment as Big Lovin's song stopped. He paused and looked out the diminutive window at the engines. Big Ol' stood next to him. The silence was deafening. He turned back to Big Ol' and instructed him to sit. Big Lovin' got on his radio and informed Burke of the situation.

The arms of the man in the cockpit that was usually cracking a joke began to flail about in a disturbing manner. His lips were moving, but it was like watching a silent movie. After the soundless commotion had stopped, a voice came across the internal radio, "Continue mission as planned."

I glanced back at Rugged, my eyes asking, *how the hell do we do the mission without this vital piece of equipment*? He just looked back at me, shrugged his shoulders, and began to work the camera.

It was great stuff. We could see everything as plain as day. However, we knew without the antenna, they wouldn't see anything but fuzz on the ground displays.

"Yes sir, these are great shots!" Big Lovin' narrated throughout the day, in such refined detail they could have drawn a picture. "You're not receiving them, sir?" he asked nonchalantly over the radios. "Hmmm. Interesting. Perhaps a bad connection?"

And there it was. Our equipment failed regularly, (recall: three downed aircraft) a failed antenna wasn't a hard concept to believe. The mission wasn't a detrimental one - simply a show-and-tell. And, we had failed. However, all of the information was recorded, so nothing was lost.

But something else was gained that day. In a world where making a name for yourself was paramount to making rank, these two officers were men of valor. They never faulted Big Ol' for the failed mission that day. Instead, they took a bullet for their crew. They had his back. They taught us what it meant to be a true leader. Respect was never demanded from our officers - it was a by-product of their personality. Each of us on CAC-9 had our fair share of bad days and stupid mistakes. That day just happened to be Big Ol's.

The Board

I stood outside of the door, leaning tensely against the hallway wall. It was cold. I dug my fingers into the cracks between the bricks, chipping away fractions of old cement and filing down my split nails at the same time. I had no idea what the time was or how long I had been standing there. I hadn't slept in two days. Every waking second went to studying. My brain was fried. I couldn't even make a trivial decision in this moment if I tried. My stomach was in knots and my bladder felt weak. I felt as if I had to use the bathroom - but I knew it was only nerves. It was sheer agony. But then again, that was the intention.

Suddenly the door opened and Roth, the nicest guy of the AW shop poked his head out with a big smile on his face. Normally I adore Roth. Today, I wanted to throat punch him. "Hey there! You ready?" He was his usual cheerful self.

I swallowed the huge lump in my throat, but it was too dry. My stomach was shot with a stab of pain. "Um, no." Maybe it wasn't too late to turn around. I had forgotten everything. I needed at least another week to study. Yes, another week would be good.

"Come on, you'll do fine," he said as he urged me inside. He was way too happy. It's like he didn't understand - like he had forgotten what it was like. But he was a *smart* operator. Things came easy for him. I don't think he ever stressed over a thing, so I'm sure his board was something he just penciled into his day right before Sunday brunch.

He held the door open and I walked into the room. *Don't put your head down. You must appear confident.* I struggled with this concept and forced myself to make eye contact for a brief second to each one. But I wasn't ready. I didn't know how I was going to handle it if I failed. There simply hadn't been enough time - but everyone insisted I have it on deployment.

"There will be less people on your board - since most people will be flying or on crew rest if you have it while on deployment." They promised.

"You won't have to bring them food if you do it on deployment since we don't have kitchens. You will still have to buy them beer though - if you pass that is," others said. *"It'll be a lot quicker since they are a lot busier on deployment because no one has the time to draw it out over an entire day - or even two as in some cases."*

And so I scheduled it while we were on deployment. And there I was - surrounded by all of these great suggestions. Still, I didn't see any of those guys with the bright ideas in here now that it was all about to start. And here I was.

I took a deep breath and began to answer each question as they came. I was drilled for the next three hours - dissecting every single little thing I knew about submarines and their engines - how they were powered, how fast they went, their drive shaft make-up, their cycles and cylinders. I didn't even know how many cycles and cylinders my own car had - but I could tell you how many each diesel submarine in the Atlantic Ocean had and which country they were from. I was quizzed on the submarine's parameters, signatures for different countries, and their tactics. Our own tactics and tools. Magic assholes (i.e. algebraic formulas). The P-3 and everything about the software system and how it functioned, when which software tool should be used in each type of tracking, the signal flow of how each box was energized, on which panel that each circuit breaker that provided power to the box was located, and aircraft emergency/safety procedures. And to my own surprise - I knew all of this information. It just came rambling out of my head and onto the white board.

After I had filled the white board for the third time with obnoxious mnemonics, Chuck came up to inspect my work. "Not bad... looks like you missed one here for spreading loss. Cylindrical, Spherical, and...?"

"Ummm..." My mind was blank and one of the easiest questions out there. I had known this since "A School" - but my brain was fried.

Chuck went on, "Com'on, what comes after C, S? Chiefs Suck..."

"Dipolar!" I smiled. "Ugh. How could I forget that!?"

Chuck sat back down and I stood in silence as I watched the board take down notes. I had to be near finished. My brain literally hurt from its raping. I had nothing left to give and I could tell they knew this.

"One more question," Chuck began as he sat back down behind the table. "You're going out to start your preflight when your SS-2 comes up to you and says that she can't fly because she has really bad menstrual cramps. What do you do?"

Hmmm. This was a test and I wasn't sure which angle he was going for at first. It was becoming a kinder, gentler Navy. He was testing my leadership skills now. He was testing a lot of things. I couldn't count how many times I had flown when I felt like ass or in pain... But as long as I was able to walk and function, there just wasn't an excuse. The entire crew depended on us to complete our missions and there just was no room for weakness.

"Well, I would say to either pop a Motrin and suck it up, or go to medical and get a down chit. Unless you are classified as medically 'sick,' you are on the flight schedule to fly."

I wanted to add 'Bitch' at the end of it, because I don't think anything would have made me more infuriated than to have a whiney female SS-2 after everything, but I thought better of it given the circumstances.

"That sounds a little harsh, doesn't it?" Chuck asked, still testing me.

"Nope."

"Alright, anyone else have any questions for her?" Chuck looked around the room. The other three guys shook their head no. "Okay, you can wait in the shop for us as we review your scores. There might be some tissues in there if you feel like you're going to cry or anything. Maybe take a Motrin." When Chuck spoke he had a deep serious voice, so one had to look at his face to see if he was joking or not. The thing is, I cannot recall Chuck ever being too serious about anything. He always wore a smile. If he wasn't so damn smart, they would've kicked him out a long time ago from some of the idiotic things he did - especially while drinking. But his previous duty was working to help design the software system that we now used in the plane. The man was a genius. And a jerk. But likable at the same time.

I rolled my eyes and shook my head as I left the room. I had never been happier to be done with something in my life. I gave it everything - if I didn't pass now - I had no idea what I would do. It would be the end of everything. If I passed, it would be the beginning.

Later that night at the bar it was, at last, my turn to buy beer for everyone as my 'reward' for passing. And I couldn't have been happier to do so.

"Congratulations, kid. I knew you could do it," Rugged said to me as we celebrated. "Now aren't you so happy that I was such an asshole to you and so hard on you? It was all for your own good."

"Well, I think so?" I said. It was a weird question that I wasn't sure how I felt about it in that moment.

He had been drinking, so he was friendlier than usual. Plus his SS-2 just passed her board with flying colors, so that reflected well on him.

"When I first found out I was getting the only acoustic female in the squadron as my SS-2, I'll admit, I wasn't really sure what to think about it. But I made up my mind right then that you weren't going to be getting any special treatment at all. In fact, I was even harder on you than I would've been to a guy. But it all paid off in the end, didn't it?"

"Well... I guess so. I passed, so that was good."

"You did awesome. I'm so proud of you."

I'm not sure if it was the beer talking, but those words from Rugged meant the world to me that day - especially since most days I felt like I was a thorn in his side - and vice versa. He drove me crazy. But he taught me to be thorough, to not cut corners, and to always put your all into everything you do. Because he always did.

Dinner. Sicilian Style.

Europe is a wonderful place for many reasons. It's bursting with history and breathtaking landscapes. The Europeans have been around for so long - they have it all figured out. They take many more holidays than us. They drink either espresso shots or wine with every meal. And they take siestas.

Because lunchtime is usually their big meal of the day, most businesses close down anywhere between 1 and 5 pm. Everyone goes home for their meal, takes a nap, and goes back to work until 9 or 10pm. The problem for us Americans over in Europe is that the Navy does not take siestas. So if we decide to go out in town, you'd best time it around the siesta - or you will find yourself wandering empty streets with all of the massive amounts of stray animals just looking for a place to grab a Snickers and a bottle of water.

That's not to say dinner is not a big celebration. In Sicily, any meal is a rea-son to celebrate - a reason to bring friends and family together. It is enjoyed and a drawn-out affair of merriment and festivity. So on the day that one of our fellow AWs, Joe, invited us all to dinner at his Sicilian family's restaurant in Syracuse, we darn near fell off our ponies in excitement.

That night someone was able to pawn their first unborn child in exchange for a government van, and a group of us jumped in and headed south to Siracusa. It was when we arrived in the city that we quickly realized what a bad choice it was to take the huge government van. As we navigated through the cobblestone streets of this city that was over 2700 years old, we turned off onto a side street that began to close in on us. We pulled in the side mirrors so as not to scrape the buildings or the micro-cars that were parked on this one-donkey road. However, the street continued to get narrower and narrower. Even when there were no more cars parked along the side, our side mirrors began to scrape the brick structure next to us. A string of cars were behind us - so backing up and out was not even an option. The city streets were so old that Jesus himself may very well have walked down them, and I sure can tell you that he would have told us *not* to attempt to drive down them in a government van.

Jesus be like, "Sailors, go get yourself a micro-Euro-car like every other Sicilian - or even better - ride into town on a donkey." (He would make a joke like that, I'm sure.)

And we'd be like, "Jesus, first off, I can't believe it's you! How's it going? I'm sure there are more important things we could talk about right now - but yes, it was some poor planning on our part to take this government van into Siracusa. Do you think you could help us out?"

And then, just when we thought we were going to be encapsulated into the tomb of a van between two large buildings, Jesus must have parted bricks. Somehow, we were able to dislodge ourselves and make it down the rest of the alley onto a bigger street. At last we had made it to our destination. It was this quaint family-owned restaurant called *La Finanziera*.

As soon as we walked in the door, we were greeted by the most amazing aromas as well as a lovely Sicilian woman who ran up to Joe, hugging him warmly. Lots of Sicilian words were spoken and then we all smiled and shook hands and hugged when appropriate. "Please, sit, sit!" she instructed and directed us to a long table full of chairs for our entire group. Quickly she scurried off and Joe whispered to us all across the table.

"Just so you know, I don't think they'll charge us for any of this - but just make sure that you eat everything they serve. In Sicily, they will take it as an insult if you don't eat everything on your plate."

Aaron and I exchanged a look. He saw the fear in my eyes. I am more of a grazer that eats constantly - but in small amounts. This was definitely going to be a challenge. He smiled and patted my leg under the table. He had my back.

I made it through the appetizers - the most succulent calamari I've ever eaten in my life. And then came the second round of appetizers. Stuffed mushrooms and baby octopus with full-on tentacles wiggling in the breeze. I gazed at the suction cups on the tentacles. For a split second, the thought of eating a baby octopus sounded disturbing, but I quickly dismissed the thought and did not allow it to come back. When in doubt, fake being okay with eating baby octopus. It tricks your stomach.

I could feel myself slowly filling up. Then came the salad. A huge plate of salad. Now, I usually feel like vegetables are a waste of time - especially lettuce, (really, what's the point? It's only pretending to be food) however the array of Mediterranean flavors in this salad had me almost wanting more. Almost. By the time I was done with it, I was comfortably full. Next was the main dish. Or so I thought. Pasta. Then a meat dish. Followed by another pasta. Soon, when they looked away, I begged Aaron to switch plates with me as his was clean.

"Oh, Babe, there's no way."

"Please, you have to, I can't eat another bite. We'll be rude Americans and never welcomed back."

Reluctantly, he agreed. And so our food torture continued. It was the most wonderful food I had ever eaten, but I wanted to cry as my stomach was near bursting - as was everyone else's. And then came the dessert. The most artistic, rich piece of Tiramisu I had ever seen in my life. Normally Tiramisu is my weakness. This night it seemed to haunt me.

Eat me. You know you want to. Just one little taste won't hurt! I never realized how rude Tiramisu could be with its espresso and liquor soaked layers upon rich creamy custard delectableness with chocolate shavings sprinkled on top. And so bite by bite, I ate that damn Tiramisu even though I just wanted to slap it. And I had never been happier to be in such pain.

The Fight

"Come on! Come here, Tripod!" Our base mascot, Tripod the three-legged dog came hobbling over below me for some leftover chips that I threw over the balcony of the second floor. It was a beautiful Sicilian night. The stars were out and the red glowing bubbles of death lava from Mt. Etna could be seen off in the distant sky. There was a calm about the night. Except for the feral cats and dogs that were mating and roamed freely around the base. (Oh, not together - you thought I meant - never mind.)

Yes, the quiet Sicilian night - except for the noise from the raging party taking place in the First Class Mess behind me. The room was bursting with people out into the hallways - including a handful of people that weren't even in our squadron.

"So Tripod likes chips, huh?" a voice came from behind me.

"He *loves* them. Well, pretty much any food that's not out of the trash can," I replied.

"I'm Steve," the stranger said, holding out his hand for me to shake.

"Julia." I replied as I shook his hand. He had a handshake that felt like I was grasping a Jello-mold, which made me wonder if he was making special accommodations shaking a girl's hand, or if he was untrustworthy. Either way, it was gross.

"Want to play foosball?" He asked. I could tell he'd already had quite a few drinks by his inability to stand steady. But I honestly couldn't think of a good enough excuse and it's impossible for me to just say no. So, I relented and went in to play with him and a few others that were already mid-game.

As the night went on, I realized how good I was at foosball. I didn't have to aim too much - I could just whack it as hard as I wanted. My competitive side took over and I began to really get into the game. *This was my kind of game!* Steve continued to bring me drinks and was acting flirtatious, but nothing too over the top that I couldn't just blow off - plus I liked having the great drink service. Suddenly, in some failed attempt to make a move on me, he grabbed one of the foosballs and shoved it down into my bra, groping me along the way.

I was caught completely off guard and stood there, dumbfounded, for a moment in my confusion trying to figure out what the heck just happened. Before I could even utter a word, Aaron came out of nowhere, grabbed him by the neck and threw him up against the wall.

"What the fuck do you think you're doing!?" Aaron yelled at him. "That's my girlfriend and you'd better keep your hands off of her!"

Now I was even more stunned at the situation - *where had he come from? What is he thinking? He is going to kill this guy.* None of this was okay.

"Aaron, let him go - stop!" I always thought I had wanted a guy that would fight for me - and now that I was in this moment, I was terrified. I was afraid of what Aaron would do - and afraid of what could happen to him. Steve couldn't move or say anything. It all happened so fast.

"Stop!" I yelled again.

"Aaron stop!" Quickly a bunch of guys came and broke them apart. I'm not sure how much time had passed - it all was a blur.

"Aaron, you need to leave now!" One of the First Classes (and Aaron's good friend) yelled out, more so for Aaron's sake. One of the guys from the other squadron had just called the cops.

Aaron let go of Steve and he scrambled away. Fuming, I stormed out into the hall.

"What were you thinking!?" I yelled at him when he followed me.

"What was *I* thinking!? What were *you* thinking?" he yelled right back.

"I didn't do anything..."

"Yeah, I know you didn't do anything. You just let him stick his hand down your shirt!?"

"I didn't even have a chance to stop him - you came out of nowhere!" I was shaking now as we were yelling at each other in the hallway. It was humiliating and horrible at the same time.

"I can't handle this. I can't handle you anymore!" I yelled and ran to my room. I just wanted the night to be over. I wanted everything to be over.

Dogfish

To keep NATO (North American Treaty Organization) forces sharp, in 1975 they developed a joint exercise called Dogfish. Besides us representing the mighty Americans, other participants included the Canadians, French, Germans, Greeks, Italians, Dutch, Norwegians, Portuguese, Spanish, Turks, and the Brits. For almost two weeks straight, our crews worked jointly with our allies in various multi-coordinated anti-submarine warfare operations with a force of ships, submarines, and aircraft. We flew around the clock and engaged in many cat-and-mouse games that worked to improve the coordination and skills of our own military operators as well as our joint NATO force operations. It was both exhausting and a blast! [http://www.globalsecurity.org/military/ops/dogfish.htm]

Of course, upon completion of this exercise, what were we to do but host a marvelously entertaining shindig for all of the aircrew platforms involved. Every country brought drinks and/or food representing their country. The French brought wine and cheese. The Spanish brought sangria - (nicknamed 'the leg-spreader of the Mediterranean') the best and most dangerous sangria I've tasted to date. The Germans brought beer and Wiener Schnitzel, and the Canadian's brought "Moose Milk." Not literally, as that would be weird - but it was a type of mixed drink similar to a White Russian. Alas, the Russians weren't there, because, well Russia always cheats at war games. Just kidding, Russia. xoxo. It was almost like a mini Epcot Center - only with war-fighters and much alcohol. Ironically, I cannot remember what we brought that year. Perhaps Cheeseburgers and Coors Lite? I seriously hope not. But clearly it wasn't anything to write home about. Or in a book.

The party proved to be a great time, and after a few swigs of Moose Milk, I headed over to the German table. I was so ready to impress them, so I let loose and recited the only line I could remember from taking two years of German in high school. "Darf ink zur toilette gain?" Which translates to "May I use the toilet?" At least I thought it did. That's what our German teacher in high school taught us to say if we wanted to use the facilities. Of course that would be the only line that came to mind. The worst part was that I wasn't even asking where the toilet was - like normal people would. I was asking them for permission.

They all looked at each other and shrugged their shoulders and replied an apathetic, "Uh, ya..."

"Danke. Ich bin Julia."

"Sie sind willkommen." I quickly learned that their German was very different from the German I learned in school. Just like the time I went to a Puerto Rican wedding with my friend, Freddie. I sounded like a formal robot. Thankfully, they were quickly forgiving of my awkwardness (in both occasions), and a good beer fixed everything (again, both occasions). I learned quickly that even a poor attempt to speak another's language is always worth the effort. Even if you mess it up - they will be grateful that you tried.

I also learned that it's a bad idea to mix all of the drinks from all over the world. Apparently, there is a reason oceans separate some of us. As the night grew on, my memory became somewhat hazier. The highlights that come to mind: Trading my shirt with a Norwegian. (It was a really great shirt designed especially for Dogfish.) Climbing over the barracks fourth-floor balcony in attempt to rescue a feral cat. Chief reaching over the balcony to grab me and throw me over his shoulder. Chief spinning around really fast and hitting my head on the fire extinguisher. Waking up peacefully in my own bed. Alone with a headache. Fully dressed. As usual. Thinking about how I really need to quit drinking so much. Missing Aaron...

I loved nearly everything about being in Sicily. The food. The people. The countryside. My friends in the squadron. Everything except for the screaming mee-mies. On any given afternoon off, we explored the nearby countryside and neat cities. We shopped, ate blood oranges and local Italian cuisine, and drank espresso shots at cafes in Catania and house wines at local restaurants by evening. We ventured up a mountain side to a mini castle in Taormina and explored abandoned churches. We drove up Mt. Etna and saw houses with hardened lava that poured right through the second-floor windows, freezing the house in time. We spent an entire day driving up to Messina to buy sets of handcrafted pottery, others toured the catacombs in Palermo. Sicily was a fabulous island and I was grateful for my time there. I also was grateful to work in the Mediterranean and surrounding areas. There was a part of me that hoped in some small way we had helped the people of the lands we flew over with our various Intel-gathering flights, although I'll never know for sure if our efforts were in vain or not.

CHAPTER 12

Sicily Part 2: DETS

During our deployment in the Mediterranean, I managed to accumulate over 800 flight hours and ended up earning the Air Medal for over 20 flights over hostile territory. It was a lot of flying, a lot of work, but also a lot of fun. Though NAS Signonella, Sicily, was our base point, we also had the opportunity to DET ("Detach" from our main deployment site) out of there into some other great countries, working some other great missions.

Nîmes, France.

Approximate distance from Deer River: 4412 miles

I see London. I see France... for some reason I couldn't get the second-grade saying out of my head as we were flying into France - an elegant place that I had always dreamed of visiting. It just so happened by good fortune, or rather not so good fortune for a co-worker of mine, that I ended up going to France. After running into a bit of trouble with the law, he was dubbed a "security risk" and was forced to stay on base for the first half of deployment, among other punishments. This created a problem for his crew that was scheduled to go to France in March of 2000. I was selected to go in his place.

I had always dreamed of traveling to France and was not disappointed. It was everything I thought it'd be. The people were classy and sophisticated. They wore all black and bathed in fancy perfume. Even the animals. The food was exquisite. I ate croissants with tiny personal jars of jelly for breakfast every morning. It was delicious and I got to pretend I was a giant. For the first time in my life, I ate cheeses other than 'cheese-products' shaped like squares and individually wrapped. I came to love 'crusty bread' and would buy baguettes from street vendors for pocket change and then just gnaw on them like a famished street rat as I walked the city. I ate enough bread and cheeses to feed a small army. I shopped in fancy French boutiques for "French Things" and had my hair cut at a salon where no one could understand a word I said. That last part was dumb and I wouldn't recommend it.

The terrain was breath-taking and the hotel that we stayed at in Nîmes was no exception. The Art Deco-style Hotel Imperator was a fabulous combination of charm and grandness. Bursting with France's fine art and culture, the lobby opened into a huge lounge with large windows offering a view of the majestic gardens that made me want to sit and sip wine with my pinky sticking out while reading a book. It was rumored that Pablo Picasso, Ernest Hemingway, and Ava Gardner had all stayed there. I could just imagine that a million years or so ago, Picasso sat just like I did, sipping wine with his pinky sticking out in those gardens, watching the pterodactyls fly overhead.

The wrought iron elevator in the lobby was only semi-enclosed by intricate iron designs as it continuously journeyed to the third floor and back. Most of the time a few of us would race up the encircling stairs and try to out-do the lazy crewmembers who took the elevator. We would wait for the elevator doors to open, as if we had been there the whole time, yell "lazy!" and run away. Though we did our best to remain on good behavior and appear that we fit in - I still could not believe the government was actually paying me to stay there! I was amazed every time I entered the lobby, but I did my best to refrain from tap-dancing on the marble whenever the urge struck my fancy.

The rooms were bright and artistic. There was a small television in the corner that played shows in the French language and showed naked women in the commercials - because no one cared about boobs there. My bedroom was roomy as it held two full-size beds, and two windows that were floor-to-ceiling with drapes that had to have weighed a hundred pounds each. Naturally, I had to put them over my head like a veil and sing "These are a few of my favorite things…"

I had my own personal balcony that each of these windows opened to with French doors. Or perhaps here they were just called 'doors.' The balcony overlooked the bustling city below, with cobble-stone paths. Every chance I got, I would rest my forearms on the iron rail until it left imprints in my skin. I would gaze out into the street and wonder what kind of a life the natives here had. I wondered how much history these streets had seen.

The city of Nîmes was located on the Via Domitia, which served as a Roman road, constructed in 118 BC linking Italy with Spain; thus, the French city had much Roman influence ringing throughout it. One of the prime examples of this was the coliseum known as Arena of Nîmes, which was built around AD 70. This arena has been used to the present day for festivals and events such as bull fighting. And although I appreciate history and cultural traditions as much as the next guy, there is much about bull fighting that I just cannot stomach.

To reach the downtown area from our hotel, we would have to pass by the coliseum. Now, I am not normally a superstitious person. (Except for my purple rabbit foot that I must wave in front of me before entering a room from the south wall.) While I can imagine the centuries of history that the stone walls had witnessed and survived, it was not a place I would have ever wanted to be locked inside after dark. I could literally feel the air quality change whenever I was in the presence of the coliseum. It was cold - not just because it was damp stone, but each time I neared it, I could feel a breeze blow through my skin, sending a chill up my spine. There were many unsettled souls that still loomed in this place. They were always watching. I had never felt such a dark feeling like that before or since, but it was made very apparent to me in that week that I passed by it, that the coliseum held many haunting secrets within its walls.

There was also a temple just down the road from us named Maison Carree that had been commissioned sometime around 19 BC - during the reign of Caesar Augustus. After the fall of the Roman Empire, the temple remained in use for various activities such as a church, residence, stables, town hall, and public archives. It later became a museum in the early 1800s. 19 BC. Over 2000 years old! It was such an amazing concept to grasp, coming from a country that was only a few hundred years old. America is such a wee babe.

Twinkies

After we arrived and needed some food, what do we sailors do? When in France... we ate at McDonalds of course. We arrived at the French McDonalds with two goals: ordering French fries, and beer. Because in France, you can get beer at McDonalds. And so we did. However, we took our beer-ordering to an all-new level. We went through the *drive-thru* and ordered a beer. There we received our "to-go" pack of beers, complete with lids and straws. And we laughed and laughed like little children at Christmas time.

We also ordered our French fries which were called "pommes frites." One cannot say "pommes frites" without a French accent. And what does a sailor put on his pommes frites while in France? Mayonnaise, of course. If you wanted ketchup, you had to specifically ask for it. Here in France, mayo was the go-to for your Pommes frites with beer. And it was amazing. It does not take much to entertain an American sailor.

After dinner, we all headed back to the hotel to rest up for our flight the next morning. Soon after I stepped into my room, there was a knock at the door. When I opened it, there stood Eugene, CAC-2's SS-3 operator, with a Sam's Club-size box of Twinkies and a case of Miller Lite in his hands. The guy knew the way to my heart.

Eugene was an eccentric fellow - and I was always entertained in his presence. He was the first Jewish guy I knew and I loved to hear about his funny religion that wouldn't let him eat bacon or celebrate Christmas - two of my greatest pleasures. I do not know how I would survive without either. He was always giving me tips on saving money too, and told me about how he would buy generic pills for his girlfriend and repackage them (including the cotton to stuff and re-gluing the top) in name-brand bottles because it was all she would accept him buying. He was clever like that. That night we just hung out in the hallway of our fancy French hotel eating our Twinkies, drinking beer, and telling stories. To this day, I cannot truly enjoy a Twinkie without a beer.

The Hole

Our missions during our DET to France were simple - we were to find and track a German and a French submarine as part of our exercise with the French military. We flew nearly every day but one, but the missions were somewhat short and we took advantage of every free minute we were granted. On one of the first flights, knowing that the mission was only going to be approximately five hours total, I did my best to 'hold it' on the flight. As soon as we landed, though, I made a beeline to the hangar in search of the nearest bathroom. I ran into one of our maintainers and desperately asked for directions. He just pointed to a door down the hall. Running in there, I stepped into the middle of the room. To the right of me was a single porcelain sink appended to the wall. To the left of me was a shower stall with a large open drain. There wasn't even a shower curtain. However, nowhere in the small room did I see a toilet. I was so confused. I turned around and went back out the door where the maintainers were close by.

"No, that was just a shower - do you know where the toilets are?" I asked them.

They looked at each other and busted out laughing. "No, you don't understand. That *is* their toilet."

"Are you fricking kidding me?" I asked. I sighed dramatically and turned back to the "bathroom," closing the door behind me. There wasn't even a roll of toilet paper. Clearly they didn't have women in this particular French military - or at least they had facilities somewhere else. I thought of how I probably would have been better off going on the plane.

And so I unzipped my flight suit and tied it around my knees. I then hovered over this nasty, smelly hole in the cement and couldn't help but think that this was *not* the glamorous side of France that I had been envisioning.

That Flight

"Jez, TACCO. Got anything for me?" the TACCOs voice broke the silence over the ICS. It had been two hours since we had been on-station and it was nearing 3am local time. Everyone couldn't help but zone-out into the darkness; whether that was out the windows or blankly staring at a screen of fuzz. My mouth was becoming raw from sucking on sunflower seeds to keep alert - a trick that I had learned my previous deployment. No matter the hour or how sleep-deprived I was, as long as I could shell sunflower seeds with my teeth, I would stay awake.

"TACCO, that's a hot negative right now…" my voice trailed off as I paged through the electronic grams on the green display. They were full of clutter from shipping noises as the Mediterranean commonly was. Trying to find subsurface contact in them was like trying to find chastity in a brothel. The weather was violent and we were getting bounced around, flying low in and out of storms. If I hadn't been concentrating so hard trying to find contact, I surely would have thrown up my dinner by now. "I'm listening to the buoys right now and they are all consumed with RFI."

"Flight, this is Three. I've got a friendly incoming at your 2 o'clock high," Eugene piped in over the noise.

"Copy, Three." Flight interjected.

Then, suddenly it was if a hand from the Heavens reached down on my display in the form of a newly filled pixel on the bottom of my gram at the appropriate frequency on the spectrum. I waited for the screen to blink as another update evolved. The line continued to grow. And when I was sure, my heart skipped a beat as I relayed the most exciting words a Jezebel (Sensor 1) operator could say.

"TACCO, Jez. I've got up-Doppler contact coming in steady on RF 22." It felt like I had just told him he was about to be the King of the Jungle. I pulled my mike back and leaned over, pointing up to my SS-2s display. "Detune everything south of RF 25."

"Roger, detuning," my SS-2 yelled off the ICS directly to me over the aircraft noise.

I managed to pull a bearing out of the mess and transferred it to the TACCO. "TACCO, did you get that bearing?"

"Just did Jez. Thanks."

"I'd say that's a pretty accurate bearing - holding steady. It's inbound to 22 - looking more and more to be a string-cutter." [*The submarine passes so close it cuts the strings of the sonobuoy.*]

"Flight, I just sent you a fly-to-point," TACCO stated. The buzz in the air had suddenly come alive. We had come alive.

"Got it TACCO. Inbound," Flight replied. I felt the plane yank hard to the left - which in all accuracy was forward for me, since I was sitting sideways as my station required.

"TACCO, IFT. P-Chutes are loaded and ready to go," the IFT called from the back of the tube.

"TACCO, Jez, we're about 30 seconds away from CPA."

"Flight, TACCO, you gonna make it?"

"Oh we're gonna make it alright," the flight station called back. We could feel the extra torque as the plane picked up speed. "Balls to the wall, baby."

"Bearings are increasing," I continued to call out. I was in my groove. We were flying low and the plane was in all her war-fighting glory. She was flying as fast as she dared, dropping and rising as she hit the air pockets in the rainstorm - but no one cared as we shook harder than a wooden roller coaster being run by a stoned carnie. We were all in our zone.

"CPA now, now, now!" I yelled across the ICS and quickly performed the calculations. "I got him going 2-7-2 at 8 knots. He is falling right on our briefed and known frequencies, I can positively classify this as our guy."

"Thank you Jez. We have attack criteria. Inbound. Three, you ready?" TACCO began going through his checklist.

"Standing by, Sir," Eugene replied. The bom bay doors opened and the plane shook with the extra drag.

"Hell yeah. Let's do this." It was like watching a choreographed dance. Everything intertwined together and all were indispensible. No one could miss a beat as the dance only succeeded when timing was delicately synchronized.

"MADMAN, MADMAN, MADMAN!" Eugene shouted the sweet words we all awaited, indicating that we had flown directly over the submarine's location.

"Weapon away on my third now. Now, now now!" TACCO released the smoke. "Oh yeah baby. And that is how it is done, gentlemen. And lady. Nice work everyone."

"Beautiful." Flight replied. "I've got a smoke in the water. France is lucky we are friends or they'd be crying in the waters right now."

"More like repenting at the Pearly Gates," Eugene interjected.

"True, true."

Our cat and mouse game continued and we were able to get in three more attacks. Finally, when our time was up and we had all the beautiful data recorded on the tapes that we needed, we called our off-station time and began our climb back into calmer skies, with a sense of accomplishment looming. There were good days and bad days in anti-submarine warfare. This was a great one.

Suddenly, out of nowhere, we lost internal power and our screens went completely black. "Flight, I've lost radar!"

"Oh shit," someone yelled.

Just then we hit an air pocket and dropped substantially in altitude - shaking the entire time. The ICS went silent. The usual soothing hum and vibrations of the propellers suddenly coughed and set forth into a horribly eerie, and unfamiliar screeching sound. It stung my ears. I frantically glanced over at the Sensor Two Operator. When I saw the blank expression on his face, I realized our fate. Something had gone terribly wrong.

The whine of the engines was agonizing. The nose of the bird began to shift at a painful angle towards the earth. I peered around the corner to watch as our usually calm flight station was in a state of chaos. The flight engineer was attempting to steady himself between the two pilots. The pilot's voice yelled over the roar surrounding us. "Set five! Set condition five immediately!"

Fighting the force of gravity, I strapped myself in. My hand alone weighed that of a car. I leaned my head back and thought, "Wow, could this be it? Was that all I had?" I began to think of my desk that I had left unordered... No one would know where to even begin with the project I was working on... I sure wish I had cleaned my car out this morning like I had been planning on doing.

You know those seconds that seem to play out in slow motion? This was mine. It was probably a total of a minute that had passed. However, one minute in the back of an airplane in complete darkness, falling and shaking like a ragdoll in complete silence - well - is an eternity. For the first time in my life, I actually thought I was going to die. All I could think was, *Holy shit, this is it.* And I prayed under my breath, *Please God, help us.*

And then, just as fast as the lights went out, everything came back on, along with all of our instruments. The aircraft steadied in a pocket of calm air. We called off-station and began climbing in altitude. That was how quickly one's fate could change in a war-fighting machine. I unclenched my fist from my chair arms and let out my breath after I had realized I was holding it.

We were fine. The plane was fine and we turned to head towards home base. It was never quite determined what it was that caused all of our avionics to short out that night. It did not happen again the remainder of the trip. In my own mind I simply concluded that every now and then life likes to keep us on our toes. It likes to remind us that we are not invincible and at any moment our path can alter. This is how we learn gratitude.

Apparently this was not our night to die.

The Irishman

The next afternoon, we went for a ride to a French vineyard called Le Jardin des Vins - translated "The Garden of Wines." I had never been to a vineyard, so I figured France would be a pretty good place to start. As the crew and I were led around the grounds and cellar, and were able to try the various wines, I managed to strike up a conversation with an older Irishman named Seamus.

Seamus knew a lot about wine which was helpful since I didn't know a thing. By this point, the tour-guide that already spoke in very broken English was clearly growing tired of my endless questions. Seamus was very friendly, as most Irishmen that consumed alcohol were, and taught me all about the wines. He told me about 'legs' and how to properly smell and taste the wines without making gross noises. He taught me the difference between the reds and whites, and why we used different glass shapes for each. Eventually it came out that Seamus was a world traveler and wine connoisseur. I found it all quite fascinating and frankly was relieved, because I wasn't sure at first if he was just another Irishman that liked to drink and make-up stories.

As all the wine tasting quickly went to my head, he poured one more tasting of the vineyards 'best bottle.' He explained that this was the vineyard's anniversary bottle and the shape of it was based on the old type of bottles they used to carry. Interestingly, there was a love story that went along with the bottle. It was the bottle that was used to transfer love notes between two forbidden young lovers at the majestic river many moons ago - unfortunately, I do believe it ended tragically, but I purposely chose to forget that part of the story. It was all very Romeo and Juliette.

One thing I will not forget, though, was that Seamus told me the price of the best bottle they served was (at the time) equivalent to about $26 American dollars. And then he went on to say that is even a little higher than he would prefer to pay. He said that he had traveled the world and tasted thousands of different kinds of wines and that you should never have to pay more than $20 for some of the best wines in the world. After that, you are strictly paying for the name. Still to this day Seamus' words remain in my ears whenever I buy a bottle of wine. And then I grab a boxed wine instead.

The Eiffel

Because I would never forgive myself if I went all the way to France and never caught a glimpse of Paris, the one entire day we had off, those that were interested planned a train ride into Paris. We left super-early in the dark hours of the morning to ride the Euro-rail. When we arrived in the city, we had about eight hours to see the city before we had to catch the rail back to Nîmes. Now clearly, squeezing Paris into eight hours was not going to be easy. But I am an idealist. So we hit the high points.

First stop was the Notre Dame. What an amazing piece of architecture, with intricate details on every piece of trim and beam. Of course, the gargoyles stole the show as they were both disturbing and intriguing. Much like a real-life haunted house or enchanted castle. Though our whole show was the exterior as the wait to get in was over two hours and we were on a tight schedule.

So over La Seine and through the city we went. Past the Louvre. Also - not enough time, but indeed a spectacular display. I had my mind set on what I had to see. The Eiffel Tower. As we walked through the city, we could see the top between buildings. She grew closer and closer with each city block. When at last we arrived, she was every bit as breath-taking as I had imagined.

Instantly I thought back to the ash tray with a mini Eiffel Tower attached to it that my grandfather had brought home from the war for my grandmother. I had always dreamed of seeing this historical landmark and now it towered over me, kinking my neck as I attempted to peer at the top.

As we glanced in front of us, we were met again with the typical tourist nightmare - a line that wrapped around half the block - all awaiting the elevator to take them to the top. I looked at my travel partner, Frank, slightly disheartened. He shrugged and said, "Let's take the stairs."

When we located the stairs, we were pleased to see that there was no line. In fact, there were very few people around. And then I could see why. There were 98 stories of stairs to climb. It was not for the faint hearted. "Alright," I said. Let's do this." And one step at a time we climbed to the top deck of the Eiffel Tower - all 1710 of them.

The view was as one would expect. Vertigo. Breath-taking. Magnificent. I snapped as many different pictures of the views as I could. The city, the river, and some just looking straight down from the top. And then I just stood there and took it all in. I felt the wind blowing and breathed in the city. *I am in Paris. On top of the Eiffel Tower - just like I told my grandma that I would be someday as I played with the ash tray.* My dream had come true.

Tunisia.

Approximate distance from Deer River: 4970 miles

By the time our crew was granted R&R, I was so physically exhausted from flying back-to-back flights day after day that the thought of touring around everyday just seemed overwhelming. I honestly would have been fine staying in my barracks sleeping, but Aaron and I decided that we needed to get away. We needed to just be together away from the drinking and partying and see where we were with things. When we walked into the ITT office (ticketing), I just exclaimed to the travel agent - please just a remote beach somewhere in which I don't have to do a single thing. So our original plans of touring Rome changed to a resort stay in Tunisia. I know, who goes on vacation to Tunisia, but I was soooo tired at that point, I would have vacationed in Nebraska. No offense, Nebraska. We had high hopes that this trip would give us the restorative time alone that we needed.

I think we both slept on the beach the entire first day and were burnt to a crisp despite wearing sunscreen. The next day we headed into the city of Tunis and did a little shopping, which is never a stress-free plan in a city. I was literally being pulled into shops by my arms. It was a very unsettling feeling.

Suddenly, an Arab man walked up to us, explaining that he was going to give us a tour. Being the young naïve pups that we were, we didn't think anything of it, other than the man was trying to make a buck (as they all were). For the next three hours, this man drug us through the city, into the back alley-ways of his friends shops (no doubt wanting us to spend money), on top of a random roof that had a great view of the city, and an old courtyard full of beautiful mosaic pieces and busts of cultural leaders. It was amazing and fascinating, and we were able to see many hidden spots of the city that the typical tourist most likely would not have seen. Additionally, we found it quite fortunate that we were not abducted that day and sold off into slavery or worse. Instead, we made it back to our hotel in time for a fabulous dinner and a belly dancing show.

When in Rome

One of my favorite things about Europeans is their lack of modesty. As a conservative Midwesterner, I admired their "baring it all" freedom. It wasn't a big deal. In Europe, bodies are just a functioning housing case for bones and vital organs. Breasts serve a purpose. They are not shameful or taboo in public, nor are they obsessed about as much as they are by the American society.

It was best described to me once from a drunken Scotsmen at a bar, "They're just boobs, Lassie, not a fuckin' fanny." I sat there confused, drinking my stout. A few days later as I relayed the story it was explained to me that 'fanny' is another term for vagina. Upon hearing this, I laughed and made a promise to myself that I would use the fabulous term 'fanny' every chance I could - because it was hilarious.

That said, it was a very common sight to see topless women sunbathing around the pool at our particular resort. I couldn't help but be tempted by the thought. *I will never see anyone here again, well except for Aaron.* And of course, he was *completely* encouraging of the idea. So, one day at the resort pool, in the company of multiple topless women scattered about, soaking in the sun's rays while, as I lay on my stomach, I unbuckled my bikini top. And when I worked up the courage to just do it, I awkwardly flipped over and shut my eyes. As long as my eyes were shut, I couldn't see anyone around me. It felt freeing - *and* terribly uncomfortable at the same time.

And then, after a few minutes went by I felt a shadow presence over me. I opened my eyes to see an Arab man peering down at me.

"Hello."

"Um, hi," I managed to get out. *Oh my god. Should I cover up, or act natural, like I know what I am doing. What would a French woman do? Ugh!*

He began speaking in a heavy accent that I really had to concentrate on to translate. He asked if we were the ones that had signed up for the camel rides tomorrow. I confirmed and then he went on to give us the details. *Extensive details.* The whole time I was trying to slowly and awkwardly lean to my other side while politely paying attention. I wanted to run away - but that would be rude.

Why isn't he done talking? How long will this take? Please go away now.

Finally, I was able to 'casually' maneuver to my stomach again for the remainder of the conversation. And after what seemed like hours, the man finally left. At that point I hooked my bikini top back on and vowed to never try that again. Yes, they were just boobs. And I admired the Europeans for not being modest. But I realized I still had too much Midwestern roots in me to go topless in public.

Camel Ride

The next day Aaron and I found ourselves riding on camels named Esmeralda and Esmina through the desert when we realized we forgot to wear sunscreen. Since this day, on the few occasions I've gone to a dermatologist and they point out that I have sun damage on my face; I have to explain to them that there was not room on the camel to carry a bag with sunscreen in it. And then they stop nagging me. Ugh, dermatologists.

So after an hour or so of wandering through the desert, we began to wonder where our leader was taking us. When one of the other European tourists on a camel next to me asked this logical question, the Arab Camel Leader quickly reassured us in a heavy accent that he was taking us to his house. *Oh, well naturally. That's not worrisome at all.*

So we arrived at the Camel Dude's house and as instructed, dismounted from the camels, leaving them tied up outside of this small house in the middle of the desert. Sounds like the beginning of a really weird action movie, right? Like we were the dumb people that spark an international incident as two American sailors are found sunburned and dismembered in the middle of the desert.

Thankfully, that didn't happen. Instead of being dangerous, it just got weird. The leader pulled out some random cloths and rags and instructed us to get dressed in them. We did as we were told, because we weren't sure what else to do. After we were wrapped up in rags from head to toe, he began playing some very foreign music and began to wave his arms around in a very strange, dancing-like manor. Shortly after, he pointed at us, indicating it was our turn to dance. What else were we to do but dance? Now I can't help but wonder if we are going to show up on a Muslim propaganda video someday for doing this. All I can say is that I'm thankful there were no camera phones back then. As the day went on, the dancing ensued until finally the leader had enough and decided it was time to go. So we disrobed, mounted our camels, and headed back to our hotel, as any good Navy sailor would do.

As it turns out, we ended up being tourists in Tunisia as well - despite just wanting to sleep. Mentally though, the trip was restorative and gave us both a break from the 'everyday grind' of deployment life. We had made some good memories. Still, when we got back to Sicily, it was hard not to fall back into our same old routines that were causing us to grow further and further apart.

Malta.

Approximate distance from Deer River: 5172 miles

When our crew was awarded with our one full weekend off, Big Lovin' made plans for us without hesitation. Upon research, he found that it would only be $200 each to take a weekend holiday (airfare & hotel) to this tiny little British island off of the edge of Sicily called Malta.

Like a doctor going in for their own surgery, it is amazing to watch military Aircrewmen fly commercially. It's as if they must put aside everything that they have been taught and surrender their fate to the hands of someone else. They are probably some of the only passengers who actually pay attention during the flight-attendant's safety lesson. Before Aircrewmen pick up their magazine to read, they have already scoped out their evacuation routes, made a plan as to what they are grabbing and who goes first. They have already looked out the window and checked the flap position, checked the engines for any leaks and the wings for any cracks or loose bolts. They have also checked out any other aircraft activity within view and will continue to monitor. They cannot help themselves.

Once our mental preflight checks 4.0 (perfect), and safety procedures have been noted, it is not uncommon for us to drift off. To this day, I get the best sleep of my life on planes and in MRIs (magnetic resonance imaging). As soon as engines start turning, it's like I'm being cradled like a baby being lulled to sleep by the sweet hums and gentle vibrations. It is near impossible to stay awake - even if I am completely rested. Usually as an acoustic operator, our time to shine was when we arrived on-station. So if it's two in the morning, more than likely, we're going to grab a half hour nap on transit if possible, so that we are well rested upon arriving on-station. I don't even try to fight it anymore.

During the flight, if aircrewmen are awake, we do not tense up when there is turbulence. Instead, it is a cue to glance out the window to ensure it is weather related, vice engine difficulties. Once it's assuredly weather, the familiarity of being yanked around is almost comforting, like the rolls of the sea to a sailor.

And when the landings come, the checklist in our head begins to fire off as soon as we feel our initial descent. We'll judge the angle of the descent, the changing pressurization, and the cloud ceiling to estimate our time of arrival. As soon as we hear the engine speeds shift, we wait for the sounds of the flaps to lower. Upon our approach, we always listen for the landing gear to go down. A most vital element to a proper landing.

We will be critical of the angle at which the pilot is approaching, and how he or she is handling the crosswinds and pitch. Our stomachs tense as we brace for impact, and do not relax until we have "weight on wheels." Then of course perform a mental critique of the landing. Some are good and effortless, and some smash the tarmac so hard, we assess they will inevitably need a hard landing inspection.

Thankfully, we survived yet another commercial flight. We safely arrived in Malta. As Chief would say, "We cheated death yet again."

First stop, baggage claim. Now, I have bags of all shapes and sizes, but for some reason, I didn't seem to have a bag that was just big enough for weekend luggage. So, for this I had borrowed a bag from Janessa.

You can imagine my surprise when everyone on my flight, including my guys, grabbed their bags up in seconds. Mine seemed to have been at the very pits of the plane belly, or so I assumed. After 15 minutes or so (which is a really long time when you're waiting) I began to grow anxious. *Okay, this is no big deal. Worst case scenario I have to buy some more clothes. I have a Visa. It could be fun... Yeah, right.* I love shopping just as much as the next person, but that's not how I wanted to spend the first day of my two-day vacation - shopping for underwear and toiletries.

I knew at this point the guys were starting to worry too. Chief remarked, "Why *yours*? Anyone of us really could care less- we'd just wear our same clothes all weekend." This was unfortunately true.

At this time, there were only two bags left on the rotating belt. One was a typical black suitcase with wheels; the other was a bright blue duffle bag. Big Lovin', being the kind and organized soul he is, decided to take action and began putting in a request at baggage claim. I described my bag again for him and he left.

"Are you sure neither one of those bags are yours?" Chief asked.

"No," I replied, getting impatient. "My bag is GREEN."

"Many bags look alike," Chief began. I looked over at him to see him reading a sign above the baggage carrousel. "Please check to ensure that you have retrieved all of your own belongings and compare your claim check numbers before leaving this area. This area is under electronic surveillance."

"Are you *sure* it's not this one?" LT Farr walked up and asked.

"No, Sir. My bag is *green*! It's a duffle bag about this big..." I motioned the sized. The blue bag that lay unclaimed on the rotating belt inched by us again. "It's just like that one there - same size and shape except it's not blue, it's..." My voice trailed off as I began to think to myself. *Wait - was it blue? I was sure it was green. It was awfully dark when I packed this morning.* "Well... it could be blue, I suppose..."

I felt my face get warm as I realized my error. I'm sure anyone could've made the same mistake. "Yes! I remember - it's blue. Quick! Grab that bag!"

I felt the heat of Chief's glare on my back, but pretended not to notice. "I'm sorry guys - it's not my bag, its Janessa's that I'm borrowing, so I guess I just forgot the color." I was trying to dig my way out of wasting the last 20 minutes looking for my bag that must have circled before us about 2 dozen times. Someone yelled for Big Lovin', letting everyone in the airport that was within ear-shot know of my humbling error.

"Many bags look alike..." Chief began in a robotic voice as he turned and walked away. I felt my face redden even more. Still, I couldn't help but feel relief as I picked up my wretched bag, trailing the guys due to the shortness of my legs. Stupid blue bag.

Cease the Night

We spent the evening touring around the island, visiting many shops. The streets were bustling and only grew busier as the night went on. Our greatest discovery, however, was a dingy Irish pub and karaoke bar. After much beer and debating, we eventually all took our turns on the microphone. LT Farr, who had way too many tequila sunrises (because they were half price), led the way on the microphone. Then each and every one took their turns.

Now, in my short years, I have flown over Bosnia and had various other "exciting" missions. I've even delivered a child without drugs, but I would have to say that singing in public was one of the scariest things I've ever done. I sang "Angel of the Morning." I even established a fan in the audience - some guy that didn't speak English, but kept repeatedly shouting my name. I still am not sure if I really sucked or not, because all of the guys dutifully said what a great job I did. Honestly, we all probably sucked that night - but I've never had so much fun sucking. You know what I mean.

After a night full of singing, people were also dancing on a cramped tiled floor crunched in between the booths and the bar. All of a sudden, they began playing an awesome swing song - the toe-tapping, finger popping kind that you just can't sit still while listening to. I'm not sure who's idea it was - probably the Guinness's. Somehow my TACCO, Stimpy, and I got up there and began to dance. I have no idea how to swing dance, but I learned that night with a great partner leading you, anyone can do it. And that's just how it went. We danced our little butts off and had a ball. Of course, it was all followed by a standing ovation… by a bunch of drunken Irishmen.

Later, we all went back to the hotel that night exhausted, but happy. Well, most of us went back to the hotel - some didn't quite make it. Some ended up wandering the streets all night because they forgot where their room was. Chief wandered aimlessly claiming, "I have no home" to whoever would listen. Many felt sorry for this poor, homeless man, not realizing his true circumstances. He woke up on a park bench with a cup full of change next to him.

Thankfully, by late morning we found him and all toured the island in school buses that looked like they came directly out of the 1950s. They were as unique as the island itself. There were historical traces from World War II, as the British troops occupied various forts and depended on the island's strategic location. The Maltese history was abundant in all of the shops as well. I'm just not sure at what point it became such a party, touristy island. The weekend was a wonderful short break from the monotony of the flight schedule. I had initially been hesitant to go, welcoming a free weekend of relaxing in my barracks. However, I'm so happy I took the opportunity to see a new place. I learned that weekend to never pass up an opportunity to travel, to sing, or to dance. I also learned the value of luggage tags and have used them ever since.

Turkey.

Approximate distance from Deer River: 5700 miles

The first night we arrived in Turkey was on a weekday night, fairly late in the evening when most shops and restaurants in the area had already shut down. Now if you haven't figured it out yet, Big Lovin' was a man of resources. He was the kind of guy that if things weren't happening, he would make them happen. That man could convince a one-legged man to climb Mt. Everest on Flag Day. Additionally, there wasn't anything he couldn't find. I'd be willing to wager Big Lovin' could find a hamburger at a McDonalds in India.

His family was native to Maine or "God's country" as he likes to call it, and they have lived there for generations. He knew the area like the back of his hand. All I had to do was to tell him I had a craving for a steak - and I'm looking for a relaxed atmosphere and somewhat authentic, rustic. He would then reply, "I know just the place. Have you been to Mac's Grill in Auburn? They have 24 marinades and will let you sample them all if you'd like!"

He always knew "just the place." I may have to drive an hour on some gravel roads in northern Maine, but I will be steered in the direction of a perfect little restaurant that no one has ever even heard of except the locals. This guy was all about the love. And food. I never had to go without candy when Big Lovin' was around - and that is important.

He was also the kind of guy that would give you the shirt off his back in a blizzard if you needed it to clean off your windshield. He was an officer that is true to himself and only ever led with his heart and the best interest of the people working for him. He has since become a Commanding Officer (CO) of an entire squadron. I can imagine he was probably one of the best COs that ever existed.

So, naturally on that wary night in which CAC-9 arrived in Turkey, there was nothing that sounded more appealing than a nice, cold beer. And perhaps some music. Music always makes beer taste better. So when we arrived at our resort, Big Lovin' instructed us all to shower and change and he would find just the place for us. In the Turkey countryside. On a Wednesday nearing 2300.

So we did as instructed while he did talking, wheeling and dealing. We all met up soon after and piled into an old van furnished by the resort? Honestly, I still have no clue where the van came from.

We drove and drove on some more one-donkey roads in this foreign country where even the donkeys didn't understand English. The van eventually came to a stop at the top of a hill where in the darkness, we could somewhat make out a building made of stones in a somewhat barn-like fashion. In fact, I was pretty sure it had been a barn at one time. It was at the top of a hill in the middle of the city of Nowhere, Turkey.

As the driver got out, the door of the barn opened, and a Turkish man, dressed simply and dark, emerged. The two exchanged words and soon the driver was waving us to come hither. So forth we proceeded into the structure.

As soon as we entered some disco music came on, almost winding up, from one of the boxes in the corner. It had to have been music from the 70s era, though I didn't recognize it as the Turkish men attempted to set the 'barn-turned-club' atmosphere. So, hearing the music, seeing 'dance floor' surrounded by about four tables and chairs that lead up to the wooden bar, we made like any good Sailors and bellied up to the bar. Drinks were passed around. It was a native beer of some sorts called Effes. Didn't matter - it was cold.

So Big Ol', Rugged, Deena, and I were sitting on one side of the bar, enjoying our drinks, when all of a sudden the song changed and something new and groovy came on.

Out of nowhere, Big Lovin' ran out onto the dance floor with astonishing eagerness. Now, realizing we had just gotten there, and I hadn't ever seen Big Lovin' get too jiggy with it until well into the night, we were all very surprised by this. Maybe it was the exhilaration of the night. Maybe it was the perfect song. But in those few seconds he busted out moves that would make MTV weep with joy. You know, back when they had music on the network. His arms were flying in the air like he just didn't care and his legs were kicking as he twisted and turned, keeping perfect time to the music. We were all unbelievably impressed. Perhaps this was why he was so excited to come out tonight. Had he been practicing these new moves?

It wasn't but seconds later when Stimpy came running out and joined Big Lovin' on the dance floor. The rhythm must have gotten him too, because you'd never seen such a pair go at it! We were all nodding and waving as we watched them shake their thing. As we continued to enjoy the scene, LT Burke came running as the others had, but this time coming towards us, screaming at the top of his lungs, "BEES! THERE ARE BEES EVERYWHERE!"

He ran past us, and the other two followed out the door. As if on cue, Rugged and Big Ol' looked at each other with fright in their eyes for a second before they took off running with myself, Deena, and the Turkish guys following immediately behind.

Luckily, the swarm of bees were able to be contained within the barn-club, as we all narrowly escaped with our lives. Big Lovin' and Stimpy escaped with only minor injuries. After that, it was pretty safe to say we were out of luck with other barn-clubs to crash, so we accepted this and became satisfied with the idea of returning to our hotel bar for the night.

Violated

The resort we stayed at in Turkey happened to be a German resort. It was gorgeous with beautiful beaches along on the Mediterranean Sea. Each night there was a buffet with every kind of food you could imagine - Mediterranean favorites, French cuisine, Italian foods, pork, beef, salads, and an entire table devoted to desserts. The European culture was much more similar to the American culture than the Turkish was. I quickly learned that though I spoke "English" - when local vendors asked if I was English, I quickly replied with, "No, I am American." This caused their faces to light up like I had just given them a plate full of chocolate cupcakes (the good kind - with vanilla filling). In their minds, Americans= money. And most often, it was true (according to their standards). While the English in these parts have a bit of ill history - you know, invading all of the countries they can - Americans love to spend their money, and by those standards, I was very American. Besides, taking over countries was so not my style.

When the crews weren't flying, they were either shopping out in town, "American, my friend, my friend, come to my shop! I have 'specially for you." Or they could be found back at the resort often angering the European guests at the resort by jumping into the pool after playing beach volleyball and covered with sand, "Damn Yankees! Get out of the bloody pool! You're full of bloody sand!" (Note: The English make the situation sound so much worse than it was - the pool was *not* bloody and it was just sand, *not* bloody sand.)

While all of this was going on, I decided to slip away one afternoon and do something 'girly.' The resort had their own spa and I had always wanted to get a facial - to see what it was all about. So I made an appointment.

The lady that I was assigned to for my treatment was German and spoke very broken English and since I only knew how to ask permission to use the bathroom in German, our conversation was very limited. However, we could figure out most things through demonstration as she showed me how to secure the robe under my armpits and pointed to the changing room.

When she began, I quickly learned that she had magical fingers that massaged every muscle in my face. I had no idea how wonderful something like that could be - or how many muscles that needed attention in my face. The time passed by and I was in a heavenly state as she put oils and potions all over my face and cucumber scented bags over my eyes. I could not see a thing, but only hear women's voices conversing in another language. Soon she began to massage down my shoulders - and then, before I realized what was happening, she moved my robe down, exposing my bare chest to whoever was in that room at that time. As I still had the bags on my eyes, I had no idea.

I began to internally panic, but did not move a muscle. She continued the massage over my exposed lady parts and I froze - unsure of what to do. I mean, these were Europeans. Exposed breasts are as common to them as pickles on cheeseburgers. I just usually preferred to keep my pickles concealed - especially after the Tunisian incident. Additionally, I never had a facial before - so I really wasn't sure if this was just how they were done everywhere. I was so confused. I had no idea what to do. *Was I being violated?*

After a few minutes she placed my robe back to its proper position and began to wash the oils off my face. Eventually she removed my eye covers and the facial was completed. I smiled awkwardly, as I had never gone to second base with a woman before and wasn't sure what to do next. I quickly tipped her and retreated back to my room. It was that day that I learned that European spas are not like American spas.

It was a cool, but humid night. The salty smell of the sea misted through the air. Otis Redding's *These Arms of Mine* could be heard playing in the night air. We sat around a Cabana table, listening to the waves crash to the slow rhythm of the music. The wind blew a chill up my spine, despite the humid night air and I felt sadness and tranquility simultaneously, almost transformed into another time. I thought of Aaron and the wedge that was growing between us. I felt smothered. He felt me slipping away and tried to hold on tighter. Instead of communicating, I pushed it out of my mind - if I didn't allow myself to think about my problems, I didn't have to be saddened over them. And so I kept going. And kept pushing him away.

I wanted to numb my mind, to not have to feel this heavy sadness anymore. As time went on, the drinks became plentiful. Our crew gleefully danced with the Turkish. They were wild rendezvous drinkers who danced even more carefree than crazy American Sailors. Our new favorite Turk was named Ufuk Tuna which we deemed the coolest name we had ever heard. Of course, Big Lovin' was able to talk him out of his name patch before the end of the trip and wore it proudly as his own. The off-duty crews were all laughing and having a wonderful celebration.

Deena and I sat next to the bar together. Suddenly another 'perfect song' came on and I had to resist the urge to dance on my barstool.

"No, no. I am not letting my Sensor One break her leg tonight," Deena said in her usual bossy tone.

"Ugh, fine," I replied all dramatically. She always thought I was much more drunk than I was because I did things sober that most people did after they had a six pack.

"What's the deal with dancing on the barstool anyways? Explain to me the desire - because I don't understand it." She said with a smile and a practical tone.

"I'm just short. It's a portable mini-stage, I suppose."

"Hmmm. Okay, I can see that." She analyzed the stool.

Deena was ten years older than me and mentioned it often. She was my usual SS-3 for the Sicily deployment and it was the first time I had another girl on my crew. It was actually quite refreshing. Finally I had someone I could talk with about 'girly' things such as shopping and make-up- though she didn't really like either one of those things. She had a heart of gold, with a guarded exterior. She had to for survival in the Navy. Her mother was Swedish and she grew up in Sweden, visiting her American dad often until she ended up joining the American Navy in her 20s. She had cross-rated (changed jobs) to AW from the ship so she was ship-tough. She later went on to become the second female AW chief in the Navy. It didn't take long for her to become my big sister - always looking out for me, as I did my best to break down her serious walls. But every once in a while I could pull her crazy side out.

I could tell she was getting a little tipsy that night as her accent, usually non-existent, would become slightly noticeable. As she drank more, she would begin blending her words, making Swedish words American by adding an "er" to the end of them and other random letters.

"Kan jab be att fe en Effes?" She asked the Turkish bartender as she brushed her striking black hair over her shoulder, unaware of her beauty. It was rare she drank beer, so I figured she had been drinking for awhile now and the taste didn't matter to her anymore. The bartender looked at her with a blank stare.

"Please Effies?" He asked and pointed to the Turkish beer. He knew Turkish, and he knew broken English - and probably some German. Unfortunately, he did not know Swedish.

When she got to the point where no one understood her, it was her signal for bed. I had only seen phase three one other time before. This was one of those nights.

"No Effes," I waved him off. "We go home now." I smiled and helped my friend down. We walked past the pool where there was a group of people skinny dipping. On the way to Deena's room I talked her out of swimming naked, riding a donkey, and keeping a stray chicken as a pet. As I dropped her off, she made me promise I would go directly to my room safely.

"Ciao panini!" She said to me as I left.

"Goodbye, sandwich, to you too, my dear," I smiled and closed the door behind me.

Somewhere in there I must have forgotten the going back to my room part, because after I dropped her off, I continued to walk along a path back to the dance floor. Somewhere in there I also must have got lost, because I came to some sort of stable where one of the other flight engineers, John, was so kindly sharing his beer with one of the donkeys. It was very random. Suddenly, some turkeys ran across the path in front of me. I laughed out loud at the situation. John and his drunk ass, and turkeys running around in Turkey. It was all so surreal and it was all so hilarious in the moment. I felt like I was in some strange music video.

As I walked further down the road and outside of the resort gates, everyone was chilling out nearby at another cabana bar. Suddenly, Big Ol' came busting out from a shop across the street wearing only a bikini. This was not a pretty sight, as he is a hairy man. He stopped to strike a pose for us all as the shopkeeper came running up behind him.

"You forgot pay! American, you no pay!" I'm not sure what possessed Big Ol' to run, but he began zigzagging in the empty street. The shopkeeper ran after him chasing him. It was the funniest sight. Soon, one of the crewmembers decided this could be a liberty risk and thought the easiest thing to do would be to go over to the man and pay for the bikini. Big Ol' was able to keep the bikini, though I believe he lost it later that night. All was well and we all went back to drinking our beer, not blinking an eye. Sometimes, when I attempt to make sense of those random nights, my head just begins to hurt and I am forced to give up. I just smile.

That Night

During this time in Sicily, my career seemed to flourish. I had advanced in rank, I had passed my board and was promoted to Sensor One, I had been selected for the award "Blue Jacket of the Month," and I was now up for a Junior Operator of the Year nomination. I was flying like a mad woman and traveling to multiple countries and 'living it up.' Things couldn't have been better. Except for one thing. While I was consumed with my career, my relationship with Aaron was slowly falling apart.

I was caught up in the things that weren't really important. I was drinking way too much and having fun with my friends and/or anyone who would party with me. We were overseas and flying round the clock. My world had become a new one - one that I didn't recognize anymore. I had lost touch with reality. Soon I was drinking every chance I could when I wasn't within a 'window' for flying. I was clubbing and thought I was having the time of my life. I was getting attention from random guys and instead of being smart about it - I was letting it go to my head.

It all began catch up with me. Aaron and I fought all of the time. He wanted a 'normal relationship.' I felt he was holding me back. From what, I wasn't sure. We broke up and got back together repeatedly throughout the majority of the deployment. It was a lot for a relationship to take. I began to lose sight of who I was. I made dumb decisions. I began making out with random people, and I started dressing like a tramp. Well, a tramp by small-town Minnesota standards. I bared my midriff. Sometimes I would wear shirts that you could see my bra through. It was scandalous. And on more than one occasion, as I danced upon a speaker, I flashed my bra to the crowd. I had become a bra-flashing, make-out whore. And though I never went "all the way" with anyone - people began to talk. Suddenly I felt like everything I had worked so hard to accomplish - my position, and respect from others was quickly diminishing. Attention from boys began to dictate my self-esteem.

During one of our break-ups, I went on a big binge drinking spree. I was making out with some random guy from the club and Jenessa walked in on us. She lost it. She laid into me about what I was becoming and how disappointed she was because she knew I was better than that. She was cruel with her words, as nothing is crueler than the truth. And although she was right - I didn't want to hear it.

I was angry and defensive and found myself running away. It was all I knew how to do- keep running when things got bad. Drink and immerse myself in things that didn't matter. I just had to get away and I didn't care what happened. I was so alone in a sea full of sailors that were fighting for my attention. So I knocked on the barracks door of the only person that I really wanted to speak to - the one that wasn't fighting for it anymore.

It was in the middle of the night and Aaron came to the door in his pajama bottoms, eyes squinting in the light. I asked him if he'd go on a walk with me and without asking questions, he grabbed his shirt and came with me.

The Sicilian moonlight lit up our path that night. I began to ramble on and on about how my life had fallen to the bottom of the barrel and all of the stupid decisions I had made. Hours went by. Aaron just listened. I told him how badly I missed him. He was the one that held me to higher standards. I wanted to be a better person when I was with him.

Finally, when I didn't think I could cry any more we just sat there in silence. Aaron often took time to formulate his replies. All I could do was just cringe, waiting for what he would say in return. I had just admitted all of my faults and mistakes that I had made. And there I stood, feeling naked, vulnerable. I had never let my guard down so much before in my life and he knew it.

And then he said something I wasn't expecting.

"I love you. I've always loved you, Julia." He put his arm around me and kissed my forehead.

"Stop. How can you possibly love me? I'm a disaster."

"Because you're my best friend. You've just lost your way. And I know the real you that's inside of this disaster. I know you better than you know yourself."

"That's not true," I sniffed.

"It is true," he said with a smile. "And no one could possibly love you as much as I do." He kissed me softly. "You need to stop this now. It's done. If you want to be together, you need to choose between your partying or us. You can't have both."

"I choose us," I said quietly.

"You promise?" he asked.

"I promise."

I felt the night air swirling around us as we stood still in that moment in time - the moment he rescued me from my depths of despair. I was not alone. I never had to be alone again.

A few nights later we were once again on American soil as our deployment came to an end. He hadn't given up on me despite how many times I had tried pushing him away. I had no idea why he loved me as much as he did. I didn't feel as though I deserved it.

I had missed everything about us. Even the messy stuff. Up until this point, I had never been in a real 'adult' relationship. It had started off as a fairy tale, as they all do. But then things got messy- they got real. It took effort every day. I had thought that was the sign of a problem and ran away. But he was still there.

I'd like to say that at this point we fell madly into each other's arms and spent our days and nights together, giving each other back massages, and feeding each other grapes. But that didn't really happen. We fought. And then we would make-up. A few days later we would fight again and he would dramatically throw my new pillows off the deck. But for the first time in my life I was actually communicating with someone, and working through our problems instead of politely moving on.

He still leaves his dirty clothes on the floor. But now when I see them on the floor, I know we are together, and I smile because I am happy. And then I yell.

CHAPTER 13

Phippsburg, ME.

August 2000

Approximate distance from Deer River: 1407 miles

American Soil! I loved everything about it. Er- America, that is. Not necessarily the dirt. Though dirt is important. Back at the end of January of 2000, we were the first crew to leave for deployment and were the last crew to come home in the second week of August 2000. It was the longest I had ever been out of my country. I had no idea what the new songs were or what the latest TV shows or movies were. Granted I had only been in Europe, but I felt as though I had been living on another planet. I was even excited to see American commercials, as the only ones I had been exposed to for 6 ½ months were AFRTS (Armed Forces Radio and Televisions Stations) - 'A-Farts' as we liked to call them. There were no advertising on them, so the 'commercial breaks' during the reruns that we watched consisted of another sailor telling you why you should go to the Chaplin if you're feeling the blues or come hang out at the base bowling alley on Friday night Karaoke night if you feel like singing the blues. At last I could laugh again at every commercial with the Budweiser Frogs - or the ones making fun of the Y2K millennium scare when everyone thought all of the computers would freeze up and society would have to revert back to the Wild West Cowboy days.

I laughed at every show. I ate American food and smiled at everyone. Even the scary looking guy that worked at the 7/11. The Dunkin' Donuts lady looked at me like I was crazy. It may have had something to do with me shaking her and shouting, "Aren't you so happy that we live in America!?" And then I bought a round of doughnuts for everyone.

Everything made me happy. Everything, except ungrateful people. When someone complained about their situation, I really went from being Barney the Purple Dinosaur that loved everyone - to Jeffery Dahmer - the one that wanted to eat everyone. Or just slap them. It was quite confusing - and I didn't even have

289

a 'family' dynamic situation to readjust to, as many of my crewmembers went through as expected.

Instead, I had Aaron - who was feeling all the same feelings. He was much more reserved about his happiness than I was. It takes a lot to make that man outwardly excited. Usually it involves fishing or hunting. Then he will scream like a little girl.

We decided to move in together during this next home cycle and found a cozy little (1.25) bedroom home in Phippsburg, Maine. The second bedroom/desk/dryer room would not allow the door to open all the way when there was a queen sized bed in it. There was a kitchen and a living room and two closets (in the whole house). The coffee table also acted as our dining room table. It was just the two of us, so really we didn't need any more room than this house offered. We barely had enough furniture to fill this house. It was more than we had ever dreamed of having.

At last we were beginning to feel like 'real people' living in a real house instead of the barracks. We wore our uniform to work but wore 'real clothes' on the weekends. On the weekends, I would paint my nails crazy colors and wear my hair past my shoulders. I was wild like that.

Every morning on my way to work, I had the privilege of seeing the sun rise over the water in an ocean inlet. I kept track of the tide schedule based on the water level and could tell if our flight was going to be able to go or not, based on if I awoke to the sounds of a foghorn. It was only a fifteen-minute drive to the beach. I loved leaving my windows open, allowing the cool, salty autumn air inside. I began to fall in love with New England in a way I had never seen it before.

We lived down the most beautiful country road with only a few neighbors in sight - including our landlord, Martha. Martha was our friendly and slightly crazy landlord. She was in her mid-50s, partially retired, and alone so she took care of her beautiful home and our small house that she rented out for extra income. She loved life and every soul in it - animal and person alike. She had lived in Maine her entire life and as a result hated to be indoors. We could always find her working around the yard that was surrounded by woods with her German Shepherds following closely behind her.

Martha loved to talk for hours with her friends. Every month when we had to pay the rent, we had to specifically set aside at least an hour, because we were not getting out of there in anything less. She made a wicked-good seafood chowder and could shell three lobsters in less than a minute. She said funny things like 'door yard' for a driveway and never pronounced an 'R.' When she asked you to give her a 'fork,' we could never contain our laughter. Martha became our mom away from our moms.

The next year our squadron spent preparing for the next tri-site deployment. Our tri-site consisted of Iceland and Puerto Rico. It used to include Panama, but in the year 2000, the hundred year-old contract deal that was made between Panama and the United States military for the property that the base was on was completed. Apparently back in the year 1900 when they signed it, they probably thought that the world would end in the year 2000. [Old American General be like - ha ha - jokes so on them! We're all going to die in 2000.] And because old habits die hard (like a zombie with a small head wound), we still called the dual deployment site a 'tri-site' deployment.

The year was spent doing crew work-ups and trainings to prepare us. And as the circle of life goes on, the 'elders' moved on and the youngers moved up. I became a crew-holding Sensor 1 and received a new Sensor 2. Burke and Big Lovin' moved on to new duty stations and Algae became the new PPC (Patrol Plane Captain) and Stimpy the new TACCO. The three of us - all the junior guys - had now moved to be the senior ones. And the best part? I was no longer the plane bitch, solely in charge of dumping the pisser after doing it exclusively for two years. Still it was painful to say goodbye to men who had become my brothers. I took comfort in knowing what a small P-3 world it was and that I knew we were bound to see each other again. I had to believe it.

Navy Jokes

Being in the military and practical jokes are just something that go together hand-in-hand, like a kayak and a paddle. Beer and hot wings. Strippers and poles. Junior people are very raw and trusting, as they should be. Therefore, it is inevitable that the senior sailors are going to take advantage of their virtue. Some people take a while to learn the ropes (myself), and a few just don't ever quite grasp the rope.

There were the typical jokes - asking a nugget to run and grab someone a can of A-1R solution, (a can of air), or to go into Maintenance and ask for some 'flight line.' They would send someone out on the deck with a sonobuoy to run all over the place to do OTPI checks (On Top Position Indicator), or just screw with the 3-P (junior pilot) in flight by running up and down the tube when he is trying to level the plane out - unable to figure out why it was resisting.

Once the AW shop sent a new guy with a 'Pad-Eye Remover' out on the flight line to remove all of the Pad-eyes. Pad-eyes are large hooks that are cemented right into the flight line. Heavy chains secure and connect the aircraft to them. This makes any movement while the plane is parked (often in inclement weather) intentionally impossible. The poor guy must have stood out on the flight line with some awkward tool trying to remove the pad-eyes all day before someone let him in on the joke. He somehow just couldn't see the humor in the situation. That was the day I learned that AWs eat their own.

I had been forewarned early on to watch my back. I did my best to. However, that did not necessarily mean that I wasn't as gullible as the next new guy - it was likely that I was much more. I was simply trusting and gave people the benefit of the doubt. Listen to me. I'm still making excuses.

On the day that went down in history as my most embarrassing moment of my life, I just so happened to be on duty as the ASDO. (Assistant Squadron Duty Officer) Go figure. It seems like so many of my stories begin there. It had been one of those days from hell on this particular day of duty. We had construction workers in and out of the building that we had to constantly escort and answer their requests on top of our normal obligations. The SDO left me in charge of the office on various occasions throughout the day, as he went to put out all of the fires.

Due to a few extensive circumstances, I was reluctantly forced to speak on the 1MC (the loud-speaker that is broadcasted throughout the entire building).

Talking on the 1MC was not as much of a regular occurrence, and is normally saved for special circumstances. Being the self-proclaimed horrible public speaker that I am, I found myself planning every teensy detail of any particular announcement I had to make so I could just read it off as I was speaking - to prevent any mistakes. After I had done this a couple of times, I began to get better at it and began to let my guard down. Soon, it almost became second nature. I got a little big for my britches. Therefore, when I received an emergency phone call requesting one of the construction workers immediately, I didn't hesitate for a second to make the timely announcement. This time I did not write it down first.

It was on that day that I, a well-respected second class petty officer in the Navy, requested over the loud speaker, in front of all of my peers and co-workers, for a "Mike Hunt" to come to the duty office. And not just once, but a second time as I repeated myself, "Mike Hunt to the duty office," just to make sure everyone heard. [If you still don't understand the significance of this sentence, you may have to read it aloud - but please for the love of god, be wary of your surroundings.]

And then…a deafening silence fell throughout the building. This place that was just seconds before bustling like a fish market in Japan on a Sunday came to a screeching halt. It froze in time and became so deathly silent, you could hear nothing but the clock ignorantly continuing to tick on the wall. Everyone in the spaces took approximately five seconds to process the information they had just heard. And then - it was as if a grenade had just gone off down the hallways with all of the explosions of laughter. All hell broke loose, and all you could hear from the office spaces and hallways was an uncontainable explosion of laughter. And yet, I still had no clue what had just happened. I went back to my paperwork.

Seconds later, both Stimpy (the SDO) and Algae, the pilot on duty, came rushing in. Stimpy was shouting, "Who told you to say that!? WHO told you to say that!?!"

At the same time Algae, my pilot, was yelling, "WHAT DID YOU SAY? WHAT DID YOU JUST SAY!?!"

I just sat there for a second, completely perplexed. *Why were they yelling at me? What just happened?* Sensing my confusion, Algae leaned closer as he spoke slowly and simply for me. "Think. About. It."

As I repeated the sentence to myself in my head, quietly, the horror struck me like someone had just slapped a wet noodle across my face. My jaw dropped as I clasped my hands over my mouth. *It was a joke! I was set up!*

"Ohmygod. Ohmygod. Ohmygod," was all I could fester. I looked up at Stimpy with terror on my face. "What am I going to do?!?"

Never have I been more mortified in my life than I was in that second. I would *never* have said a word like that - let alone over a 1MC in front of my entire squadron. There wasn't an emergency! I picked up the receiver that lay off the hook on my desk and held it to my ear. Of course, it was dead. I was still stunned. *Who would have set me up like that?* I mean, admittedly, it was impressively horrible!

Stimpy and I spent the rest of the day trying to undo the damage and explain the situation to every member of the squadron that thought they should poke their noggin into the duty office just to have another laugh. We also spent the entire day trying to pinpoint who the guilty, anonymous caller could have been.

Eventually, it was determined that an itty-bitty nugget, fresh to the squadron was put up to it by a few of the guys in my shop. One might say he and I got off on the wrong foot. I later learned he went off to become a pilot, and a pretty good one at that. So I would like to say I am very happy for the little bastard. Mostly.

"Hey! Where have you been?" Deena asked.

"I just got back from lunch," I replied. "Why, what's up?"

"Did you get a chance to say goodbye to Chief?" Deena asked. "I know he was looking for you."

"No, I thought he wasn't leaving until tomorrow."

"No... he checked out this morning. I think he left already," she said in her usual matter-of-fact tone.

My heart dropped. *I didn't even get to say goodbye.*

"Go check in the Maintenance Office. They could tell you if he's around yet or not, but I'm pretty sure he's gone."

I opened the hangar doors and walked swiftly down the hangar bay, trying not to get upset. No matter how hard I tried, I could never contain my emotions.

Suddenly the doors to Maintenance opened up and Chief stood there in his flight suit with his backpack slung over his shoulder and helmet bag in the other hand. "Hey!" he called out. "I was looking for you!"

"Yeah, Deena said you had already left."

"Well I'm about to. Can't wait to get out of this hell hole," he said with a rare half smile.

"What are you talking about? You're going to miss this place so much."

"Yeah. Maybe a little."

I shrugged my shoulders and tried not to look sad. Our whole crew was leaving and everything was changing. I still wasn't used to this sort of thing. Chief had taught me so much about the Navy. How to fuel and do weights and balances. That you never leave a man behind. That the best kind of beer was free. And the second best kind of beer was cold. The three biggest lies were the duty driver is on his way, and guys will call you in the morning and... The list went on and on.

"Well good luck to you, I guess."

"Thanks kid," he said with a smile. "I'll miss you. You've come a long way," he nodded, as if to reinforce his thoughts. "You know, not many AWs take the time to learn how to take fuel samples."

I smiled.

"You're doing good. Keep it up. And stay out of trouble, ya hear?"

"Yes, Chief."

"I'm pretty proud of you," he said and smiled a full, real smile.

And just then the seas parted and the rays of the Almighty shown down from the sky to signal the end of the world. Just kidding. That didn't really happen. But it may as well have. I never, in all my life imagined that those words were capable of being uttered from those lips that were usually pinched in a bitter-at-the-world frown. I thought of showing my shock, or acting dramatically surprised. But instead I just hugged him goodbye. Because I was going to miss seeing his grumpy face and foul mouth every day. And I realized I probably wouldn't have come out of these past couple of years alive if it weren't for this hard-to-please man. I owed him everything for that.

Enlightenment

The night was slow and dramatically drawn out like a cat yawn. I sat at my desk, spinning my pen with my right hand. I hated silence and the night shift caused silences so loud that one could count the seconds ticking away at the clock that clung to the pale brick wall across the room.

At last the Duty Officer returned to his desk adjacent to mine after making his rounds. I nearly jumped at the opportunity for some conversation. I flooded him with questions about his upcoming plans for the weekend. It soon evolved into talking about his children. I enjoyed listening as much as storytelling. Almost.

The time began to pass much quicker. An hour. Another. Pretty soon we took a stab at current world events. I couldn't help but get excited as I do when my passion about a subject leaks out. My opinions and viewpoints poured on out like a rambling brook. In turn, I listened intently to his. Another hour passed. I felt refreshed. Cultural stimulation at its finest in the wee morning hours.

Then, he crossed his arms across his chest and leaned back in his chair. He frowned and cocked his head to the side and said the words I would never forget.

"Petty Officer Maki, you're a smart girl." He paused, and I was about to thank him when I sensed there was more to come. "Why are you enlisted?"

Enlisted. The word was spoken like a foul taste in his mouth. Had I heard him correctly? *Don't react. Don't react.*

I answered slowly, carefully choosing my words. "You… think… I enlisted because I wasn't smart enough to go to college?"

"I said you were smart, but isn't that why most people enlist in the military instead of going to college?" His demeanor was as casual as a Sunday picnic. It was why I had previously let my guard down.

My fists began to clench. "No, Sir." I was nearly whispering by now. "Actually, my father begged me to go to college up until the day I got on the bus headed for boot camp. He promised to find a way to pay for it. Whatever it took."

I shifted in my chair.

He looked even more perplexed as he considered the thought.

"I enlisted because I wanted to get out there," I continued. "I wanted to see the world and the Navy seemed the easiest and quickest route to do so at the time. I am going to college right now. I just decided to enlist first."

"Oh. Okay." He paused for a moment as he studied my face. "Did I offend you or something?"

I had enough conversation for one night. I began spinning my pen on my desk again, not bothering to look up. "No, Sir. Actually, you enlightened me."

Stitches

I stood outside the bathroom and took a huge gulp of air and raced into the head, as I had limited time. I flung the toilet seat up and unhooked the awkward lid from the plane's portable pisser with my opposite hand. As I lifted the lid, I could feel the warm stench release into the air - despite holding my breath. I turned my head away and poured the dark urine mixture into the toilet, doing my best not to splash. When I really took the time to think about what I was doing, I would gag. With my left foot I reached up and flushed the toilet and quickly resealed the lid. I quickly ran out of the bathroom, proud that I had made it the whole time holding my breath. I was a rock star at holding my breath these days.

I brought the pisser back to the aircraft head that I had adorned with perfume page inserts from my Cosmopolitan magazine in attempt to deodorize the place. It was a failed attempt. I quickly vacuumed the plane, threw my SV2 (survival vest) on to bring it back to the PR shop, grabbed the trash, my helmet bag, the pan that I had brought brownies for the crew in and my backpack. I was in a hurry, trying to haul everything at once as I had my first college class of the new semester tonight and was excited that we had landed in time to make it to class. I took three steps down the ladder when I realized my SV2 had caught on the ladder handle. Thankfully, the IFT was standing behind me and observing my predicament, he unhooked my SV2 from the handle.

The next few seconds were somewhat of a slow motion blur and I lost my balance and came crashing down the ladder - approximately a 12-foot drop to the cement flight line below. I couldn't even tell you if I bounced off the steps on the way down or fell directly onto the cement. Somehow though, my helmet flew out of my bag and across the flight line. My plate broke in half, and my chin made direct contact with the cement, creating a huge gash in it. My chin - not the cement. I stood up slowly, dazed and in too much pain to care who saw this time. Blood was dripping all down the front of me. I grabbed my chin to stop the bleeding and Ron, who happened to be on this flight, came running up behind me, grabbing my scattered items.

"Oh my god. Are you alright!?"

"Yeah, yeah. I'm fine. I just need to get a tissue or something for the bleeding." Leaving all my stuff behind, I stumbled into the women's head and began washing my face, picking small rocks out of my chin. It was a smaller gash - just bleeding quite a bit, but manageable. I was able to cover it in tissue and walked back into the hangar to retrieve my gear so I could head out to class - despite the strange daze that I felt.

"Maki, stop- let me look at that." I turned around and Algae was standing there. "You okay?"

"Yeah, really, I'm fine."

"It doesn't look fine," he said peeling off the tissues. The bleeding had already slowed down quite a bit, so I was convinced it wasn't a big deal. "Do you need a ride over to medical?"

"Medical? I have to go to class. It's really not a big deal."

"Class? Are you kidding me? No, you're gonna have to skip it tonight. You need to go to medical."

"Seriously, Sir. It's not that bad. Please, I can't miss class tonight," I pleaded with him.

"I'm sorry - but I won't feel comfortable until you get checked out by medical. That's an order."

"What? An order?" He was pulling rank on me for something like this? *Well I never.* "Do you understand?" He asked, interrupting my thoughts.

"Ughhh. Fine. Yes *Sir.*" I sighed and tried not to sound disrespectful despite being angry. It was a fine line. Like not being allowed to talk back to your parents when you're 20. I couldn't believe I was being forced to go to medical again.

The duty driver ended up driving me and waiting as I received three butterfly stitches. By the time I got back to the hangar to retrieve my gear, the plane had been put to bed and my college class was way over.

As I walked down the hall to the AW shop to grab my bags, I heard a voice call out from one of the officers from another crew. "Petty Officer, you'd better get your hair within regs."

I turned around slowly, with my blood stained flight suit that no doubt smelled of sweat and traces of urine from dumping the pisser. It was true - my hair was falling out of its normal pinned up position and touching my flight suit collar. I looked like hell. My body hurt and was covered in bruises.

"Yes sir," I said with a defeated smile and turned back around. I was pushing my tears back from being disciplined over my effing hair. Because if I didn't smile in that moment, I would have lost my mind and started screaming or crying. I didn't know which would have been worse.

The TORPEX

Every home cycle our crews do all sorts of work-up exercises to prepare for the upcoming deployment. There are various evolutions involved in this process in which the crews are graded. The most impactful one of these is the TORPEX. The TORPEX (Torpedo exercise) is where we track a loud noise source called a SLED and execute our simulated attacks upon the source. Thankfully our crew, CAC-9, was stellar at this and had a perfect streak going from our previous years. Naturally, we knew we were the belles of the ball.

The evolution was a fairly simple one. Fire up the system. Pick one of the lines that are blaring across the display. Put the frequency in auto-tracker since it is so loud. (Unlike real submarine data). Relay the speed and course to the TACCO. Let TACCO perform the attacks as appropriate. It was so simple that a monkey could do it. Any monkey, that is, except for an overly-cocky one that thought she knew everything about catching bananas- er subs.

I thought for sure that I would be better off tracking the frequency line myself rather than rely on the software system to do it for me. I didn't trust it. So I decided to manually track the source myself. And all was going great. I was sending dead-on bearings and calling out perfect course and speeds for quite some time. We were ready to perform our first (and most important attack). Stimpy called out, "Attack on my third now. Now, now, now!" and released the weapon accordingly.

All was great. That is, until I saw on the third "now" a dynamic event occurred and the SLED changed course. Unfortunately, this was time-delayed so our attack was on an incorrect course and speed. Had I used the auto-tracker (as I was advised), the system would have called this event almost immediately and we would have realized it before the attack. Our grade for the event: 2 out of 20. Our crew had failed the evolution. And it was my fault.

That night I went home and locked myself in my bedroom. I wanted to run away. I had caused my crew - my crew that had always had my back - to be the laughing stock of the squadron. *How could I ever face them or anyone in the squadron again?* I, the 'Junior Operator of the Year' award recipient had single-handedly brought my entire crew down with me. No doubt they all despised me right now. I wished they had just yelled at me, but instead we all just silently departed the plane, debriefed, and went home. I had never hated myself so badly than I did in that moment. I cried the ugly cry into my pillow and just laid there for hours feeling sorry for myself.

Suddenly, my phone rang, knocking me out of my trance. "Hello?" I asked, trying to sound as normal as possible.

"Hey Kiddo," my dad's voice greeted me cheerfully. "What's going on?"

"Oh, not much," I sniffed.

"What's wrong?"

"Um, well, I've just had pretty much the worst day of my life. My entire crew failed an evolution because of me. And I have no idea how I'll ever be able to face anyone at work again." I tried to hold the tears back, but it was impossible.

"Aaah. I'm sure it's not that bad."

"Dad, believe me. It's bad. I've never failed so badly before in my life. I can't go back there."

"Well, kid, sometimes... sometimes we just don't come out smelling like a rose." I knew he was trying to make me feel better, however, I don't think anything he would have said could have helped in that moment.

"I know Dad, I just, I can't really talk right now. I'm sorry."

"Okay. But it's going to be okay. I promise. You just need to put one foot in front of the other tomorrow, no matter how badly you want to run away. Just keep going."

I took a deep breath. "I know." It wasn't what I wanted to hear. I wanted him to say, why don't you just go AWOL and come and live with me? You can drive dump trucks for me and live at home. You won't have to see any of those people again.

But he didn't. Instead he simply said, "Alright, Kiddo. Love you."

"Love you too. Bye."

The next morning, it took every ounce of my being to get up, get dressed, and go to work. But I did. I felt the whispers as I walked down the hall. I couldn't make eye contact with anyone. Overhearing casual conversations made me just want to scream. I recalled a time when I used to have casual conversations. Yesterday morning. Now it seemed so ridiculous when there were so many more important things in life to worry about. Like being the laughing stock of my squadron.

Of course, the other AWs thought it was hilarious and immediately made fun of me. Because that's what they do. But it was too soon. I didn't want to hear it. And as the day went on, and they continued to heckle, it slowly became easier to listen to. In fact, I think it would have been so much worse if people didn't state the obvious. "So I heard you bombed the bombing."

"Yep. Pretty much," I said, nodding my head.

"Haha- guess they wouldn't want to send you in if we were being attacked," Whiner remarked.

"Guess not," I replied, straight faced.

"Eh, they'll take everyone they can when we're getting attacked," another interjected.

"Dude - did you see the tits on the girl Dean hooked up with last night?" Whiner asked.

And just like that they moved on. Because that's what humans do.

Our crew was given a second chance to take the test to pass the evolution. On this flight, I used the auto-tracker and [surprise!] we got a perfect score. But the damage had been done and the scores were averaged into each other. Thankfully, our crew had an amazing sense of humor and just embraced it. We ended up designing our crew patch with a huge barn and a torpedo on the ground next to it. (Couldn't hit the broadside of a barn.) And they forgave me. Because that's what humans do.

Anna

About half way through my home cycle, I received the most exciting news. My best friend since second grade, Anna, was accepted into art school in Rockport, Maine. She would be only about an hour away from us. It was amazing to think that both of us Deer River girls would be living so close to each other out on the East Coast.

Working around the inconsistent flight schedule was challenging, but every chance I could get, I would drive up to visit her on the weekends. We were living such separate lives now, but still had the ability to pick up like we never were apart every time we would get together.

If one thought I was a naïve, small-town girl, next to Anna I looked like Lindsey Lohan - but with less eye make-up. Anna was a petite, blond hair, blue-eyed Scandinavian girl with a face full of freckles and a laugh like a chipmunk. A cute chipmunk that is; not a psycho one. She was everyone's friend and often drew in the type of people that wanted to 'protect' her from the world. She was going to school to study black and white photography back when the world still used this crazy thing called film.

For two girls that grew up together, jumping off rope swings into the lake and dancing on the high school dance team together, her world couldn't have been more different than mine. It was full of pot-smoking liberals that wanted to change the world, as most 20-somethings did. While we in the military were out doing counter-narcotic operations, they were back home smoking it. While they were demanding peace, we were sharpening our skills at launching weapons. While they had girls that took pictures of their vaginas and called it art (no exaggeration), we had guys that set "Condition 4" while flying naked except for a helmet. (Again, wish I was exaggerating here.) I often felt like we were Forrest Gump and Jenny when I would go to visit. Only Anna didn't sing naked. Not since elementary school anyways. We fought for peace, and they did peaceful protests. In my opinon, they were both oxymorons. Ironically, underneath it all - we all essentially had the same dream.

One night I went to one of her college parties that they threw on campus (which was actually a collection of old, beautiful Victorian-style New England homes). As I walked into the smoke-filled room and weaved my way through the mellow crowd, I sat on the baby poop-colored davenport next to a few students. The room was an avocado green and the walls looked as if they hadn't been painted in decades. The Grateful Dead was playing on the CD player and everyone was wearing hip-huggers. As the music played on, "*I will get by, I will survive...*" all I could think of was, *holy shit. I'm in the 70s*. I was such a fish out of water, but I had never experienced such a calm gathering in my entire life.

A few weeks later, Anna happened to be visiting me when I decided to return the favor and take her to a Navy party. As we walked in through the doors, we were both instantly greeted with hoots and hollers and kindly invited to do a keg stand. Politely declining, as the line was too long, we continued to walk into the living room in which Guns and Roses were playing "I Used to Love Her, But I Had to Kill Her" so loudly that we could barely hear each other speaking when we were six inches apart. Off to the left a couple of girls were dancing in just their underwear on the coffee table. I made a mental note to join them later. A crowd gathered around the kitchen island that was littered with every type of hard liquor bottle known to man. Seven guys were doing shots alphabetically and if they couldn't find a liquor that started with that letter, they would eat anything they could find around the house that started with that letter. They seemed to be stuck on "T" and when someone shouted Theraflu, (they must have just run out of tequila) I quickly ushered Anna out the back patio. We arrived just in time to watch one of our friends take a running leap through the bonfire with his wife coming up from behind yelling at him to get in the car because he was getting out of control. Key word being "getting."

Off in the distance there were silhouettes of naked bodies skinny dipping in the ocean. Some people had passed out in lawn chairs strewn about, while others were dancing behind them to their own beat. It was a beautiful scene of happy sailors enjoying their off time. My theory was that we didn't get as much off time, so when we did, we had to play three times as hard.

"Thank you so much for bringing me. I will never forget this," Anna said, smiling.

I smiled back, thinking how far I'd come, as this scene didn't even shock me anymore. Instead it just felt comfortable. "Of course. I'm so glad you're here."

Great Flights

Not all of our flights were exciting anti-submarine warfare missions or intelligence missions. Many, many hours were spent going around in circles "in the bounce pattern" as an observer on pilot-trainer flights. These flights usually consisted of "minimum crew" which was two pilots, a flight engineer, and an observer. As an observer, we were responsible for the entire tube of the plane for normal operations as well as emergency operations. Sometimes the flights were completely uneventful and just consisted of dozens upon dozens of take-offs and landings. A good day in flight was when the two were an equal number.

A great day in flight was some of the days where we were burning hours and would get to expand our usual pattern. On one particular winter night in Maine, our designated pilot decided to go a little off of our usual bounce pattern and requested a flight clearance to go down the coastline.

That night we flew down the Eastern Shoreline, taking in the lights of the various coastal cities. And then we reached New York City. With permission, we circled around and up Manhattan and then followed along the twisting waters of the Hudson River. The Empire State building stood tall off our portside wing.

The twin towers glowed majestically. We passed over bridges and hundreds of boats below us. The city that never slept lit up below us like a sparkling dance. From this height, everything was at peace. And as we made our way into the Bay, there stood the most beautiful sight of them all. The Statue of Liberty. The iconic sign of America's gates of freedom, welcoming its visitors, and representing everything that was great about our Nation - and we were looking directly into her eyes.

As I walked off the plane that night after our flight, I could not help but look around the flight line where all of these big beautiful planes were resting under the starry night sky. They were decades old. They were worth billions. And we, four kids all under the age of 25 had the privilege of taking them into the sky. We were given the gift on a daily basis of seeing the world from a perspective that most never will. I wanted to always remember that moment and freeze it in my mind, as to never take my horrible and amazing job for granted. I was going to have days that I failed, and I was going to have days that were wonderful. Today, it happened to be a great day to be a part of the world's most powerful Navy.

And then one day in June...

"Ah, are you sure that's a good idea?" Anna asked Myron as she sat in the back seat of his F-150, trying not to hit her head on the gun rack. He was from Texas, so it was only natural that he had a gun rack in his truck. I loved his truck. It was raised with big tires and he had made a huge, homemade bumper for it, because apparently wooden bumpers are better. When I asked Myron if he would drive me to my wedding, it felt like I was bringing a small piece of country - like where I grew up - to my East Coast wedding.

"This? Oh don't worry about it. It's only my second one," he said as he popped open a can of beer and took a long drink. He was wearing his good cowboy hat, dark jeans, and a huge, shiny belt buckle - a sure sign of dressing up for a country boy. "Here. Take a drink. You probably need one."

It was true. I could definitely use a beer right about now to calm my nerves, but I really did not want to arrive at my wedding smelling like beer. "Just one sip," I replied taking the can and drinking a long, refreshing gulp. It was nearing 90 degrees outside, which was completely unusual for June in Maine. Still, I was so grateful for such a beautiful, sunny day. It made all of the outside pictures that we had taken so perfect.

In the backseat I had my best friend in the world and my little sister. They both looked beautiful in their lilac colored dresses and their hair pinned up with daisies. We were on our way to the little old church and I was about to get married in. I looked down at my bouquet of daisies and wildflowers. I could not believe this moment was actually happening. I was so scared and so excited at the same time. All of the planning had come down to this moment. *Just breathe.*

As we pulled up to the church that sat on a hill, overlooking the Kennebek River, I saw my other bridesmaids, groomsmen, the photographer, and my dad, all waiting for me. Everyone else had filtered inside, as the church, built in 1802, only had one main room with four stained glass windows along each of the sides. From the first moment I went to this church, I knew it was the church I wanted to get married in - and I pictured the flowers I would put in vases in each window. And now that today was here, each windowsill was filled with wildflowers.

On cue, the music began - a piano version of "Love" by John Lennon. Each of my bridesmaids walked down the aisle until it was just my dad and I, alone, and waiting for our signal when the music changed. He was so handsome, dressed up in his tux, and all freshly shaven. I had never seen my dad in a tux before. All I could do was smile, so that I did not cry. The music switched to the song, "I Can't Help Falling in Love" by Elvis.

"Are you ready?" he asked with a smile.

"I'm not sure. I'm so scared."

"You're okay," he smiled. "I'm here."

I smiled back, took a deep breath, and then just put one foot in front of the other. As we walked into the church, everyone was standing. I was surrounded by every person that meant the most to us. Aaron's family from Michigan, my crew, Martha, and my entire family had made the trip out to Maine from Minnesota, Kansas, and California. My aunts, uncles, cousins, grandma - even Pastor Vicki had flown out from Suomi Church to perform the ceremony. Anna, the maid of honor and Tayte, the best man. And they were all looking at me right now, with expressions of joy in their eyes and smiles on their faces. I had never felt so much love. And then, I saw him. The man that was waiting for me at the end of the aisle. The man that was about to be my husband. Aaron smiled at me as our eyes met and he caught his breath. Instantly, all of my worries and nervousness melted away. And all I felt was love.

Honeymoon Call

"Hey! How are you guys doing?"

"Um, we are good," I replied, as I answered our cell phone. It was early in the morning - early when on vacation. I was worried when I saw Tayte was calling our phone, so I answered it promptly. "Hold on, I'll get Aaron..."

"Oh - no, actually, I was calling to talk to you. I'm really sorry to bother you guys on your honeymoon. I wasn't going to call. And then, I just couldn't wait any longer."

"What is it? Did something happen?" Now I was really confused.

"No, no. I - well, this is going to sound really strange, but I was wondering if I could get Anna's number from you?"

"Anna's number? For what?"

"Well, I just - I just can't stop thinking about her. We had so much fun at your wedding, and if it's okay with you, I'd really like to ask her out."

"Ah, I don't know - I just, um..." I wasn't sure how to say it. "She's not exactly like the kind of girls you normally date."

"I know, I get that. And that's why I can't stop thinking about her. That's why I want to call *her*."

"Okay... I just don't..."

"Julia, I know what you're thinking. But you don't have to worry. I'm not going to hurt her. I promise - this is different," he said. I could hear the sincerity in his voice.

"You promise?"

"I promise. Trust me."

"Okay..." Cautiously, I gave him my best friend's number, hoping it was the right thing to do.

Eleven months later, our best man and maid of honor were married on the beach just a few miles down the road from where Aaron and I were married. This time we were the best man and matron of honor. Because destiny is a funny thing.

CHAPTER 14

Puerto Rico.

August 2001

Approximate distance from Deer River: 2530 miles

Not quite two months after we were married, Aaron and I left for opposite ends of the globe. He to Iceland, me to Puerto Rico. He packed a parka, and I packed a bikini. Both of us believing that we got the better location deal over the other. Three months. I could make it three months until our crew would be flying up to Iceland for the remainder of the deployment. I had no room to complain when everyone else around me had to wait six. Still, it was hard to be away from my new husband.

However, being in Puerto Rico did make it a little easier. I couldn't get over what a tropical paradise it was. Of course, it was the only place in the Caribbean that I had been, so I really had nothing to compare it to. Still, I was in awe. The waters were a brilliant blue-green and so clear you could look at the ocean floor fifty feet down and it appeared as if it were five. The water was as warm as a bathtub and I couldn't get enough of it. And despite the weather being swelter-ing, the ocean did not fail to refresh, making it all better. However, when we were under obligation to work in this weather, I was singing a different tune. Usually "Summer in the City" as it is the only song I knew about heat.

For our pre-flights, we would bring along an extra t-shirt to switch out the one that we pre-flighted in under our flight suit that was now drenched in more sweat than a field mouse in a snake aquarium. We arrived in August, and while we Navy folks stationed out of Maine felt as though we could not breathe when stepping outside into the air that hung with humidity, the locals were beginning to observe a fall cool-down - roughly to around 85 degrees. On the flip side, they were stocking the store shelves with fall and winter wear up in the San Juan mall. Seriously. As in a time where I felt I had not brought enough tank tops and went to the store to search for some, all I could find were stacks of sweaters and shelves lined in boots. Boots!?! I needed more flip flops and could only order them online and had them shipped from the states. Thank Heavens, the Internet was catching on - and I discovered this new magical website thing called Amazon. It was a candy-store for adults.

Our missions in Puerto Rico were once again different. This time we were performing counter-narcotic operations, stopping drug-runners that were driving "go-fasts" or speed boats that were loaded with smuggled drugs into the United States. Because the P-3 possessed long flight duration capabilities, we were an excellent patrol and search tool. We were given a large 'box' or area over the ocean in which we would fly up and down a grid, searching for any unusual activity or suspicious looking vessels. When such vessel was located we would then contact the Coast Guard to move in by ship and catch the 'runners.' Upon seeing the Coast Guard and realizing the gig was up, the runners would make a last ditch effort and often set their own boats and drugs on fire and jump into the ocean, knowing we kind Americans felt obligated to save them. And if the evidence had been destroyed, well then we couldn't arrest them for anything. Though most likely Big Jose back in Brazil would not take too kindly about losing a boat full of good treats - but that was a matter between Little Pyromaniac and Big Jose.

The Porch

Our barracks in Puerto Rico were made of cool, cement walls that seemed to have been constructed a hundred years before we inhabited them. Most days the central air-conditioning worked. On occasion, it failed. The surrounding yard was littered with coconuts and cockroaches that scurried across the cement in the afternoon light.

On a starry, sultry night, you could find many of the maintainers that just came off a long 12+ hour shift, littering the ragged couch and wicker chairs that lined the porch. Most sat with a 'cold one' in their hand all were relaxed - soaking in the moment of friendship among co-workers who became a temporary family away from family. Every night when I came home at a 'normal' time (which didn't happen often as we flew round-the-clock), I welcomed this sight as a piece of familiarity. I was comforted by the camaraderie and loved the companionship during a lonely time. There were many jokes, many sea stories, and always AC/DC playing in the background. It was a pure collaboration of characters hanging around and communing on the famous porches of Roosevelt Roads, Puerto Rico (aka Roosey Roads).

I'm not exactly sure when it was that I first heard the term. It had to have been during one of the nights I was passing by. I didn't hear it in vain. I couldn't have, because I could not recall a time of any hurt feelings or any other feelings than those of intoxication and free spirit. That being said, I don't even know how the term stuck in my memory. I do know, however, that I thought it was just a funny thing to say, as I think animals are funny. And the thought of a bunch of monkeys sitting around on a porch had to have been the funniest scene ever. So off the top of my head, I may have innocently used it a few times before in passing. I had no idea that it could've been used in a negative sense. I would have never - had I known.

It wasn't until one day I was in the lobby, talking on the community phone to my love that was at the top of the globe in Iceland. It just so happened a couple of the guys that had clearly 'had a few' came stumbling past me, throwing out what was no doubt some crazy words, and kept on going. This struck me as funny and I laughed out loud and stated to Aaron, "Oh, my gosh Aaron, you should see them. They are just a bunch of porch monkeys! But like monkeys with clothes on - which is even funnier!"

Instantly the phone went silent on the other end. Aaron suddenly changed his tone and quietly asked, "Julia! Do you know what that means?"

"Um, it doesn't MEAN anything. It's just a funny word for these guys 'cause they have been acting like complete animals on our porch."

"Nooooo... that is a derogatory term for black people," he replied slowly - like I was the biggest idiot out there.

"What?! No it's not! That's the dumbest thing I've ever heard." I didn't believe it. *Of all the stupid things. Who makes funny things like monkeys into something insulting? That's just stupid.*

Then there was a long pause. "Julia, how long have you been saying that?"

He asked cautiously.

"I…don't know…I can't remember." I instantly felt horrible. He went on to explain it to me somewhat - so I could try to understand. Still, I didn't. I mean, I understood, but it just didn't make sense. There were no words. I just had no idea. I could only hope if anyone heard me, they weren't offended by my ignorance.

The Catamaran

My favorite day in Puerto Rico by far was the day I had a Saturday off and Whiner was looking for someone to go with him on a Catamaran trip. Since the opportunities to actually get out and explore our local surroundings were rare, I jumped at the chance. For only $40 each a beautiful catamaran would take a group of people out snorkeling for the afternoon. Also included was lunch and of course, all the rum you could drink. What could be a better way to spend the afternoon? Even if it was with Whiner, my friend that drove me insane.

So we set sail over the Caribbean blue waters and toasted our glasses of rum-filled, fancy cocktails, pretending we were pirates. We arrived at the first diving location just after lunch. Not only did we swim after a few drinks, we also didn't wait an hour after lunch and forgot to put on sunscreen. Those were crazy times back then and we just broke all the rules.

Snorkeling was the most amazing thing I have ever done. It was like I was swimming in a beautiful aquarium with happy fish that were every color of the rainbow. The happy tropical fish swam alongside me like we were old jolly friends going for an afternoon stroll. I pretended that I was a mermaid with my flippers as I elegantly floated through the waters. I told jokes to the fish and they just looked at me with a shocked expression on their face - because fish don't laugh. I learned that one the hard way. Soon our time together came to an end. I bid them farewell, promising to visit again as soon as I could. Again, they just looked surprised with wide eyes and round mouths, as I waved and returned to the Catamaran which I had now renamed *Queen Anne's Revenge*.

After one more drink, we arrived at our next location, which was a coral reef.

I was so excited - I had always wanted to see a reef in real life. However, I quickly learned the hard way what a moody bitch coral reefs really were as it tore into my flesh numerous occasions. At this location, we had been warned about the jellyfish and it didn't take long to figure out why. They were everywhere. And so were the tropical fish. Every shape and color one imagines when they think of tropical fish. They were everywhere! I dove down and was careful not to touch the reef and continued to dodge the jellyfish. It was then that I had one of those out-of-body experiences in which I realized what this was all about. I had done it. I was officially trapped in Super Mario Brothers Undersea World.

Whiner and I had brought along under-water disposable cameras and did our best to capture the scenery. While I was thankful we had attempted to capture the day in photos - the camera did not do the location any justice. Most of our pictures turned out looking as though we had smeared Vaseline all over the lens. And despite waking up in regret from the hangover and sunburn from hell we had the next day, I will never forget the vibrant medley of colors and creatures that exist in this amazing world that is under the sea. It was my happy place.

Birthday Surprises

I am a firm believer in the magic of one's birthday. So after I left home and became an adult, the realization of your birthday being just another day to everyone else was a hard reality to accept. I'm not quite sure I ever have. I find it so important to gush over others in the one day a year that is all about them. (Reference Johnny's fake birthday celebration.) So, when my birthday happened to fall on a day that I was on deployment in Puerto Rico, far away from my family who were all back home and my husband who was a world away, I had no one that would gush over me. A selfishly sad realization.

I am not sure if it is 'adult code' that you are supposed to not say anything about your birthday and just pretend that you don't care, because I find that incredibly difficult to do. Or maybe it is just guy code or something. Whatever it is, I really try, but have the hardest time following this rule and tend to tell everyone I see (including gas station attendants, pet store clerks, etc) that it is indeed my birthday, all the while I am beaming as if it is a proud accomplishment. Yes, it is true. *I am* the one who was born on this very day.

During the entire day of work, I was sure to let everyone know so they could meet me at the club to celebrate. I think more than anything I was just afraid of being alone and sad on my birthday. I planned to go out to dinner with the enlisted guys on my crew, but was delightfully surprised when the entire crew was at the restaurant waiting to surprise me. They even had a cake! Somehow they knew how very important in was and meant the world to me. We had a fabulous seafood dinner at a restaurant on the water. Then we made our way to Woody's, the famous club on base in Roosey Roads (well, the *only* club on base, really).

Nearly the entire squadron had come to the club that night, or so it seemed, as it was, after all, a Friday night - although when you work seven days a week - that minor detail doesn't seem to matter too much. And of course, when it is your 23rd birthday at a club full of your friends, staying sober is quite a challenge. As the night went on, things became somewhat hazy, though I did my best to keep a clear head. I didn't want to miss a moment. So we all danced. And sang. And drank. And were merry until the wee hours of the morning. And just when we didn't think we could have any more fun, Horton (the new SS-3 on my crew that replaced Deena) grabbed my arm, insisting that I come with him, and I was whisked away by some of the guys on my crew into a car.

"Where are we going?" I asked, smiling, happy. Although slightly disappointed that I didn't have a chance to say goodbye to everyone in the club.

"Don't worry about it. You'll have fun." Horton answered, blowing his cigarette out the car window. Well, of course, I knew I'd have fun. I was extremely happy at this point. So much that I think I would have had fun at a dental appointment. So I just hung my head out the window, and resisted the overwhelming urge to climb out onto the roof.

Well, the surprises kept on coming as we pulled into this dimly lit shack on the side of the road outside of the gate. It was a building I passed every time I left base, but had never had the guts to venture to. Or perhaps the opportunity. Though I had heard the stories.

"What? Oh no. I am *not* going in there." I objected upon arrival.

"Quiet." Horton simply stated with a sniff, "Or I'll make you slap yourself."

He could be so rude sometimes. He grabbed my arm to drag me along behind him. And though my morals were conflicting, [*Grandma Henning would not approve*] really, what choice did I have at this point? After I was done having an internal dialog of my conflicted conscience, I got out of the car and followed him.

Maybe it wouldn't be a big deal to see grown women taking their clothes off? I wanted to be the cool chic that went along with the boys to the strip club, acting as if I hardly noticed anything. However, these guys knew better. They were trying to shock me and strip club de-virgin-ize me into every aspect of the crazy sailor world. It had been long enough, they decided. If I was going to be a true sailor, I had to at least go to one dirty strip club.

Reluctantly, curiously, and pretty drunk, I entered the door of *Papa Joe's*. Or better known by the Navy guys as *"Papa Ho's."* As the doors parted, I felt somewhat like I was crossing through the wardrobe closet into the secret world of Nim. Upon first glance, it appeared as any other bar. There were round table and chairs, a bar filled with a motley looking crew, smoking, toking, and joking with shots of whisky on the rocks decorating the bar they were propped against. Off to my left were the typical pool tables and dart boards that looked like they hadn't been replaced since 1963. Some lonely American cowboy song was playing in the background. Although it was located in Puerto Rico, this place was clearly designed for sailors. To my right was a makeshift 'stage' that I couldn't help but think was definitely not looking up to safety codes - let alone two poles the ran from ceiling to stage.

So this was where it all happened. It was true then. They really used these firemen's poles. I'd seen movies, but you just never can tell how much is Hollywood. I felt so guilty for just being there - like at any minute someone was going to come out and yell at me.

We went up to the bar. "Dos cervezas, por favor," I said to the bartender. Living in Puerto Rico was helping my Spanish. I knew the basics anyways. Hello, how are you, friend, money, pretty girl, goodbye, toilet, and how to count - but that was from Sesame Street. And there was that one night in San Juan in which I learned "¿Dónde está mi gato" (where is my cat?) from a poor lady that had lost her cat. We spent the majority of the evening helping her look for it until she found it locked in her garage. It was all very random and I was told later not to help people look for their cats in San Juan. It could be a set-up, as the place was crawling with gangs after dark. Apparently, these gangs didn't like cats.

"Caunto años tiene su hija?" Paul asked the bartender, thinking he was hilarious.

The bartender leaned forward and looked him straight in the eyes and replied, "no, Amigo, no."

"A game of pool?" Horton asked around, attempting to keep us from getting kicked out of the bar. Everyone nodded and filed our way over to the pool table and began a game. If I haven't mentioned it yet, I am terrible at bar games. I think the problem lies in the fact I hate to aim. (Hence the reason I liked Foosball so much) I'd rather just pick up the stick and shoot it. I'm not sure why. It's the same with bowling. And golf. Someday I want to be this cool pro that just walks up and shoots and keeps going and all of the appropriate balls go into their desired pockets. Until then, I'll keep practicing, not aiming.

So there we were, shooting pool, when all of a sudden good ol' Hank Williams was rudely ripped from the juke box mid-song, and a scratchy rendition of Def Leopard's "Pour Some Sugar on Me" came across the speakers.

[*Step inside, walk this way. You and me Babe, hey, hey!*] And then, low and behold our performer of the hour emerged, and naturally, wearing a quite scantly-dressed school girl outfit. It was one of my favorite old songs and for a second, I really had to resist the urge to run up there and dance with her. It was perfect - she had a stage (because she was short, I'm sure) and I, of course, quite intoxicated firmly believed I was, yet again, the best dancer in the world at that moment. Still, I respected the fact that this was her show. Later, I was quite happy I made this decision.

Then there was the pole. Somehow, in one fell swoop she wrapped her leg around that brass pole and twirled herself right to the ceiling. *She must have rocked in gymnastics!* I thought to myself, and judging from the few shouts from the men in the room, I figured they must have been thinking the same thing.

Without missing a beat, and with another quick swoop, she was upside-down, and her button-down white top fell ever so gently to the floor to reveal the most amazing sparkly bra-top. It shimmered rainbows under the spotlights as she made herself go around the pole again and righted herself. I thought it was great that this woman had a bit of a poochy stomach on her. Horton made a vocal cringe at that moment. I slapped him on the arm, suddenly feeling like I needed to stick up for plus-sized strippers everywhere. I personally thought it was nice to see a performer that actually looked like a real woman. Apparently, though, I was informed that most guys don't come to strip clubs looking for real-looking women. And apparently Papa Hoe's women all were very real - stretch-marks and all. Also apparently, once a woman is naked, as this woman soon became, guys don't notice stretch marks anyways - and their interests perked up as the show went on.

Just as I was starting to get into the show, once again, I felt conflicted. I began to think how this girl was someone's daughter, or even mother. Hell, she may have been a single mom that had to work in this place - just barely getting by. She couldn't possibly be happy doing this. Maybe she just needed someone to help her. And so, as the show went on and the woman lost all of her modesty, I couldn't help but relay all of these thoughts to the guys around me.

Finally, my flight engineer, scolded me, "Maki, shut up already - you're ruining it."

I didn't want to ruin the fun night. But I couldn't help it either. So, I stopped. I drank my drink. And kept thinking. "Fine, I'm sorry. I can't help it. It's just that...

"Stop!" Horton cut me off. "Here, give her this dollar." He handed me a crisp dollar from his fancy wallet. Horton was always fancy. "I want to see you give this to her." I wasn't sure if he was just trying to get rid of me, or was actually entertained by the idea of me giving her a dollar. He laughed. "Tell her it's for her college fund or something." He sniffed. He always sniffed after he thought he said something clever.

I sniffed, and took the dollar from him. "I'll give her your dollar." (As if it'd be a challenge or something?) As I walked over to the stage, they followed from behind. Matt was already at the stage holding out his one of many dollar bills at this point.

So I stood there, in front of her and held my dollar out just like I'd seen the other guys do. She was doing some maneuver on the ground now. When she saw my dollar, she began doing a cat walk on her hands and knees towards me, slowly, like a lion suddenly decided to investigate something mesmerizing out in the tall, thick grasses of the plains.

As she approached me, she stood up on her knees. She carefully pulled the dollar from my fingers and shook her head no at me. I was confused. *Did she want my dollar or not?* Then she demonstrated by placing the dollar in her teeth ever so carefully, that this was how I was supposed to elegantly and obediently present her my gift as if she was the Queen of England - that is assuming the Queen happened to strip on Friday nights in Puerto Rico for some extra pocket change.

In two seconds, my mind jumped to thoughts of, "Oh hell no." Two more seconds later I thought, "Oh, what the hell," as I began to hear shouts and cheering from around the bar. So, very delicately, I placed the dollar between my teeth (luckily I had been drinking so the thoughts of where this dollar had been failed to enter my mind). I leaned forward and Miss Topless came forward towards my mouth, and all the way to my ear. I froze - having no idea what was going to happen.

Slowly, and delicately, she put her lips to my ear and ever so slowly pulled back, her cheek traced mine until her mouth was right next to mine. I could feel her warm breath on my lips. It smelled of whiskey. She held it there for what seemed like an eternity, perhaps expressing her gratitude. Or perhaps just putting on a good show. *Well this is interesting.* I could hear the guys cheering in the background. *Oh she's good. She knows exactly what she's doing.* Then, without missing a beat, she swiftly but seductively grabbed my dollar between her lips, carefully making steady eye contact the entire time.

And then, as effortlessly as she came, she retreated quickly and slid onto her next customer, working her way down the line. I suddenly let out my breath, unaware that I had been holding it. It was then that I realized, she knew exactly what she was doing, and that she would be fine without any help from me.

September 11, 2001

Although it had only been a month and a half, we were flying round the clock, and could not wait for our crew's R&R days. They were coming up quickly - on the schedule for September 12, 2001. Algae (breaking the rules as usual) scheduled his flight to head to New York a day early.

Everyone always asks, "Where were you on September 11?" September 11, 2001. It was a day in history that for those who lived it - they will never forget it. For some, it changed their lives entirely. For others it changed their perspective on life. It was a day America was attacked and was suddenly vulnerable to a new generation. Our people suffered. Our economy was brought to its knees. Thousands wept, millions mourned. It was a day that changed the world.

On that particular morning, we had an early preflight that began sometime around 3:00a.m. It was already a sweltering, humid day as usual in sunny Roosey Roads. Preflight was unusually uneventful and we departed successfully at our scheduled 6:00am take off. We just happened to be doing counter-narcotics operations in the Caribbean that were a good three hours or so transit to our on-station location from home base.

We were all in good spirits despite the painful hour. We all had tickets in hand for our R&R. Everyone's thoughts continued to drift into future plans. Since I would be seeing Aaron in one month, my friend from high school, Jenny, was flying down to stay with me in Puerto Rico and we had arrangements to tour the island together. Algae had already left for the airport that morning, headed home to Long Island. So far, all was on track as the military always reserves the right to give and take anytime it pleases - we just had to get through this day.

We had only been on-station for a short time when we found our first target. We began imaging the craft. (Circling the plane around it and taking pictures from various angles - trying to capture anything unusual for identification purposes.) Upon completion, we found nothing suspicious and moved on.

Stimpy had just finished transmitting our progress to home base when we received the most disturbing radio call. "Lima Charlie, you are to RTB [return to base] immediately. Repeat: you are to RTB immediately." We were unable to ask any questions.

Right away, we wondered if we had imaged the wrong guy. *Perhaps it was one of our own undercover and we had blown their cover? Or maybe one of our own aircraft had gone down?* The thought was unfathomable and made me sick to my stomach. *Why the lack of information?* It was killing us. Here we were - eleven crewmembers in the middle of the Caribbean Sea - hundreds of miles from any land or civilization, and all we knew was that something had gone terribly wrong.

The flight back home was extensive and grueling. Our thoughts were toxic, but we did our best to push them out of our mind. Someone randomly threw out that maybe China had attacked us. We laughed at the absurd idea; however, we would soon come to realize that our worst nightmares, minus a few details, were not that far from the truth.

Upon landing at home base, we noticed that every bird was parked on the ramp. There were no pre-flights, tests, or post-flights going on, and even more unusual, no APU's were running. This meant that no plane was even turned on, so no maintenance personnel were even working on them - had the planes been broken and unable to fly. The entire flight line and base echoed an unnatural silence. A very unsettling sensation took over my body as the plane was jolted to a halt. We sat for a moment, unsure of what to do next, afraid to move.

As soon as we were safely off the runway and onto the ramp, a familiar voice was heard over the intercom. "Crew's released." The pilot that was filling in for Algae routinely stated as we rolled down the flight line to our parking spot outside of the hangar. "Apparently we're a turn-around flight [another flight would follow immediately in the same plane] so we don't have to put the plane to bed."

Anxiously, I unfastened my seat belt and waited for the propellers on the four engines to make their last rotation. Upon completion of this, I released the door and began to lower the ladder. A few familiar faces were already starting to gather on the deck, waiting for the ladder to be extended all the way down. The crowd was suspiciously unusual. Finally, the wheels on the ladder hit the deck. Immediately a familiar face in a flight suit and SV-2 made his way up. "Hey Jim! What the heck's going on," I asked him as he stepped into the plane.

Jim didn't even pause for a breath as he began to shout to us over our APU, "The Pentagon has just been hit! And the World Trade Centers too!" I didn't understand. *Why would he joke about such a morbid idea?*

"Hit? What are you talking about," I asked.

"Come on, man. What's going on?" Someone behind me shouted.

"Seriously. Some planes crashed into the towers and just now the Pentagon. They've grounded all flights except for those assisting in emergency aid. We're taking this bird up to Pennsylvania and loading up doctors and nurses to bring to the city."

No one spoke for what seemed like an eternity. What could we say? We did the speediest turn-around in P-3 history, helping the next crew get off the ground swiftly. As I carried my gear into the hangar, still in a state of confusion, I stopped in the first shop I came to, the PR shop.

Everyone was gathered around an old 13" television set tuned into CNN. There it was on the news, plain as day: speculation about the worst terrorist act in history. Over and over again the image of the planes crashing into the World Trade Centers was shown until it had burned into our minds. They showed a sea of firefighters and policemen picking through smoking rubble. They showed the people covered in ash. People in bandages on stretchers. The bodies falling from the sky. People crying. Screaming. Grieving. Like millions of others that day, I was so shocked that I could not hold back the tears. People were dying right before our eyes and there was nothing we could do to help them. *How could this happen? Why did this happen?* The words "unbelievable," came from a voice somewhere in the room.

At once, my thoughts began to think of those I may know in harm's way. I didn't have any family in New York or Washington D.C. that I could think of. Then I realized that there would be a crew coming off of leave today before ours went on tomorrow. People would be flying back from all over the place today. *Oh my god, Algae! He flew out this morning!* Suddenly I wanted to throw up. I was flooded with panic and trepidation for all of my fellow sailors that would be traveling at that moment.

We were sent back to the barracks right away and the base went into a lock-down. No one could get on, and no one could get off. The phone lines were constantly occupied, as everyone frantically tried to call their loved ones. Everyone was glued to the TV in search of answers. I remember the newscaster wrapping up the day by trying to bring comfort to the country. He said that all we could do now to honor them was to go home and hold your loved ones a little tighter. Except that I was half the world away from my loved ones. All that we in military had that day were God and each other.

No one that lived it will ever forget that day. We won't forget the faces of grieving. I won't forget the sadness and disbelief on the faces of those in our squadron who discovered that their loved ones were gone. We were an East Coast squadron, and many who picked orders there had family all over New England. I'll never forget the disturbing images that haunted every station on the television for weeks. I'll never forget the evocative pictures of survivors looking for their friends. It was a time that our country came together to mourn. Life for Americans and the rest of the world were changed forever on that day that we were attacked.

The Aftermath

Of course, our leave was cancelled, except for Algae who had thankfully made it as far as Florida and then was stuck in an airport terminal for 3 days. But he knew - like the thousands of others that were stuck in airports all over the country - he could not complain. They were miserable, but they were alive.

The base remained in the highest security. Everyone was glued to the TV as the stories began to unravel. It was a devastating tragedy. But the amazing thing about tragedies is watching the good come out in people. If you look hard enough, you will always see it.

Overnight, our country's patriotism was restored. Kids marched straight down to the recruiting offices and enlisted. Flags were being flown from every window. Our country's support for the military grew. A few days later, there was a lady at the exchange passing out ribbon loops in red, white, and blue stripes to pin to people's shirts. I was wearing my flight suit at the time, so I just looped it into my dog tags where it still remains, tattered and worn.

Our leave was finally granted a month or so later and anyone who hadn't planned on going home originally, ended up booking a flight to see their loved ones. And about half the guys on the crew came back to receive phone calls a couple weeks later announcing their wives were pregnant. In fact, all around the country there was a mini baby-boom. Everyone had received that wake-up call from Old Man Mortality. Life was short. It was also in one of my phone conversations with Aaron that he announced his desires for us to begin planning our family when we saw each other next. Initially shocked at the suggestion, I quickly realized how contagious babies are once the idea gets planted in your head.

I pondered the idea for weeks as four other crew members were currently expecting babies or planned to try for them when we got home. The thought terrified me. I had always had big plans that didn't have room for kids for a long time. But I was beginning to get the feeling that the time when they would fit into our lives was coming. I had to choose if I wanted a career in the military or if I wanted a family.

Then one day, during a flight I was sitting in the galley with the guys. Someone had brought on a Cabela's magazine and I did my favorite thing to do when I saw a boring magazine. Flip through and make up stories about the people in them - usually with a Southern accent, of course.

"Shirley, you must come see my dandy trout I just caught in this mini-creek I just discovered. Tom, Tom, that's a fabulous trout - but I must bring little Susie to grandma's on this fabulous 4-wheeler and in our amazing rubber boots! Aren't they shiny? So shiny Shirley! Well you have fun but don't forget to be home in time to cook my trout. You know I've never learned how to turn the stove on. Oh Tom. You're truly despicable. I love you."

All of a sudden I looked up as my Sensor Two, Matt started clapping. "Just so you know, you're going to make a great mom someday," he said with a smile.

I smiled.

El Salvador.
October 2001
Approximate distance from Deer River: 3125 miles

Our squadron rotated the crews on short DETs out of El Salvador during this deployment. Our missions continued to be much of the same counter-narcotic operations we were doing in the Caribbean. The country's prime location on the west coast of Central America made for an ideal home base for drug-runners out of Columbia. El Salvador is known for its pristine beaches and gorgeous volcanic backdrop. Unfortunately, we never were granted the opportunity to see these views. A few crews before us were allowed to take an escorted trip into the city, however since we arrived post 9/11, the threat level was too high to allow us to leave the base or our hotel.

Thankfully, our hotel had everything we could possibly need. Three abundant buffets every day. A fancy pool. Comfortable bed. And a fully-stocked bar run by an amazing local who we came to call a friend over our stay. He would bring in homemade foods and drinks to share and we tipped him generously. He was our link to the rest of the world there, as we were surrounded by gates and cornfields with a creepy shack and scarecrow off in the distance from my window view. I tried not to let my imagination go too wild with that one and kept my curtains closed for the majority of my stay. After all, we were in our comfortable American bubble.

When we landed from our missions, we had to change in trailers on the flight line into civilian clothes and take a bus to the Comfort Inn hotel, which was surrounded by a fence and armed guard. It was about a 15-minute drive or so off of base. It was in those 15 minutes that I had my only daily glance at the country, outside of protected gates.

This impoverished country had been besieged by the devastating Salvadoran Civil war from 1979 to 1992, so traces of it lingered everywhere. This war between the military-led government and a coalition of left-wing guerrilla groups had left much of the population with what they could carry in their arms. The land that was mostly agriculture dominated was full of rubble and abandoned buildings. There was very little civil order. There was no certainty. And the people had been living in fear for decades. Children grew up not knowing the comfortable, safe feeling that we took for granted.

Upon arriving in this country, I felt shallow and ashamed. Here I was busy worried about which dance or cooking class I was going to take next, or if I had a pair of brown shoes to match my new purse - they had to worry about if they were going to be able to bring home enough food for their family that day to feed them one solid meal.

I thought back to the days I spent as a child dreaming of becoming a princess in a huge castle where I was rich and had everything I ever needed. When I saw this place, I suddenly realized that I *was* rich. I was born into a life of luxury - not one of survival. When something broke - I bought another. If food spoiled, I threw it all out. If I was hungry, I went to a restaurant and ordered food. When I was cold, I turned up the thermostat or went to a store and bought a coat.

Of course they stared at me. I was spoiled and didn't know it. I had come into their country, without a care. We had more food than we could eat in a sitting at our hotel. Our military protected us. I wasn't sure how to make sense of it. Why did I get an armed guard while being transported between the base and hotel when a 7-year-old little girl had lost her family and lived alone on the street? How could I just accept that there was nothing that I could do? I realized how desperately everyone in our country needed to see a third world country to understand our blessings. It changed everything. I made a promise to myself in that moment that when I had the resources to do so, I would help. Somehow. If I ever had children, I would take them each on a mission trip somewhere before they were grown so they would know too.

Iceland. Again.
November, 2001
Approximate distance from Deer River: 2820 miles

And then? One hot November day in Puerto Rico, we hopped aboard our trusty ol' flying machine with all of our belongings and made a one-night stop in Brunswick. While all of the guys were out making cookies with their beautiful significant others, I was lucky enough to have Martha waiting for me at the terminal to go indulge in some home-cooked Maine lob-stah. Oh Martha. Her mothering embrace melted away my sorrows and loneliness. And though it may not have been as climactic as the rest of my crew's night, it was a wonderful evening and a great chance to catch up with my adopted mom. And as I listened to her tell me stories in her amusing accent, I smiled, because for a moment I was home and very soon I would be reunited with my love.

After dinner and a good night's rest in my own heavenly bed that felt like angel kisses in comparison to the barracks' bed, I swapped out my previously packed bag of sweaters, leaving behind my sun dresses, and caught the next P-3 heading up to the Arctic Circle. Everyone on the crew was smiling that day. We all had a half-way-through deployment refresher and knew that every day was another day closer to coming home.

It was different landing in Iceland this time. I wasn't going into an unknown world ahead of me. I actually had someone waiting for me on the tarmac that was as joyous about my arrival as I was. It had been three months. I had nothing to complain about compared to the rest of my crew. But three months had felt like an eternity. The world as we knew it had changed in those three months and so had we. While there was a colossal amount of enlistments into the service after 9/11, I personally was beginning to feel the opposite. I had been away long enough. I was getting tired of living out of a bag and by a flight schedule. It made planning for anything near impossible - including going to college. I was ready to put roots down somewhere and be with the most important person in my life. The end of my enlistment was coming up and I was ready for a family. I knew I didn't want to have kids on active duty. I couldn't leave them for 6 months or more at a time - though I respected the decision of those that did, I just knew it wasn't the life for me anymore.

Congratulations

The phone call came in the middle of the day in the duty office four weeks later. I was "studying" in the AW shop as usual, so I didn't think too much of it when the ASDO told me there was someone on the line in the duty office for me. I ran down the steps and picked up the receiver that was stretched over the one long desk that was shared between the SDO and ASDO.

"This is Petty Officer Maki," I spoke into the phone.

"Hi Petty Officer Maki. This is Commander So-and-So, from the command hospital."

"Oh, yes?"

"I just wanted to call you and let you know your blood work came back.

Congratulations, you are pregnant."

What!? That's impossible. It's only been 4 weeks of "not taking precautions" and "seeing what happens." Instantly I looked around me at all the people carrying on their own separate conversations in the duty office to see if they had heard her voice over the phone. No one seemed to look up - so perhaps I was safe.

"Oh, well. Um. Thank you so much," I said, as if she had just given me her new recipe for peanut butter cookies. I was in disbelief, lost for words, and concentrating on keeping my tone even and my face expressionless. *Well shit. I guess this is "what happens."*

"Okay well do you want to make an appointment now for a trans-vaginal sonogram to confirm the heartbeat and age? Or would you rather call back to schedule it? I also need to get you a prescription for pre-natal vitamins."

Again I scanned the room, wondering if they heard the word trans-vaginal. "Actually, I can call back."

"Okay then. Sounds good. Well you take care then and I'll see you soon."

"Thank you ma'am," I said quickly and hung up the phone. Then I just stood there. *Did she really just say I had a baby growing inside of me? I didn't feel any different. Maybe she read the test wrong. Wasn't it supposed to take a while to get pregnant?* And in those few moments of trying to wrap my head around the idea, the thought never occurred to me that it could possibly affect my job. After all, I had just gone flying the day before yesterday - the day before I took the test at medical. It certainly didn't affect the outcome of the pregnancy test.

I wanted to tell everyone, but didn't dare tell a soul yet. I remembered that people didn't tell everyone right away. *But I had to tell someone. Aaron! I had to tell Aaron, of course. And then I have to buy an instruction book or something on being pregnant.*

I knocked on the door to his shop that had a big "AT" written on it and poked my head in. "Hey. Is Aaron in here?"

"Aaron!" Jay yelled behind him over the TV. Clearly, they were "hard at work" as they were watching this new crazy show that had just came on called "Survivor." It looked ridiculous and I could only assume it wouldn't last long. "Your old lady's here." Aaron whipped around in his chair and walked over to where I was standing.

"Hey. What's up?" He asked smiling.

"Your world as you know it is about to change completely and forever," is what I wanted to shout to him. Instead I just asked, "You got a few minutes?"

"Sure, what's going on?" He never could wait.

I didn't want him to guess anything so I lied. "Oh, I just need to talk. My mom just called and things are crazy back home," I said as we were walking down the hangar bay. "Here, come in here," I led him into the stairwell where it was completely separated by doors - loud doors, so we would hear immediately if anyone was around. I couldn't risk the wrong ears overhearing.

"Oh, is it your sister again?"

"No..." I paused, looking at him. Then away as I was trying not to smile. Then at the ceiling. Then back at him. I thought of all of the fabulous lines I could deliver and make this the most magical moment that he would remember forever. Then I realized it was me about to talk - and I could never do it with a straight face. I had to just tell him. *TELL HIM!* My brain was yelling at me. I took a deep breath. "So... I'm pregnant! You're going to be a dad! Eeeeee!"

He stood there for a second, absorbing the information. And then Mr. I-don't-get-excited-unless-it's-about-hunting replied, "Wow. Really? That's great!" And smiled politely.

I stood there slightly confused and asked, "are you excited?!"

"Of course, I'm very excited," he said with a smile again.

I jumped up and put my arms around him as we stood on the landing on the stairwell in front of big glass windows, hugging. "Whoa - careful," he said and put me down - pointing at the Commander through the window that was walking up to the building. "We're in uniform. If he saw us..."

"Aaron, ohmygod. We are married and we're having a baby! I don't care if he saw us hugging in uniform," I said smiling. "I'm so excited!"

"Me too, Babe. That's really awesome." And just when I thought he was going to give me a high five for a job well done, one of the doors burst open and someone began making their way down the stairs.

"Well, I'd better get back to the shop," he said. "We can talk more tonight."

"Okay, sounds good." I smiled and shook my head as I thought how different we were. But that was what made us great. I would need his level head and calm demeanor if we were about to become parents. *Holy crap. We're going to be parents!* And then, before he turned the corner to go down the stairs he looked back at me and smiled back. I knew everything was going to be okay.

That night we took turns calling our parents. My family squealed with excitement over the phone. His politely said how pleased they were - that it would be very nice - much like getting a coupon in the mail for a free ice cream cone. Later in the night we called Tayte down from his room and told him our news. It was so nice to be able to tell someone in person and see the excitement on his face. A week later he bought Aaron the book, *My Boys Can Swim,* because apparently they could - very well.

A few days later, I went in for my sonogram and confirmed the little heartbeat was actually there. In that tiny moment frozen in time, like mothers everywhere, I fell in love with my baby. She was mine to love and protect. The feeling caught me by surprise and brought tears to my eyes. It was real. I was *really* having a baby.

"Everything looks great so far," the doctor confirmed. "I just have a bunch of paperwork for you to bring back to your command and we'll have to update your Page 13 regarding your flight status."

"Whoa - my what?" I sat up on the table with a thin sheet of paper covering my lap.

"We'll just have to update it stating the reason you will be 'downed' for the next 8 months or so - until you get a clean bill of health after the delivery."

"Wait - why wouldn't I be able to fly? I read the instructions a while ago - women can fly up to their third trimester."

"Oh yes. Well that has recently changed," the Commander stated as carefree as if she was telling me that the day's weather forecast had changed.

"But I *have* to fly - at least for another month and a half. I'm on deployment. I don't understand how it could change anything this early on. I went flying last week. No one can even tell that I'm pregnant - heck, I can't even."

"I'm sorry - that is the current instruction."

I suddenly felt the weight of the world on my chest. I *had* to fly. I had to finish out my last deployment. My crew was depending on me - they wouldn't be in a ready status if I didn't fly. "There isn't anything I can do?" I asked her.

She paused for a moment. "Well, you can always request a board with two or three flight surgeons present. They can review your health record and write you a waiver if they see it suitable. Is that something you would be interested in doing?"

"Yes, definitely. I mean, I think so. I have to think about all of this now. This kind of changes everything." I didn't know what to do. I had been so excited about this. We planned this baby, thinking I would be out of the Navy well before she was born. It just never occurred to me that it would interfere with my job in my remaining months. I wouldn't even be showing by the time deployment was over. Suddenly I was afraid to tell anyone. I was afraid when they found out I couldn't fly that I had done this on purpose as many girls did in the beginning of their Navy career to get out of the military. There was a stigma attached to being pregnant in the Navy. But I didn't think it would affect me at this stage in my career. I only had 6 months left in my enlistment. And flying was my job.

Unsure of what to do next, I broke the news to Aaron who encouraged me to talk to my LPO (Lead Petty Officer) and let him know what was going on. So I did. Thankfully, he was very supportive. And then I told LT Spencer - one of the only four female officer aircrewmen in the squadron at that time. Together the three of us broke the news to the Skipper. I respected the Skipper greatly (it wasn't Squishy anymore) and wanted him to know before he found out through the paperwork route or rumor mill. Knowing that crew readiness was essential to the squadron, he thought going to the board and requesting a waiver to fly would be the best option.

The guys on my crew took the news very well. They were surprised, as I had always said I hadn't planned on having kids for a long time. But they were excited for us. Still, I couldn't help but feel like I had let them down. I began putting together my paperwork to request a waiver to fly.

A week later, the novelty of being pregnant began to wear off and was quickly replaced with awful morning sickness. But not just morning sickness - *all day* sickness that was never relieved by vomiting, but instead lingered on all day like the feeling of being carsick 24/7. "Petty Officer Maki, can I talk to you?" Algae asked me one day.

"Sure," I said and we walked out into the hangar bay where the background noise of APUs running on the ramp blocked out most of our conversation to onlookers. The smell of the exhaust now made me ill.

"I know that you are very determined, and I've always appreciated that about you, but I'm not so sure it's a good idea for you to fly right now."

"Why do you say that?"

"I just know if it were my wife, I wouldn't want her to fly. I mean, we don't know what the constant pressure changes, or G-forces can do, or how much radiation is being constantly put out by our gear. There are just so many things to think about. "

I swallowed as I listened to him. It was upsetting because I didn't want to hear it. "Okay, well thank you for telling me your opinion."

"It is just my opinion. But you have to think, maybe there is a reason they stopped granting women permission to fly while pregnant," he continued and I looked up at the high hangar ceiling, thinking back to just a month ago when my friend, Gut, took me up in the man-lift to the top of the P-3 antenna - nearing the top of the hangar - just for fun. I loved taking risks and having adventures. And now I wasn't even supposed to go on the plane anymore? *Had I just ended all of my chances for an adventure again?*

"Are you alright?" Algae asked with genuine concern on his face.

I wrinkled my nose to keep my eyes from watering up as they did when someone asked me if I was okay. "Not really. But I will be. I'm just - I'm just really sorry for all of this." I looked down at the ground.

"It'll be okay," he said, smiled, patted my shoulder, and walked away because even though he was my big brother that had been there through some of the best and worst moments of the last few years, he was an officer and was not allowed to hug me.

Later that day I did what I always do when I had a major problem to solve. I asked everyone who had an opinion that mattered to me what their thoughts were. Tayte, Stimpy, Matt, Horton, Janessa, and Whiner... All of them told me that they didn't think I should risk flying right now. Especially the guys on my crew. So everyone that I would be affecting most by not flying, were the ones who advised me to think about my baby first - because she would be what was the most important in the end. I knew they were right. But it was a tough pill to swallow.

Then there was Aaron who's opinion mattered the most, but ultimately promised to support whatever I decided because he did not want to be the one to tell me not to fly anymore, knowing it was like giving up a piece of myself. Naturally, the baby's safety was his number one concern. And so, I never got the waiver. I sat on permanent duty for the rest of the deployment working 12-hour days, seven days a week. I couldn't help but feel judged as another girl who got pregnant to get out of her job. But it didn't matter. Because for the first time in my life, it wasn't just about me anymore.

I never did get to fly again on active duty. Maybe it was for the best that I never knew my last flight would be the last - or I would have been a blubbery mess the entire time. I also missed out on a DET to Spain. I couldn't help but have moments of shame when I felt I was being judged because I was a female in the service in maternity clothes, followed by moments of joy as I'd feel my baby girl moving.

One week before my due date in August 2002, I gave birth to the most beautiful baby girl I had ever seen. She was ours to love forever. As she lay on my belly looking up into my eyes, not crying, but absorbing the world around her, I knew that as difficult as it was to give up flying at the time, I had made the right choice. She was now my world and what mattered the most in our life. Our new adventure had begun.

CHAPTER 15

We arrived back home to Brunswick from our deployment in January of 2002 and the cycle began all over again. The squadron would spend the year of home cycle training the next crews for the upcoming deployment. New crews were formed with the people who were going to be around the next year and a half. Old friends left. New ones came to the squadron.

I found joy in training the new kids coming into the squadron. While I was pregnant, I worked as an instructor in the flight simulators, training the crews and helping them with their qualifications. I sat in as an instructor on Sensor One boards. One of my favorite questions to ask the guys was the one that was presented to me on my board. "What do you do if your Sensor Two says that she can't fly today because her cramps are too bad?" I watched them trying to read me, often expecting me to want them to go easy on the girls. I often found myself explaining to them that they were not doing them any favors. Special treatment never helped anyone. Only equal treatment created equal respect.

I thought back to some of the great leaders I had along the way. I felt like they were being so hard on me at first, but in reality, this is what they had been trying to teach me from the beginning. If you are going to call yourself an aircrewmen, you needed to be able to launch the 200-pound life raft. You needed to be able to carry the bag of bulletproof vests up the ladder. And you needed to figure out a way to pee standing up (or modify as necessary). There just was no room to half-ass things in the military. People get killed when you half-ass your job.

I found such fulfillment in training others that I almost did not miss flying. Almost. I finally was able to fill that void that lingered when I felt like I was not contributing. And though I could not be in the sky hunting submarines, I found it rewarding to teach new 'nuggets' the secrets of the cat and mouse game and witness the satisfaction in their face when they 'got it.' Everything had come full circle.

Freedom

The sun was just peeking over the pines in the distance. As its rays touched the dewy grass, the blades almost sparkled, looking as if they were covered in frost. But it was too balmy for that. Not a sound could be heard but the morning birds chattering. The silence was unusual, as there always seemed to be an APU running as Maintenance never seemed to sleep. It was a humid summer morning in late June. It was the day before I was officially discharged from the Navy.

As I walked out onto the ramp, careful not to step on the pad eyes, all of the planes were lined up, chained down in their resting position. They went by names as simple as Lima Charlie 320, 912, 915, 586, 571, 207, and 002. I thought of the places 915 had taken me; she always favored our crew. And what a crabby old pain in the ass 586 had been - sitting in the hangar for months with a cracked wing. But she recovered just fine and ended up being one of our best birds. 320 sure gave us a run for the money - constantly leaking oil. 571 was always ready to please - though she protested in the hot weather. And 002 was a newbie to our squadron, so I did not know her as well. Somewhere in the last five years, I had come to love these stinky old planes. They held my life in their hands every day. They showed me the world. They protected, defended, and rescued. And they expected nothing in return.

I walked slowly between the two rows of aircraft. There were six out on the line and one in the hangar as the squadron was gearing up to go back on deployment. This deployment they would be doing without me. The missions had begun to shift yet again as things were heating up in the Middle East. I was torn between the sadness of saying goodbye to it all, but excited for the adventures that lie ahead of me. It would be a new phase in our lives. But leaving this one behind was already much more difficult than I ever imagined.

I breathed in the salty Maine air and could smell a hint of the JP-5 fuel residue. I smiled at the beautiful sight in front of me as the sun was rising over the P-3s on the ramp. And then just above the tree line in the distance I heard that old familiar sound, the hum of four propeller engines. A few seconds later, she emerged. Another P-3 from our neighboring squadron was circling in the flight pattern. As she flew on overhead and out to the Atlantic, her engines rumbled a deep resonance, and the sound gave me chills of excitement. *It was the sound of freedom.*

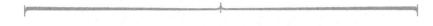

Several Years Later...

"I just don't know how to let go of the guilt, you know, that I didn't do enough."

"I know exactly what you mean," Don said, sipping his whiskey on the rocks. Growing up, he had been like my second father. He was Anna's father and had been the only other house I spent almost as much time in as my own. The day was nearing 90 degrees so sitting on the porch, having a drink seemed like a perfect way to spend a Saturday afternoon. "You know all the 'Vietnam Veteran' hats that you see the guys at the VFW and American Legion wear?"

I nodded my head.

"I have never been able to bring myself to wear one - because I wasn't there. I mean, I was in the Army during Vietnam, but they sent me to Boston to do Morse coding," he laughed. "I didn't serve my country in a war."

"But you were in the service during Vietnam. You were supporting them from the stateside," I argued with him. And then I thought for a moment and shrugged. "But I get it. I feel the same way. I got out before Iraq and Afghanistan and I don't know what to do with that guilt of not doing enough. Not being there."

"You remember my neighbor that flew the float planes on Chase Lake?" Don asked me.

"Yeah, I remember. Anna and I used to go take care of his dogs, didn't we?"

"Yep. That's the one. Well, he flew fighters in Vietnam. And I've had this same conversation with him. Do you know what he told me?"

I shook my head this time and took a sip of wine from my glass.

"He said that it wouldn't have mattered what you had done - you would still have that feeling of guilt. He did two deployments flying into Vietnam. Countless missions and thousands of flights. He feels guilty he didn't do *three* tours in Vietnam. No matter what you did, no matter how many people you saved, no matter how many years you served, most veterans will feel that it's never enough - that you could have done more."

I felt tears well up in my eyes as he spoke. For the first time, I could make sense of the nagging feeling in my stomach. I finally understood it.

What They Don't Teach You in Deer River

In the end - just what all did I get out of the Navy? I got my heart broken. A few times. I got some bones broken and a few stitches. My feet fell flat and my back has been messed up since the ladder incident. I was yelled at on several occasions. I cried many days and felt pain so deep I didn't know if I would recover. I felt the guts of loneliness on many, many nights. I spent months at a time working shitty hours, weekends, and holidays. I buffed more decks than I can count, cleaned hundreds of toilets, spaces, and aircraft. I have had other people's urine spill all over me and have taken out the trash for years straight.

But in five short years I was able to step foot in 13 different countries. I watched the sun rise and set over three different oceans and countless seas. I have seen glaciers, volcanoes, mountains, canyons, deserts, and everything in between that our beautiful earth has to offer. I have laughed, loved, traveled, ate too much, and drank too much. I have seen how the wealthy live and the poor beg to survive. I have seen suffering and I have seen rejoicing.

Above all, I have had the privilege to work next to the bravest our country has to offer. The ones that signed a blank check that can cost as much as one's life. I have made friends as close as family - friends that would have laid down their life for me. I owe everything to these men and women who looked after me; who taught me. They taught me responsibility and accountability over my own actions. They taught me to not take life too seriously, to not pass up an opportunity to make fun of someone else, but to make sure they are laughing with me. They taught me that I must be willing to laugh at myself - and if I look for things to be offended by, I will find them. They taught me that it is much easier to look for the good in people. They taught me to work hard but play harder. They taught me that when it comes to spending time with friends and family - quality is much more important than quantity. They taught me that life is short, to take chances and to do great things whenever possible. We just don't know when it will be our last flight.

The Navy was my opportunity to have an adventure. However, I came to realize that life in general was its own adventure. Most often we never end up where we think we're going to - or even where we think we would want to be. And just when we think we have it all figured out, things happen, we struggle, but grow even more. Our goals change. And we often end up in a much better place than we ever imagined possible. We cannot dwell on the mistakes of our past or regret the paths we did not take. We can only look back at our pasts to learn from them. It was the path we were on and grew to become the person we are supposed to be. And in the end, I learned that the greatest adventure is always the one that lies just in front of me.

I will always feel blessed to have been brought up in a town like Deer River. It's true that there were a lot of things in the big world that I was sheltered from, growing up in my small community. But Deer River gave me the strength I needed to go out into the world, knowing that I always had a place to come home to. It was, and always will be, where my roots are. And because of these roots, I was able to fly.

PHOTO ALBUM

Left: Me in France!
Below: Our crew patch after the unfortunate Torpex incident

CAC-9 in Malta

Just a normal day in the air. (Horton & I)

Pinning on my
Second Class Petty
Officer Crow

The infamous SLAM missile littered with our signatures

Aaron and I all spiffy in our dress whites
together at a Change of Command

Aaron and I on our wedding day, June 16, 2001

ACKNOWLEDGMENTS

Thank you to all of my great friends and family who have helped make this book possible. Thank you for listening to me ramble on about writing it for years now. It only took 13 years. But I'm quick like that.

Thank you Robin for your amazing editing skills! I could not have completed this without you. Well, I supposed I could have, but it would not have been the same.

Thank you to ©*Photography by Anna Lise' Riley* for your creative ideas and photography that resulted in the cover photo. Thank you to Aaron, Tayte, Rob & Stacy for lending me your backsides to grace my book cover. I will forever cherish them.

Thank you, Mom, for all of your significant editing help. Thank you for all of your encouragement - not just with the book, but for my entire career. Thank you for being the rational, sensible person you are - as long as it was before 8pm in which you haven't yet turned into a gremlin. Thank you for the letters, phone calls, and prayers. Mostly, thank you for believing in me.

Thank you to my little sister, Liz, for your amazing photography work (©*Studio 308 Photography*) and for your patience during my awkward photo shoot. You truly have a gift of capturing the beauty in nature and diminishing the awkwardness in the individual. I'm glad I could help you perfect this skill.

Thank you to my little, little sister, Kaye, for inspiring me to start this book when you joined the Navy. My initial intentions were to teach you all my lessons of what and what not to do upon enlisting. I was going to show you so hard. But as time went on, it was clear that you did not need my advice. You paved your own path and did beautifully on your own Navy journey. You know, the one without per diem.

Thank you, Dad, for always listening to me ramble on and on, for accepting those midnight collect calls from other countries when I needed you most, and for never mentioning the bill. Thank you for always offering me a gun when you worried about my safety. Thank you for always believing in me and for gracing me with your wisdom. "Be good. And if you can't be good, be careful." I think that advice kept me alive - or at least out of jail.

Thank you to my very best friend in the world, Anna, for your countless hours of help and inspiration to keep going when I just wanted to punch the computer. Thanks to you I only did twice. Thank you for knowing the right words when I could not think of them. Thank you for the kick when I was stuck. And thank you for choosing me back in second grade to be your best friend forever.

Thank you Claudia, Joey, and Cecelia for giving mom 'quiet time' so that I could write. I hope you will always be inspired to follow your heart and to remember that anything is possible if you are willing to work hard enough for it. I love you with every piece of myself. Even my second toe (the ugly one that never healed right after I broke it).

And above all, thank you Aaron for putting up with me on a daily basis. Thank you for interjecting your amazing spelling and grammatical skills that I tend to lack. Thank you for always giving me your honest opinion (sometimes a little too honest), and for your encouraging words when I needed them most. Oh, and thank you for making your amazing guacamole whenever I have the craving. Mostly, thank you for choosing to spend your forever with me.

CREDITS AND CONTRIBUTORS

Publishing: Tactical 16, LLC
CEO, Tactical 16: Erik Shaw
President, Tactical 16: Jeremy Farnes
Cover Photo: Anna Lise' Riley
Cover Design: Kristen Shaw

ABOUT THE AUTHOR
Julia A. Maki

Julia A. Maki grew up in northern Minnesota and enlisted in the Navy as an Aviation Warfare Systems Operator aboard P-3Cs. After the Navy, Julia settled in Maryland with her husband where they both ended up working for the Department of Defense as civilians. They have three children together, which initially inspired her to write children's books about the military. Her first book, *My Mom Hunts Submarines* was Julia's way of telling her children about what she did while in the Navy with the underlying message, "There isn't anything you cannot do." Her second book, *All Hands on Deck! Dad's Coming Home!* was inspired by her sister's job in the Navy aboard the USS Stennis. It is a book for children that have parents that are deployed in the military. *Still My Dad* was written for children with parents that are wounded veterans, but can be applicable for anyone facing a disability. *From the Sky* was inspired by the amazing things she saw while flying all over the world. Finally, *What They Don't Teach You in Deer River*, is Julia's memoir and first novel.

When she is not writing, raising a family, or working, she finds her passion in volunteering for organizations supporting veterans.

ABOUT THE PUBLISHER
Tactical 16, LLC

Tactical 16 is a Veteran owned and operated publishing company based in the beautiful mountain city of Colorado Springs, Colorado. What started as an idea among like-minded people has grown into reality.

Tactical 16 believes strongly in the healing power of writing, and provides opportunities for Veterans, Police, Firefighters, and EMTs to share their stories; striving to provide accessible and affordable publishing solutions that get the works of true American Heroes out to the world. We strive to make the writing and publication process as enjoyable and stress-free as possible.

As part of the process of healing and helping true American Heroes, we are honored to hear stories from all Veterans, Police Officers, Firefighters, EMTs and their spouses. Regardless of whether it's carrying a badge, fighting in a war zone or family at home keeping everything going, we know many have a story to tell.

At Tactical 16, we truly stand behind our mission to be "The Premier Publishing Resource for Guardians of Freedom."

We are a proud supporter of Our Country and its People, without which we would not be able to make Tactical 16 a reality.

How did Tactical 16 get its name? There are two parts to the name, "Tactical" and "16." Each has a different meaning. Tactical refers to the Armed Forces, Police, Fire, and Rescue communities or any group who loves, believes in, and supports Our Country. The "16" is the number of acres of the World Trade Center complex that was destroyed on that harrowing day of September 11, 2001. That day will be forever ingrained in the memories of many generations of Americans. But that day is also a reminder of the resolve of this Country's People and the courage, dedication, honor, and integrity of our Armed Forces, Police, Fire, and Rescue communities. Without Americans willing to risk their lives to defend and protect Our Country, we would not have the opportunities we have before us today.

More works from Tactical 16 available at www.tactical16.com.

Ashley's High Five for Daddy
By: Pam Saulsby

Death Letter
By: David W. Peters

Line in the Valley
By: Chris Hernandez

Proof of Our Resolve
By: Chris Hernandez

The Pact
By: Robert Patrick Lewis

Love Me When I'm Gone
The True Story of Life, Love, and Loss for a Green Beret in Post-9/11 War
By: Robert Patrick Lewis

And Then I Cried:
Stories of a Mortuary NCO
By: Justin Jordan

Losing the War in Vietnam
But Winning the War to Reclaim My Soul
By: Frank DiScala

Zuzu's Petals
By: Kevin Andrew

Thank you to the following sponsor for supporting this project:

Veteran Integration Program, Peer Navigators
The Veteran Integration Program specializes in assisting in the transition process through employment, education, and training.

The Veteran Integration Program is part of Mt. Carmel Center of Excellence: a Beacon of support for Military, Veterans, and their families by providing wellness, transition, and resources.

www.mtcarmelveterans.org

CPSIA information can be obtained at www.ICGtesting.com
Printed in the USA
BVOW04s1655201016

465523BV00005B/9/P